# FROM "CHE" TO CHINA:

# LABOR AND AUTHORITARIANISM IN THE NEW GLOBAL ECONOMY

Vandeplas Publishing: Labor Law Series 2

# FROM "CHE" TO CHINA:

# LABOR AND AUTHORITARIANISM IN THE NEW GLOBAL ECONOMY

BY

## STEPHEN F. DIAMOND

**VANDEPLAS PUBLISHING**

UNITED STATES OF AMERICA

From "Che" to China: labor and authoritarianism in the new global economy

Diamond, Stephen F.

Published by:

**Vandeplas Publishing - October 2009**

801 International Parkway, 5th Floor
Lake Mary, FL. 32746
USA

www.vandeplaspublishing.com

Vandeplas Publishing: Labor Law Series 2

ISBN: 978-1-60042-090-0

# Table of Contents

# Introduction

The trade union is widely assumed to be the quintessential democratic institution.  It is credited with introducing a measure of democratic accountability inside the modern industrial workplace but also with serving as a "workshop for democracy" in the surrounding political environment.  Thus, as workers become actively concerned about their own working conditions they shape their labor organization through democratic means – organizing, debate, elections, and collective bargaining with employers – and that, in turn, stimulates a larger interest in democratic values.  Motivated unionists carry the lessons of workplace democracy into the larger political arena, participating in political parties, debates and elections.

Thus, modern industrial relations theory, once a dominant force in economics, law, sociology and political science, was as much about politics as it was about workplace conflict.  At its heart industrial relations theory hoped to devise a seamless framework whereby the trade union, formed in the heat of class conflict, could mature into a central legitimating structure for a peaceful democratic capitalism.  Plant level union activity would motivate workers to engage in political institutions in the outside arena and to bring to that arena the tools they had developed in the workplace.  In turn, as their presence impacted political developments more broadly, the institutional context in which capitalism functioned would evolve bringing needed reform and flexibility back into the workplace.  Thus, industrial relations were seen as being consistent with the innovation and modernization processes of late 20th century capitalism.

The idea that labor organizations could be part of a dynamic and sustainable *authoritarian* regime has received far less attention from industrial relations theorists.  In the Cold War era, the high water mark of industrial relations theory, it was assumed that "trade unions" such as they were in regimes like the Soviet Union or pre-1989 Eastern Europe were merely "transmission belts" for the state with little autonomous power or responsibility.  For the most part this was not an inaccurate assessment.  But what much of industrial relations theory missed, and what social science theory in general has been almost pathologically blind to, was the development of neo-Stalinist regimes that devised a completely different approach to the question of labor organization and economic and political development. Particularly in the authoritarian regimes that emerged outside of the protective cover of the Soviet Red Army, more inclusive institutional forms were developed by neo-Stalinist movements in order to compensate, so to speak, for the absence of direct Russian power.

Thus, while Soviet Stalinism emerged in response to the failed experiment of the democratic Russian revolution of 1917 and the regimes like those of East Germany, Poland, and Czechoslovakia were established as part of the post war Soviet occupation, the third world neo-Stalinist regimes were largely home grown affairs and had, to a certain extent, to fend for themselves. They required new institutional forms whose purpose was no less authoritarian but whose means of operation was distinctly different. In their rise to power these movements often made a populist appeal to the labor movement while upon the seizure of power their message would shift towards an argument that the role of the labor union had fundamentally changed. Thereafter, the role of the "trade union" was to carry out state and party goals but not necessarily by simply imposing those goals on a prostrate population. Instead these political institutions engaged in an argument with the population in order to foreclose any opposition to the regime. There is, then, a sense in which the neo-Stalinist regimes mimicked the industrial relations approach by attempting, in their own way, to legitimate the authoritarianism of those regimes in the workplace through their own unique approach to "trade unions."

The essays collected here explore the mutual dynamic of a declining industrial relations order and a continuing presence of authoritarian neo-Stalinism on the global scene. The first chapter, entitled "Will the Real "Che" Guevara Please Stand Up?" lays out the theoretical terrain on which neo-Stalinism operates within the labor movement. Ernesto "Che" Guevara is best known today as the charismatic leader of the Cuban revolution who attempted to spread that revolution to Africa and Latin America. Guevara was, as well, however, an architect of the authoritarian politics of the

Cuban regime. And the Cuban regime, in turn, inspired numerous other movements around the globe for the next two decades. In particular, of course, the Cubans were directly involved in training and supporting some in the leadership of the Sandinista movement in Nicaragua. Thus, this essay traces as well the next stage of neo-Stalinist theory inside the Sandinista revolution that took place in 1979, twenty years after the triumph of Castro and Guevara.

The second chapter, "Killing the Patient: Shock Therapy and Labor in Eastern Europe," is based on a talk delivered to a symposium organized by the MacArthur Foundation and the Social Science Research Council in Prague, Czechoslovakia in 1993. This time was, of course, a critical turning point in east European history. The talk was an attempt to bring to bear the experience of the declining industrial relations order of the west to an eastern European audience that was putting great hope in the possibility of constructing western-style democratic institutions after the fall of the Berlin Wall. The process of globalization was beginning to be felt first hand in the United States labor movement and thus the experience of the debate over labor rights in the new North American Free Trade Agreement, or NAFTA, was relevant. While the Czech Republic, now separated from its poorer neighbor Slovakia, has done relatively better than other east European regimes, at the time there were strikes and protests taking place throughout the region against the "shock therapy" reforms recommended by western advisors like Jeffrey Sachs as these were beginning to have their intended destructive impact. Many of those countries still suffer the effects.

The next three chapters deal with the impact of China's emergence in the global economy on organized labor. China, of course, is the largest of the world's authoritarian regimes. While globalization advocates have argued strenuously that the economic modernization of China would bring with it democratic reform, this has not turned out to be true. The reform process began more than thirty years ago and a decade into the process the efforts of Chinese students and workers to bring about democratic reform was met with bloody repression. The brutal memories of the June 4, 1989 massacre by the People's Liberation Army still hang over the collective consciousness of the Chinese population. Incredibly this has not stopped the emergence of an entire industry of what can only be called intellectual apologists for the regime who continue to argue that it will or in part already has evolved towards universal democratic norms and institutions. Perhaps most striking is a subset within this milieu of "labor intellectuals" who are attempting to establish a formal working relationship between, on the one hand, the American labor movement, long hostile to Stalinism and its offshoot, the neo-Stalinist movements of the third world, and, on the other hand, the Chinese state's labor organization, the All China Federation of Trade Unions, or ACFTU.

The chapters here take a decidedly different approach. Chapter three, "Bridging the Divide," was written in the wake of the unprecedented events that took place during the meetings of the World Trade Organization in Seattle, Washington, in November 1999. At the heart of the confrontation there between advocates of the globalization process and opponents from the labor, environmental and human rights movements was a question about whether labor rights were genuinely universal and thus of relevance even to developing countries who depend heavily on low cost labor to win an advantage in global markets. The WTO meetings were quickly followed by an intense debate over whether the United States should suspend the labor rights conditionality it nominally imposed on China in order to allow China to enter the WTO freely. The debate quickly demonstrated the fragility of the alliance between labor unions and other groups that had joined forces in the Seattle demonstrations. This essay proposes an alternative approach to international labor rights in order to demonstrate the importance of those rights to workers in both the advanced and developing economies.

Chapter four, the second of the three essays on China, "The 'Race to the Bottom' Returns," confronts directly the heart of the argument made by some labor intellectuals to justify their relationship with the Chinese regime. The assumption made by these intellectuals is either that there is no race to the bottom in working conditions underway as a result of globalization or that regimes like that in China are attempting to block such a development with worker friendly economic policies and legal reforms. Thus conventional academics like labor law scholar

William Gould[1] and labor economists Gary Fields[2] and Robert Flanagan[3] argue that "race to the bottom" advocates misunderstand what is happening in the international economy and that in fact globalization benefits workers overall. They are most keen to defend the free trade policies adopted by the United States over the last two decades lest the world revert to a destructive form of protectionism led by narrow-minded trade unions.

Another group with closer ties to the labor movement itself such as labor educators Kent Wong and Elaine Bernard as well as labor historians David Brody and Nelson Lichtenstein contend that while there may indeed be a race to the bottom evidenced by the explosion of sweatshop labor in places like the *maquiladora* zones in Mexico or the coastal export processing zones of China, there is reason for optimism about responses to this process.[4] They point to anecdotal evidence that they contend indicates that Chinese workers actually are free to engage in union activities. Brody and Lichtenstein argue that the ACFTU is not much different than the so-called "company" unions that played a minor role in the mass wave of unionization that took place in the 1930s in the United States. They view arguments that support the development of the autonomous and widespread activity of workers outside of the ACFTU as a kind of "conjuring" trick that has no real hope of success. Wong and Bernard go further and actively take part in efforts to create links between American unions and the ACFTU. Fortunately, to date, those efforts have come to very little.

"The 'Race to the Bottom' Returns" argues that only a cartoon version of the actual process of globalization can lead one to conclude that it is a benign event for workers in the United States and abroad. In addition, it notes that the hoped for reforms by the Chinese regime must remain only that. Rather, the Chinese government realizes that its authoritarianism is intimately linked to both its successful restructuring of the older state owned industrial sectors of the economy as well as its encouragement of the new coastal sweatshop sector. Any examples of apparent labor freedom in China, though more than likely illusory, have to be set against the regime's intolerance of any movement that can threaten its claim to legitimacy.

Finally, Chapter Five, "The PetroChina Syndrome," returns to the theme of the decline of industrial relations theory yet rooted in the China debate. Through a case study of the restructuring of a major Chinese oil company this essay asks what impact globalization is having on the previous attempts at using industrial relations to legitimate capitalism. The argument here is that far from being inconsistent with the globalization process, Chinese authoritarianism is well suited to the spread of capitalism around the globe. But both China and the advocates of globalization may at the same time be spreading the seeds of their own eventual destruction since the vacuum left by the former legitimating ideologies advocated by both sides of the Cold War has yet to be filled. The recent collapse of the global financial system will certainly offer a real world test of this proposition.

# Chapter One.

# Will the Real "Che" Guevara
# Please Stand Up?

<u>Introduction</u>

As one approaches the heart of Managua, Nicaragua, from the country's only international airport, it is impossible to miss the giant statue, sculpted in classic socialist realist style, of a soldier thrusting an AK-47 rifle into the air. A slogan etched into the base of the figure read: *"Sólo los obreros y campesinos llegarán hasta el fin."* "Only the workers and campesinos will reach the end." This Sandinista slogan, fashioned from the words of Augusto Sandino, the insurgent politician who battled U.S. marines in Nicaragua in the 1930s, is intended to remind Managua and its visitors of the Frente Sandinista de Liberación Nacional's steadfast belief that theirs was a revolution made by and for the workers and peasants of Nicaragua.[1]

It might come as a surprise then to realize that the harassment, intimidation, arrest, and even killing, of workers and peasants who peacefully criticized or protested Nicaraguan government policies was a regular event inside Nicaragua during the FSLN's first period in power, from 1979 until 1990. In late 1985, for example, Alejandro Solórzano, a leader of the pro-Moscow Nicaraguan Socialist Party and, at the time, head of the major Nicaraguan Construction Workers' Union, was arrested and held in jail by the Nicaraguan government for twenty-four hours. His crime? He had begun a hunger strike to protest the ceiling set by the FSLN on annual bonuses awarded Nicaraguan workers. Solórzano was one of the first victims of a renewed Emergency Law put in place by the Frente allegedly to help the nation's battle against the *contra* rebels.[2]

Widely respected human rights and non-governmental organizations documented many such actions. A report by Amnesty International released in early 1984 described the detention in November 1983, of five transport workers' union officials for alleged violations of the Public Order and Security Law. That law was part of a package of restrictions on civil liberties imposed by the government when a State of Emergency was first declared in March of 1982. The law forbade many traditional trade union activities, including the right to strike. The strike ban was lifted in August of 1984 in the run-up to Nicaragua's first post-revolution national elections, but was re-imposed in October 1985.

Three of the five transport unionists were released in December of 1983, but two others remained in custody pending trial on charges of "sabotage" and "attempted assassination." Under the emergency law, a strike, the weapon considered fundamental to the effectiveness of a trade union, can be considered "sabotage." Amnesty concluded its report on Nicaragua by observing, "union members are frequently subjected to arrest and short term detention." A March 1986 update by Amnesty concluded that these actions constituted "a pattern of intimidation and harassment."[3]

The New York-based Americas Watch group reported in 1984 that trade unionists active in the social Christian oriented Nicaraguan Workers Central (*Central de Trabajadores de Nicaragua*, or "CTN"), one of the larger independent labor federations in the country, were arrested in 1983 for alleged "violent anti-government activity." But the report noted that there was "suspicion that the real reason for their arrest was their otherwise lawful exercise of freedom of speech and assembly." This report noted that some of the arrests were "apparently for holding meetings and conducting CTN business." In a separate incident, also described by Americas Watch, 18 members of the CTN were arrested near Esteli and Jinotega in the rural northwest region of the country. Eight of these unionists were later released, but the ten others remained in custody at the date of the report's publication. One of these ten "died in custody under unclear circumstances."[4]

Finally, the Geneva-based International Labour Organization (ILO) issued in the spring of 1984 a 33-page report detailing the findings of their investigations of violations of trade unionists' rights in Nicaragua. The report included the results of a fact-finding tour of the country in December 1983. The report was updated during the June 1984, meeting of the ILO and supplemented by several follow on reports.[5] The report described allegations of illegal arrests, beatings, threats, and union busting carried out by members of the various Sandinista organizations, including the militia, the police, the Sandinista Workers' Central (*Central de Sandinista Trabajadores* or "CST"), and the Sandinista Defense Committees. The response of the government to these charges was also recorded.

The ILO expressed "its serious concern at the large number of arrests of trade union leaders and members...and wishes to point out that measures designed to deprive trade union leaders and members of their freedom entail a serious risk of interference in union activities and that, when such measures are taken on trade union grounds, they constitute an infringement on the principles of freedom of association."[6]

Government representatives refused comment on many of the allegations, contended that in other situations the facts were too vague to justify response, and argued that many of the actions taken against the independent unionists were for "counter-revolutionary" activities. The Legal Advisor of the FSLN's Ministry of the Interior, however, told the ILO's representative in response to questions regarding unionists detained without grounds that "there may perhaps have been abuses on occasion."[7]

This limited selection of FSLN behavior could have been repeated for almost any period of time while the FSLN was in power during the 1980s. Rather than giving full support to the independent and democratic organization of the working class and peasantry, the FSLN did everything in its power to channel workers and peasants into organizations established from above, by the new Sandinista state and party apparatus. This evidence indicates an apparent conundrum: the FSLN professed a strong commitment to workers' interests, yet seemed intent upon the suppression of *independent* expressions of these interests.

The above incidents shared two important characteristics: one, the activists expressed criticism of the regime; and two, the activists organized themselves into *independent* trade unions to express that criticism. Allegedly, the regime encouraged criticism through its system of participatory democracy. There were extreme limits to the genuine freedom of expression *within* that system. But Nicaragua's independent unions were outside that system and were subject to particularly high levels of harassment under FSLN rule. What did the FSLN have to fear from an independent trade union movement? Why did the FSLN need to establish its own party and state-controlled labor movement? This chapter attempts to answer these questions by examining the general theory and ideology that lay behind the FSLN's labor relations' policies.

These are not just theoretical or historical questions. The Sandinistas recently returned to power in Nicaragua, with their long time leader Daniel Ortega elected President. Similar authoritarian, if populist, regimes are in power today elsewhere in Latin America such as Venezuela, Ecuador and Bolivia. In each of these countries there is talk of a "new socialism." Advocates of Sandinista style politics laud the re-emergence of this so-called "left" in Latin America as evidencing renewed hope for workers and the broader poor.[8] These movements are considered a "rebellion against neo-liberalism."[9] In Asia the Chinese communist regime remains in power in part because of its ability to retain a tight grip on its workforce through the All China Federation of Trade Unions, or ACFTU. Now, China is spreading its power globally through investments in Africa and elsewhere and its ideological influence is even affecting the U.S. labor movement where some labor leaders are lauding their new links to the ACFTU.[10] Thus, despite the collapse of the old Soviet Union and its satellite eastern European states in the early 1990s, bureaucratic and authoritarian movements remain a powerful social force in the post cold war world. Even anecdotal evidence adduces this conclusion: the ethereal image of "Che" Guevara is found around the globe, even in

4

the Middle East where he is admired by fundamentalist elements.[11] In fact, our understanding of the Sandinistas and the new authoritarianism of the post cold war era must begin with the intellectual influence of Guevara and the Cuban revolution he helped lead.

## The Ideological Background

The Cuban revolution was an important model for the shaping of Sandinista ideology and policy. It is also to the Cuban revolution that one can turn to begin to unravel Sandinista trade union policy. In the theoretical perspectives laid out by Guevara and the organizational structures established by Fidel Castro lay the building blocks of FSLN policy towards its base among workers and peasants. The core tenets of Guevara's "theory" of revolutionary trade unionism were laid out in a speech to the Cuban working class in the summer of 1960. The July 26 movement had taken power in the first month of the previous year, without a great deal of labor unrest. But Castro immediately unleashed a five-day general strike to establish his credibility among Cuba's workers. With the complicity of the pro-Moscow People's Socialist Party, he then moved to take control of the relatively large and anti-Communist, independent Cuban labor movement. Guevara's speech, entitled "On Sacrifice and Dedication," laid out the basic political argument behind these bureaucratic moves.[12]

Though there is no evidence that the Sandinistas were directly influenced by this particular speech, the closeness of the arguments made by Guevara to those made by the Sandinistas responsible for trade union policy is telling. No one denies Guevara's general impact on the leaders of the FSLN. Further, only the portraits of Sandino and the Nicaraguan poet Rubén Darío outdid the ubiquitous presence of the image of Guevara in Sandinista Nicaragua.[13] Finally, the key Sandinista who was in charge of party trade union policy during the 1980s, Comandante Víctor Tirado López, explicitly acknowledged the debt of the Nicaraguan revolution to the thought of Guevara.[14] Tirado López was the FSLN leader with the greatest seniority on the FSLN's National Directorate after Tomás Borge. He came to the FSLN from the Mexican Communist Party soon after Castro's 1959 victory.


The Chimera of Industrialization

Guevara opened his remarks to his audience of Cuban workers by placing the question of industrialization at the heart of his agenda, defining it as "the road to collective well-being in this age of economic empires." This would be "an exceedingly difficult road" for Cuba. In particular it would be difficult for the industrial working class. The Cuban peasantry were already "beginning to receive the fruits of [our] victory - they are completely with the Revolution." Unfortunately, because the working class had yet to receive "the fruits of industrialization, the fruits of the revolutionary movement's determination" they had yet to fully comprehend the importance of this process.

Guevara's remarks targeted the political attitudes of the working class towards the development process as a particular barrier for the regime to overcome:

> [W]e are starting, with hopes for a great effort, on the road to industrialization. At this moment the role of the working class defines itself. Either the working class completely comprehends all its duties and all the importance of this moment and we triumph, or it does not realize them, and industrialization becomes one more of the lukewarm attempts America has made to save itself from the colonial yoke.

To Guevara whether a tiny island nation of a few million people can triumph in the age of "economic empires" would depend on the sacrifices of a few hundred thousand industrial workers!

Guevara made, as well, what has become a standard argument in the literature of national liberation movements: that the reason the Castro-led revolutionary movement in Cuba was based in the countryside was due to the weakness of the working class. "Cuba," he said, "like all underdeveloped countries, does not have a forceful proletariat." Further, Guevara stated that workers in the industrial sector are privileged relative to the peasantry and, hence, the "solidarity of the working class" has been "destroy[ed]." A paradox in Guevara's thinking should now be apparent. On the one hand, the working class was too small and divided to overthrow a tinhorn dictator like Batista, but, on the other, it was thought capable of lifting an underdeveloped nation into the world economy.

## Class Divisions Remain

Despite its weakness and privileges the working class remained a problem for the new regime because of its tendency to view itself *as* a working class. Guevara argued:

> [T]he working class still retains much of the spirit, that made it see only one difference: between the worker and the boss - a simplistic spirit that led all analysis to precisely one great division: workers and boss. And today, in the process of industrialization, which gives such great importance to the state, the workers consider the state as just one more boss, and they treat it as a boss. And since this is a state completely opposed to the State as Boss, we must establish long, fatiguing dialogues between the state and the workers, who although they certainly will be convinced in the end, during this period, during this dialogue have braked progress.

Hence, Guevara wanted to undermine the "spirit" (class conscious and militant, rather than simple) that had made the Cuban union movement a success under the old regime.

Whether or not the new revolutionary State was a "Boss" is central to understanding the tension between a national liberation movement and a trade union movement. To Guevara, and to the FSLN some years later and to similar movements today, because the vanguard organization had taken state power *in the name of* the working class and had established some form of input into decision-making for workers, then workers were no longer allowed to view the State as an adversary.

Instead of fighting for workers' basic interests, defined democratically from below by the workers themselves, it was now the role of labor leaders to implement State policies elaborated by the revolutionary vanguard. "What should be clear...is what Fidel said the other day: The best labor leader is not the one who fights for his comrades' daily bread. The best labor leader is the one who fights for everybody's daily bread, the one who understands the revolutionary process completely, and who, analyzing it and understanding it in depth, will support the government and convince his comrades by explaining the reasons for the revolutionary measures." This is, of course, "transmission belt" trade unionism so familiar to students of Stalin's Russia.[15] But one should pay close attention, as well, to Guevara's concept of "everyone" when he argued that labor leaders should "fight for everybody's daily bread." At first glance, it sounds as if he was appealing to the longstanding concern within trade unionism for social justice. But, in fact, he was, as we will see below, attempting to erase the concept of a distinct relationship between the individual and society. This is essential groundwork for the evolution of a totalitarian ideology. Democratic trade unionism, on the other hand, fights for each individual's rights and out of that fight builds a *social* movement. Hence, such a movement is able to make a fundamental contribution to a progressive, industrial society.

Guevara's aim was to prevent the emergence of an alternative road to social change in Cuba. One tactic of national liberation movement theory was to set up a straw man in the image of so-called "bread and butter" or "business" unionism. The Sandinistas would refer to such unions as "economistic" or, even, "castrated."[16] The reference was quite often aimed, in the developing world at least, at the unions established with the aid of the United States-based AFL-CIO.[17] Generally, these unions first emerged, quite naturally, in the factories and on the plantations of U.S. multinational firms. Because of this association it was assumed by the guerrilla movements that these unions were incapable of building a strong opposition to politically repressive regimes in the Third World.  There was a kernel of truth in this argument.  In many instances in post-World War II history, unions tied to the AFL-CIO have, because of the American labor movement's frequent willingness to subordinate workers' interests to the general U.S. foreign policy, limited their trade union organizing to bread and butter issues that were not likely to threaten pro-Washington political regimes.

But the FSLN's or Guevara's critique of this stance ignored the potential for building a broader movement out of battles over apparently small, individual issues, whatever the intent of policy planners in the AFL-CIO's Department of International Affairs in Washington.  Hundreds of members of such unions have begun "simple" bread and butter struggles and found themselves jailed, tortured and even killed by Third World regimes.  To spotlight the potential in such "narrow" efforts, one should recall that an event as important as Russia's February Revolution began when women workers demanded bread.  More than sixty years later, the dismissal of a widely respected woman shipyard worker in the Polish port of Gdansk sparked a strike that led to the formation of the national labor movement Solidarity.  In neither case was a so-called revolutionary vanguard the essential ingredient - only "bread and butter" unionism defending "individual" interests.  Should not a revolutionary regime allegedly established in the name of the working class, fully expand and open up the opportunity for individual workers to express themselves, from below, through democratic institutions of their own making?

This, however, was not Guevara's agenda.  His aim was to turn the energy and creativity of the industrial working class into grist for the mill of the State.  This "does not mean that the labor leader should become a parrot," as Guevara argued, "simply repeating what the government says through the Ministry of Labor, or through any other majority.  Of course, the government will make mistakes too, and the labor leader will have to call attention to them forcefully if those mistakes are repeated and if they are not corrected."  He foresaw a role for some independence on the part of labor leaders - but only to point out mistakes, not to question the basic direction and organization of State power. This "is nothing but a procedural problem," Guevara concluded.

What, then, is at the top of the Government agenda for their new labor leaders? First, and foremost, workers must sacrifice without protest:

> It is inadmissible, and it would be the start of our failure, for the workers to have to go on strike, for example, because the employer-state - and I am talking about the process of industrialization, that is, of the majority participation in the state - adopted so intransigent and totally absurd a position as to force the workers to strike. This would be the beginning of the end of the people's government because it would be the negation of all we have been upholding. But the government *will*, on occasion, have to ask sacrifices of certain types of workers. ... [A]t some time or another, we will have to face up to those [revolutionary] duties and temporarily renounce some of our privileges or rights at a given moment, for the common good.

It is here that the trade union plays a key role:

> That's the job of the labor leader; to recognize that moment, to analyze and make sure that the workers' sacrifice, if it is necessary, be the smallest possible one, but at the same time, to show the worker comrades that the sacrifice is necessary and to explain why, and to make sure that everyone is convinced.

Guevara, then, ruled out any independent policy role for the trade union leadership. They are not to voice independent or individual working class demands much less consider promoting alternative roads to national development. They are simply to implement sacrifices - convincing workers to work harder, longer and with less money - precisely the opposite of the role that these unions played prior to Castro's revolution. Perhaps most ominously, they are "to make sure everyone is convinced." That is, they must now take on the role of disciplinarian, on behalf of the State, of their own membership.

It should be emphasized that Guevara did not want to transform the role of the labor movement in order to eliminate it He recognized openly that the State *needed* a labor organization among workers - but not an independent and potential adversary. Rather, to paraphrase the sectarian American socialist Daniel De Leon, Guevara wanted to build a cadre of "labor lieutenants of the state." One advantage of this system we have already noted: the ability of the labor leader to point out procedural mistakes by the State. Now a second role, much more significant, is added: the need to implement through persuasion and discipline, the sacrifices the State says the workers must make in the name of national development. "A revolutionary government cannot demand sacrifices from above; they must be the result of everyone's will - of everyone's conviction," Guevara argued. "Industrialization is built of sacrifices. A process of accelerated industrialization is no lark, and we will see this in the future." This role for some type of new labor movement is the first step in the establishment of a human resources policy in third world revolutions. Under the Sandinistas, the need for such a policy would stimulate the use of the more sophisticated program of participatory democracy inside Nicaragua's unions and workplaces.

## Revolutionary Development to Supersede Capitalism

Guevara then moved on to place his initial outline of the proposed new role for labor in a larger context. "By what means," he asked, do we intend "to develop our economy?" He examined the free enterprise system and asked his audience to compare it with the system of "revolutionary development." The former is anarchical, enslaving, and monstrous, Guevara said. "But there is another system. It is the system in which we face up to ourselves and tell ourselves, 'we are revolutionaries, the revolutionary government, the people's representatives'. And who do we have to make these industries for, who has got to benefit, if not the people? And if the people must benefit, and we are the people's representatives, we, the government, should carry the weight and direction of industrialization, so that there will not be any anarchy."

A form of "rationalization from above" lay at the heart of Guevara's conception of the new system. "When we need one screw factory, there will be one screw factory. When we need a machete factory, there will be *one* machete factory, not three. Let us save the nation's capital." This approach was to be taken towards wages, as well as capital investment: "We should never reward the worker *or* the professional, with a higher salary than the prevailing one, than the just one, in order to gain a social advantage or to destroy someone, because that is a non-revolutionary procedure. But we will always try to keep the workers' salaries as high as the industry will allow, always considering full employment our first duty, and after jobs for the unemployed, more work for the underemployed."

The irrational also emerged in Guevara's argument. With one sentence he revealed the central purpose of this "rationalization process" of saving capital and maintaining a general ceiling on wages: to begin the illogical process of industrialization in one country. "... [W]hen we need a basic industry, *although it does not make money, although it is not the best business*, we will build that great basic industry, because that is going to be the base for the entire road to industrialization." (Emphasis added) The central justification for changing the purpose and structure of the trade union movement, for implementing wage freezes and strike prohibitions, and for limiting freedom of expression, was to allow the State the freedom to pursue, Don Quixote-like, industrial windmills!

## "Great Duties of the Working Class"

Having provided his working class audience with a general outline of the goals of the new State and the role of labor unions in the pursuit of those goals, Guevara moved on to outline three "basic duties of the working class." Keep in mind that these duties were announced from above by the new regime - they did not emerge independently from discussions among union members themselves.

"[A]fter analyzing the problems this country has had, we discover what are the basic duties of the working class," Guevara began. "Of course there are many duties, but in economic terms there are three great obligations, three obligations that sometimes even conflict with the common denominator the working class has made of its aspirations and its struggles against the ruling class, because one of the great obligations of today's working class is to produce well."

Guevara immediately preempted what he presumed would be the natural response of his audience, the audience that incorrectly viewed the new State as a Boss. "When I say `produce', the workers can say `that is just what the bosses said, and the more we produced, the more money we gave them, and the less they needed some comrade, and we caused the unemployment and increased concentration of wealth'." Guevara responded directly to the first of these concerns, though rather vaguely. But he ignored altogether the second argument - making clear that a new kind of concentration of wealth would be essential to his system of revolutionary development. "That is true," he continued. "That is why there is an apparent contradiction. But production right now has got to be, precisely, the production of wealth *so that the state can invest more in the creation of sources of work,* and it has got to be the type of production that does not cost anyone his job. We have got to invent constantly, develop popular initiative, in order to create new sources of work, sources that will demand the greatest possible development." (Emphasis added) In Guevara's view, then, the concentration of wealth in the hands of the State is the only solution to the problem of unemployment - the working class is caught in his developmental dilemma.

Linked to working harder in Guevara's system was the second "basic duty," the promotion of thrift and savings among industrial workers. Every penny saved, was a penny earned for the State. "I wanted to save this document. The comrades at CMQ gave it to me, and it is an outstanding example of what the working class should do. It is nothing more than the idea of saving the spools of all the country's typewriter ribbons, not the ribbons but their spools, to avoid having to import these items. This is another of the great duties of the working class, which is tied to the duty to produce, to save, always to develop its initiative so that not one centavo is spent unnecessarily. The wasted centavo does not help anybody, and if it is not put to work it will never help the workers. And each centavo saved is put into our foreign trade, or into the National Treasury. That is, it makes possible the development of another source of work."

Guevara then linked these two basic duties to State-centered development: "Production and thrift are the basis of economic development - production and thrift, I repeat, for the benefit of the workers. You cannot ask anyone to make sacrifices, to be more careful, to work harder every minute for someone else's benefit. It would be unjust to demand that. We *are* asking this wherever the state takes direct control of a factory's operation. More and more, the major factories - the ones we will build, of course - will be state-owned. The State's role will increase and the duty of the working class will increase too."

## The Totalitarian Outlook

The third and final "great duty" of the working class is consistent with a central concern of Guevara's - that the State *needs* a vigorous labor movement, though one of its own making. "[T]he third great obligation of the workers, besides producing and saving, is organizing. Organizing, not in the old sense of organizing as a class against another class, but to organize in order to give more to the Revolution, which is to give more to the people, which is to give more to the working class."

Then, in a brief, but remarkable analysis, Guevara elaborated the link between his concept of the new union movement to a totalitarian image of the future Cuba: "[E]veryone is being transformed into a worker, everyone who is directly concerned with production, and we have got to go on developing thus and thinking of the nation as a whole." Here was what the new workers, "cogs" in Guevara's new machine, must achieve by carrying out the "great

14

duties":

> [W]e have got to do exactly the opposite of what we have been used to doing. They had us used to a circle. We could cite the union, if there was a union, and then the neighborhood, the family, and then the individual, one person, who was the most important. Sometimes you could consider your child the most important; generally you considered yourself the most important. We have got to try to consider ourselves, the individuals, the least important, the least important cogs in the machinery, but with the requirement that each cog function well. Most important is the nation. It is the entire people of Cuba, and you have got to be ready to sacrifice any individual benefit for the common good.

Guevara then returned to the specific role of the union and union leader in this totalitarianization process:

> And thus successively, each human grouping is more important than the individual; the whole group of a sector of the working class is more important than a work center's union, and all the workers are more important than one. That is something we have got to understand. We have got to organize ourselves anew to change the old mentality. Change the mentality of the union leader, whose job is not to shout against the boss or set up absurd rules within the order of production, rules that sometimes lead to featherbedding. The worker who today collects his salary without earning it, without doing anything, is really conspiring against the nation and against himself.

The worker, the union, the union leader - each were to flow together, hierarchically, harmoniously, in order to carry out a State-centered development process. Only if this was organized from above, with the consequent surrender of independent organization, personal initiative and freedom of expression, could the eventual goal of industrialization, of "revolutionary development," be met. The glue holding this process together would be a totalitarian ideology that puts concepts like "the nation" and "the people" ahead of individuals and ahead of democratic institutions and decision-making. "Hostile" unions or workers who "have not discovered the real meaning of the problem....should disappear, because our job, the job of industrializing the country, the most important job of present-day Cuba, cannot be done, by any means, with the will of only a few or with the genius of a few, or of one man."

## Sandinista Ideology and the Trade Unions

The basic goal of the FSLN has always been to break Nicaragua out of its mode of economic dependence and backwardness by development from above through authoritarian means. We now can examine the attempt to achieve that goal in direct relation to the Nicaraguan working class and trade union movement. There was no Nicaraguan "Che" Guevara: neither in the sense of an outstanding romantic hero, nor in the more immediate sense of a plain-speaking theoretician of national liberation movement policy able to articulate such a policy for a working class audience. One explanation for the lack of a "Che" as theoretician may be simply that one was been necessary. It could be argued that the Sandinistas needed simply to build upon what Guevara already outlined quite concretely. They did not need to repeat what has already been stated. There is some evidence for this in the various pronouncements in FSLN literature about "building on the great works of Marx, Lenin, Mao and 'Che'."

A more instrumental view would advance a second explanation. Given the sensitive political situation during the period of Sandinista power in Nicaragua, where the private sector and the political opposition maintained a strong presence, the Sandinistas often "pulled their punches" publicly, appearing to soften or actually reversing moves towards strong State-centered development. This was one symptom of the "balancing act" which lay at the heart of the FSLN's relationship with its mass base and the private sector. A third possible explanation was that the social problems the FSLN faced were vastly different than those of Cuba and hence required genuinely different tactics. Thus, one extreme view expressed by Sandinista activists was that Nicaragua did not yet, in the first decade of FSLN rule, have what they called as "well-developed" or "well-defined" a situation as Cuba.[18]  The FSLN did not have complete control of Nicaraguan society in the manner of Castro and the Cuban Communists.  Others suggested this euphemistically:  Cuba was already genuinely socialist while Nicaragua was only on the road to socialism.  I believe this argument is the strongest explanation for the absence of a *publicly articulated* Guevaran trade union policy, but I would add an important corollary.  The lack of genuinely strong and independent trade unions in Nicaragua during the 1980's made direct ideological confrontation with such a movement unnecessary.[19]  Sandinista activists usually only faced disgruntled or apathetic individual workers in their workplace organizing efforts, not standing unions independent of the FSLN.  Hence there was a need to pay attention to problems like the motivation of individual workers and the rationalization of production, rather than the need to confront recalcitrant trade union opponents with a strong independent base.

But in place of an outspoken Guevara, the FSLN had several layers of intellectuals, party cadre and activists who clearly understood, if only implicitly, Guevara's "theory of revolutionary trade unionism."  A survey of their arguments gives us a unique look at neo-Stalinist theory as it faced an ongoing revolutionary process.  At a theoretical level are the writings of revolutionary intellectuals like Orlando Núñez Soto, Director of the Center for the Investigation and Study of Agrarian Reform in Managua.  A longtime FSLN cadre, Núñez's writings on the "class forces" in the Nicaraguan revolution were well known among Sandinistas and influenced a wider debate among national liberation movement theorists throughout Latin America, the United States and Western Europe.  Similarly, Carlos Vilas, an Argentinean who worked with the FSLN for many years, developed an overall perspective on the question of class and revolution.

The work of Núñez and Vilas aimed to understand the overall dynamic of the Sandinista revolution.  In their view, that process has a great deal of relevance to revolution throughout the Third World.  In turn, they hoped that Third World revolutionary movements could impact political and economic developments on a

17

global scale. Like Guevara, they, too, wanted to take on the "age of economic empires" with a form of "revolutionary development." To the field of international politics, such a perspective may seem outdated, simply a hangover from the "days of rage" or Paris, 1968. Because of the growing disillusionment with the state-centered development projects of the Soviet bloc, it may at first seem surprising to find a vigorous and intense debate emerging around such issues in the Third World and among supporters of such political views in the developed industrial world.

But despite widespread opinion in the West, it is clear that "free market" ideology, not to mention the capital investment which must lie behind this ideology, has been far from successful in winning the battle for the "hearts and minds" of the billions who live in the developing world. The capitalist world has yet to show its ability to solve the global problems of hunger, hyperinflation, debt, unemployment or environmental destruction. Though Russian-backed traditional "Stalinism" has largely been eviscerated from the former Soviet bloc, it is clear that a form of "neo-Stalinism" is taking a tentative one step forward in this part of the globe and continues to remain potent in Asia.

Hence, there continues to exist a "market," so to speak, for a cataclysmic, or revolutionary, alternative - one that feeds off of the ongoing crisis of capitalism, in spite of the strength of capitalism relative to traditional Moscow or Beijing style Stalinism. As José Luis Coraggio, an Argentine who worked in Sandinista Nicaragua for many years, and two U.S. social scientists, Richard Fagen and Carmen Diana Deere, argued in an essay during this period, the power of "socialism" in the Third World draws directly from the failings of capitalism:

> The attraction of socialism to many groups and sectors in the third world often does not derive directly from either the theoretical power of Marxism or the organizational successes of revolutionary organizations and parties. *What keeps the socialist vision alive in the context of underdevelopment is the lived history of the failure of capitalism.* The failure of peripheral capitalism to deliver improved standards of living,

social justice, and minimal quality of life to large sectors of the population in the small, peripheral societies gives the socialist vision a dynamic that would not be predicted from a cool analytic look at the successes and failures of actually existing socialisms in the third and second worlds. Poverty, unemployment, rampant class privilege, dictatorship and disregard for basic human rights, foreign penetration and exploitation, are the deep subsoil in which the dynamic toward socialist solutions is cultured and takes root. At a very basic level, millions understand that markets operate to their disadvantage, even though they may not have the conceptual vocabulary to express this clearly.[20]

It is to this deep inherent discontent that the message of neo-Stalinism is driven home:

The socialist promise to replace a flawed and misallocating market rationality with a more rational and just social rationality (through planning, public ownership, etc.) has a large and potentially receptive audience (one might say a *natural* audience) in the periphery. So does the promise of democracy. When nationalist, antiforeign, and "you have nothing to lose but your chains" arguments are added to understandings of this lived reality, the appeal of socialism rooted in self-determination is potentially very powerful indeed. Socialist organizers understand these realities and the potential power of these appeals, just as their enemies fear them.[21]

It is important to see the debate within Sandinista circles about their ideology in this overall context, for it is this context that gives so much fire to these "theoretical" efforts. In fact, it might be argued that the crisis of traditional Stalinism has actually freed the national liberation movement theorists from the excess ideological baggage of a close association with Moscow. It will be our concern here to analyze the overall perspective now emerging and to examine most closely those tenets of that perspective that relate to labor and trade unionism.

At a more concrete level are the speeches of Comandante Victor Tirado López, the FSLN National Directorate member who was in the 1980's responsible for the Party's trade union and labor organization work. Tirado López spent much of his time as a FSLN leader traveling around the country meeting with workers and union leaders in a variety of settings.[22] Finally, there is the FSLN's trade union cadre itself. These were the hundreds, perhaps thousands, of staff members and activists of the major Sandinista unions and party institutions who actually organized and implemented the FSLN program inside unions and the workplace.

A General Theory of Neo-Stalinism

One of the most intriguing documents in this debate is a small book co-authored by Núñez and an American, Roger Burbach. It is called: *Fire in the Americas: Forging a Revolutionary Agenda*.[23] It was first published in Spanish in Nicaragua where it was granted that country's highest Social Science award, the Carlos Fonseca Prize. It was then published in English by Verso Press, an imprint of New Left Books, in its newly begun Haymarket Series, which aims to stimulate political debate within the left about North and Latin America. Núñez we have described above. Burbach is the Director of the Center for the Study of the Americas, a small independent think tank located in Berkeley, California. The book's analysis of a potential road to power for left authoritarian movements has proven to be surprisingly prescient – pointing to the methods to be used by Venezuela's Chavez, Bolivia's Evo Morales and Ecuador's Rafael Correa. In fact, Burbach's Center is now at work on an update of the original text, tentatively titled *The New Fire in the Americas: Popular Challenges to Failing States and a Faltering Empire*. According to the Center's website, the new book's "central thesis is that there is a new rebellion in the Americas, one that provides hope and inspiration in the midst of a world ravished by imperial wars. It is a fire that is burning on many fronts, with differing intensities, one that flares up at unexpected moments in unpredictable locations throughout the hemisphere."[24]

The original text's subtitle sounds rather ambitious, even

presumptuous, but it should be taken quite seriously. This work represents perhaps the clearest statement yet published of what may be called a "General Theory of Neo-Stalinism." In the words of Pablo González Casanova in his introduction to the English language edition: "By systematizing the thought that now runs so deep in the continent, [this book] will help to spread that thought more widely and to draw out implications for emancipatory action."25 The authors lay out the basic conditions and principles they believe should lay behind the road to and control of power by a bureaucratic anti-capitalist movement. In their own words:

> Today the major challenge is to develop a political strategy and a theoretical approach that can bring together the diverse social movements in the Americas, break down their historic isolation, and challenge the dominant order. It is our belief that by drawing on the political experiences of the diverse societies of the Americas, from Chile and Argentina, to Peru, Nicaragua, Mexico, the United States and Canada, the left can collectively begin to develop the theoretical approaches and strategic priorities that will lead our movements into the twenty-first century.26

Their argument has four distinct components. One, their advocacy of a neo-Stalinist revolution emerges in the face of what they see as the dual crisis of Soviet-style traditional Stalinism and Western U.S.-led imperialism. Two, this dual crisis has led to the emergence of a general striving for "democracy," whatever that may mean to its various independent advocates. Three, the disparate movements found around the globe for an authoritarian anti-capitalism need a new set of tactics, an alternative to the Soviet-inspired "dictatorship of the proletariat," now widely regarded as inconsistent with the general striving for "democracy." In its place, the authors posit a system of political alliances drawn from what it sees as the four basic "forces" of a revolutionary movement, under the hegemony of a vanguard party.

Finally, fourth, the authors lay out an integrated structure that should be put in place to firmly establish and manage a neo-Stalinist society. The key elements in this system are: a) a vanguard party; b) a network of mass organizations loyal to the vanguard party; c) a commitment to political "pluralism," allowing both the expression of conflicting views within the mass organizations and the establishment of non-vanguard parties - serving as a political barometer for the vanguard and as a steam valve to let off dissident social pressure; d) a system of participatory democracy as a means of both stimulating and harnessing the social will; and e) a mixed economy where the so-called "commanding heights" of the economy (foreign trade, banking, major industrial plants and agricultural properties) are held in the hands of the state, but private markets and initiative are allowed to stimulate competition and, hence, productivity in other sectors of the economy.

The dual crisis of the United States and the former USSR is not seen as an equal one. In their view, the capitalist West has fallen into a general economic and social decline that severely limits its political appeal. The East, on the other hand, appeared to them (just a few years before the collapse of Stalinism) only to be suffering a crisis of political credibility, caused by a certain narrowness in strategy. "The US empire and the capitalist regimes in much of Latin America and the Caribbean are in crisis, a crisis born of severe economic distortions on a global scale and of the exhaustion of the old political approaches used to contain mass movements," they write. "The resurgence of US militarism in the 1980s - the New Cold War and the 'Reagan Doctrine' - are reflections of this crisis. They are attempts to hold back the tide of social change and democraticization by marshalling the resources of the empire to maintain an *ancien régime*."[27] Or, "Due to the ever deepening fiscal crisis in the United States, the days of the Alliance for Progress - when the United States, could send billions in economic aid to prop up pro-US regimes - are long gone. Also gone are the times when US multinationals and banks rushed to Latin America and the Caribbean with tens of billions of dollars in new investments and loans. Today the United States can offer little economic assistance, only austerity programs and limited bail outs for a few US-proxy governments like Honduras, Jamaica, El Salvador and Costa Rica."[28]

Regarding the socialist world, Burbach and Núñez speak of a "crisis of orthodox Marxist theory."[29] This crisis is linked directly to a critique of "the weak links in the ideological armor of the established socialist societies."[30] These societies "have tended to adopt rigid and non-democratic forms of the 'dictatorship of the proletariat.' In society after society we find the party and the state setting policy with only minimal consultation or participation from the masses." But instead of firmly breaking with this history, the authors justify it as an inevitability: "In most revolutionary countries, even after the imperialist challenge was met, the material needs of society and the drive for economic production led to a continued emphasis on centralization and the growth of a bureaucratic state."

They only distance themselves from the worst aspects of such a system: "All this was compounded when the parties of these societies began to codify and put forth a reductionist or simplistic theory of the dictatorship of the proletariat, i.e. one which justified the concentration of power in the highest levels of the Communist party. This model was then adopted by most of the new revolutionary states in the third world, thereby perpetuating the growth of a deformed socialist state."[31] Even this effort at developing a critique did not prevent the authors from defending these countries as "socialist" nor from noting that this "does not mean that there were not democratic tendencies at work. In some socialist countries a certain positive tension does exist between the democratic aspirations of the mass organizations and the authoritarian tendencies of the party and the state."[32]

One is tempted to point out that claims about the existence of "democratic tendencies" in these societies are somewhat weakened in the face of the massacre at Tiananmen Square or the fall of the Berlin Wall. But such a response would miss the strength of the argument made by Burbach and Núñez. The validity of "*Neo*-Stalinism" lies precisely in its attempt to distance itself from the traditional Soviet-style Stalinist model of both the road to power and the consolidation and management of that power once won. A major step in this process is taken by their critique of Latin America's own Moscow-linked Communist Parties. They write:

> The submission of the Communist parties in the Americas to the policies of the Comintern, reflected a fundamental weakness of Marxism in the Americas - its inability to develop and sustain an indigenous revolutionary strategy. While broad class alliances were certainly necessary at different stages in the 1930s and 1940s, they should have been determined by the needs of the struggle at the local or national level, rather than being dictated for all by the Comintern. The problem was that during the very years when the Communist movement reached its apogee in this hemisphere - the 1920s and 1930s - it failed to produce its own body of Marxist theoreticians capable of developing political programs and strategies suited to the specific political conditions faced by Communists in their respective countries. There were organic intellectuals in the parties who made invaluable contributions, such as Mariátegui in Peru and Julio Antonio Mella in Cuba, but in large part the intellectual work that emerged in the Americas was a mere adaptation of political ideas and strategies developed in Europe."[33]

The distancing process continues with a critical review of the management of power by traditional Stalinism, especially in the Soviet Union, once such power was established:

> A serious problem for revolutionaries today stems from the fact that since the early part of this century Marxism-Leninism has been identified with the evolution of post-revolutionary society in the Soviet Union. The party and state structures that were implanted in the Soviet Union were generally viewed as the model for other revolutionary societies to follow. Given the problems that developed in the Soviet Union - Stalin's domination, and purges of the Soviet Communist party, the program of forced industrialization, the liquidation of the Kulak class - the close identity of Marxism-Leninism with the Soviet experience soon created tremendous ideological and political problems for

revolutionary movements elsewhere. To this day the leaders of the capitalist countries use the Soviet experience to discredit Marxist revolutionary movements.[34]

To broaden the credibility of their effort, the "neo-Stalinists" accept the "new challenge" of democratic reform now said to be offered by U.S. imperialism:

> In this political and ideological battle a major tactic of the United States is the sponsoring of controlled democratic elections and the restructuring of governments to give them a reformist facade. Central America is the showcase for this project: there the United States is directly financing elections, bankrolling its favorite politicians (usually through the CIA), and placing US advisors in key government ministries in an effort to modernize the state bureaucracies....The left must meet this democratic challenge head on if it is to win the larger war against imperialism. Denouncing dictatorial governments and mounting guerrilla movements against them will no longer be sufficient. There will be few easy targets like Batista, Somoza, or Duvalier. In many parts of the third world the struggle will be fought over democracy, over whether the United States and its reformist allies - be they Duarte in El Salvador or Aquino in the Philippines - can contain the democratic aspirations of the masses and prevent revolutionary alternatives from developing. And the left, to meet this new challenge, will have to take up the democratic banner in a way that it has never done before.[35]

In a moment, I will examine the structure that these authors propose be put in place to win the "battle for democracy" while carrying out a "neo-Stalinist" revolution. But this perspective begins first with a new approach to analyzing the social structure of a potentially revolutionary society. It is out of this analysis that the proposal for a new structure will emerge.

Building on the independent work of Núñez, *Fire In the Americas* argues that today's revolutionaries must look beyond the narrow "class struggle" between workers and bosses in the economic arena. "The fundamental forces that drive capitalism today are still the same as those that Marx described in *Das Kapital.* But the social structures of capitalist societies and their state apparatus are significantly more complex than in the nineteenth century. Exploitation in both developed and underdeveloped capitalist societies has now reached the stage where it affects a wide array of social groups ranging from women and ethnic minorities to youth, Christians, the elderly and the middle classes. In the underdeveloped countries, the rural-urban migration combined with the lack of employment opportunities creates an explosion of urban poor."[36]

Beyond the traditional categories of worker and peasant, the authors describe a new "third force" within this new social complex that they believe is central to revolutionary change in the developing world. "To link political strategy and theory, it is necessary to locate the `motor' of the revolutionary process. In the advanced capitalist societies, it is the working class that embodies the basic contradictions between capital and labor. In most underdeveloped countries, however, it has often been the peasantry that constitutes the largest single social force. ... We believe that important transformations have occurred in most societies that make it imperative to expand this system of class alliances. While Marx and Lenin were both aware that other social sectors - especially factions of the petty bourgeoisie - could play a role in the revolutionary process, neither developed a program for their incorporation."[37]

It is this incorporation of "petty bourgeois" sectors as a distinct element in the revolutionary movement that the authors see as critical. "History compels us to broaden revolutionary theory and practice. Diverse political experiences, ranging from the Cuban revolution and the political ferment in the United States in the 1960s, to the May 1968 rebellion in France, and the 1979 Nicaraguan revolution, have made it increasingly clear that the impetus for revolutionary change no longer comes only from Marx's working class or Lenin's worker-peasant alliance. Today a *third* social force comprised of a variety of groups - the middle classes, the intellectuals, the urban poor, the petty bourgeoisie, and the ethnic and social movements - often plays a highly original role in social change. ... The ubiquity of exploitation, combined with new potentials for liberation, have been central in creating a third social force comprised of the middle class intellectuals, progressive Christians, and the social movements (feminists, ethnic and minority movements, gays, etc.). ... [T]hese groups sometimes have a greater potential for sparking a revolutionary process than either the workers or the peasantry. Today they are ripe for a new social vision, a vision that will liberate human nature."[38]

The neo-Stalinists argue that a vanguard party is required to hold these three forces together. It is the vanguard which can provide "direction and guidance",[39] they argue, noting that "focusing on the masses and rejecting the need for a vanguard party" is 'tailist' and 'revisionist.'" Such a position "ignore[s] the reality that the popular classes are almost inevitably influenced, if not dominated, by the values of the established order." A revolutionary movement requires "strong leadership. ... to deal with these mass attitudes. ... with backward ideas in the movement." In addition, a vanguard is necessary to handle "internal social tensions within the movement itself." These latter are all the more likely given the less coherent nature of the third force in comparison with an organized working class or peasantry.[40]

But in recognition of the inherently disparate nature of the third force, they argue for a policy of tactical alliances between various fronts and coalitions, with members of the vanguard fighting to take leadership roles in these movements. They criticize the "authoritarian structures" found in "most socialist countries." Further, they point to the "verticalist and undemocratic" practices of vanguard parties as "weaknesses" which must be "overcome."[41] They suggest that the vanguard party be a "mass front in which the base has a role in deciding the direction and program of the party." They argue for "political pluralism" within the vanguard itself, as well as within the entire revolutionary movement.

But their discussion of these apparently democratic reforms of traditional Stalinist organizational principles is laid out in only the most general terms. There is no discussion of the actual decision making process within such organizations. They note that Marx himself described the direct democratic control that the participants in the Paris Commune had over their leadership - including the right of recall, direct elections and the abolition of state functionaries - but they stop short of suggesting the implementation of such measures in their neo-Stalinist movement.

## The Neo-Stalinist Apparatus of Power

In the exercise of power, there would appear to be very little to distinguish neo-Stalinism from its traditional parent. The strongest tendencies towards terror and repression are often absent, but the basic social structures are the same. A vanguard party is in command, perhaps modified by the neo-Stalinist definition of pluralism: consultation with, not control by, the mass base of the revolutionary movement. Using Nicaragua as an example, Núñez and Burbach note: "Today [1987] the positions of the Sandinista Front on national liberation, anti-imperialism, the mixed economy, political pluralism and non-alignment all reveal a broad ideological orientation. The revolutionary movement is multi-class, multi-ethnic, multi-doctrinal and politically pluralistic. And the party itself is not headed by a single strongman, but by a national directorate comprised of nine individuals who discuss the issues with broad input from the base before reaching agreements by consensus."[42]

The process of "input from the base" was, of course, structured through the network of mass organizations, all open in their *a priori* declaration of loyalty to the vanguard party. Burbach and Núñez note that the Frente Sandinista did not declare a dictatorship of the proletariat upon taking power "as previous revolutions have done"[43] but, instead, broadened the revolution's "democratic content" by forming mass organizations which it then granted voting power on a national Council of State. This move, described above, took place in 1980. It gave the FSLN overwhelming control of this national interim governing body. In essence, it insured that the FSLN's nine person National Directorate ran the country directly, but with its broader, "pluralist" image intact.

In this development it might be argued there exists a shade of difference with traditional Stalinism. The lack of a Red Army to back them up, on the one hand, and the ever present pressure from the "democratic" colossus to the north, on the other, ensured some greater life in the Sandinista mass organizations than might otherwise have been found there. But the experience of other non-Red Army backed Stalinist regimes *outside* of the U.S. orbit indicate that such "life" is also occasionally present without ever placing centralized control in doubt. One thinks of the Yugoslavian self-management system, for example.

In fact, this "life" is essential if these organizations are not to atrophy, withering away and becoming the kind of empty bureaucratic machinery so widespread under traditional Stalinism. The aim in these cases is to overcome the fundamental failure of traditional Stalinism - that totalitarian tendencies mitigate, first, against providing central planners with the basic information they need for decision making and, second, undermine the generation of the motivational energy required by workers and lower level managers for carrying out the plan.

Burbach and Núñez see the system of *participatory democracy* as the key to maintaining vigor in these organizations. In their brief discussion of this system the authors lay bare, however, the totalitarian nature of even so-called democratic structures: "It is essential to recognize that democracy limited to the political party system is not democracy at all. *It must instead permeate to all aspects of civil society.* Democratic practices must prevail in union, cultural and religious organizations (for believers and non-believers alike); in community activities, education and even international relations. The components of consultative and participatory democracy are well known in many socialist societies. They involve the formation and development of distinct mass organizations for the workers, the peasantry, the teachers, youth, women, and so on. Participatory democracy also means that many of these organizations should have substantial responsibilities in the workplace: in the factory, the field, the office, and the school. Social and economic equality can only be achieved if the workers (broadly defined) play a role in running the economic and bureaucratic institutions that affect their lives."[44]   Thus, through the mass organizations the state bureaucracy and the party apparatus can map out their widespread intrusion into all aspects of the lives of their country's population.

Outside of the formal Sandinista orbit, the FSLN also attempted to establish a form of neo-Stalinist "pluralism."   Rather than force opposition parties out of existence, common in some traditional Stalinist societies, these authors argue that the Sandinista experience demonstrates how their existence "provide[d] an escape valve for the more discontented elements, and simultaneously serve[d] as a political barometer for the revolutionary parties to make adjustments in their course if the non-revolutionary parties gain momentum."[45]

It is in this context that the neo-Stalinist profession of support for pluralism and elections must be understood.  Because fundamental control of society is guaranteed by the vanguard's stranglehold on the security apparatus, key economic sectors and organizations, and its ideological dominance, it feels it can *afford* pluralism.  In fact, pluralism can serve as a warning signal in case the vanguard has lost touch with the general population.  After all, Burbach and Núñez write, "the bourgeois democracies, when they feel secure, have allowed the Marxist parties to compete in their elections, and there is no reason why nonrevolutionary parties should be excluded in a vibrant and dynamic socialist society."[46]

Once again turning to Nicaragua as an example, they note that although initially some sectors of the FSLN saw the staging of national elections in 1984 "as a formal procedure that meant little for the development of the revolution" they soon saw tremendous advantages reaped from the process of mass mobilization that followed the onset of the campaign.  "[A]n internal dynamic was set in motion," Burbach and Núñez write, "that compelled the entire Front to take the elections seriously and to expand the country's democratic processes.  The mass organizations of the revolution, and particularly the Committees for the Defense of the Revolution, launched a program of dialogue and internal education that significantly raised popular consciousness around political and economic issues. As a result, the *Frente* won a resounding victory in the midst of a counterrevolutionary war and a deteriorating economy. The elections demonstrated how a revolutionary government can *solidify its hold on power*, not by adopting increasingly dictatorial measures, but by building mass democratic support."[47]

This concludes our examination of the General Theory of Neo-Stalinism. It began with a recognition by its authors of a dual crisis in both the capitalist and Stalinist worlds. The former is suffering from a long-term social and economic decline, while the latter need only recover from certain political deformations. The widespread emergence of a demand for "democracy" is seen as a tremendous opportunity for a revival of "socialism," independent of its dubious heritage in the Eastern bloc. As an alternative to the traditional class struggle between workers and bosses, leading to a narrowly-built dictatorship of the proletariat, the neo-Stalinist analysis finds society divided into three key forces: workers, peasants and the all important third social force made up of disparate elements including the urban poor, intellectuals and those among the petty bourgeois disaffected by capitalism.

A new broad-based program of alliances and coalitions is proposed to pull these three forces together. A vanguard party is required to lead this movement. Out of the mass fronts established on the road to power will grow the mass organizations, loyal to the vanguard, which will, upon the seizure of power, begin to exercise control of society through a system of participatory democracy. Given the secure hold the vanguard has on the state, political pluralism and even parliamentary-style elections are a possibility and may even have a distinct advantage for securing greater hegemony for the new regime. Underpinning this political system is a mixed economy that guarantees that the state controls the key areas of the country's wealth, while allowing limited markets and private ownership to supplement the bureaucratically-managed state enterprises.

## Núñez' Third Force: A Key Proposition of the General Theory

As mentioned above, a central component of the *General Theory of Neo-Stalinism* is the premise that the societies that are potential locales for a neo-Stalinist revolution are not broken into the traditional categories of class conflict. There is neither simply the struggle between worker and boss, nor the tension between landowner and peasantry or rural proletariat. Instead, a new "third force" is considered central to socio-economic organization. The General Theory proposes that this new social class can, indeed must, play a central role in organizing a social revolution. The fundamental purpose of this analysis, developed by Orlando Núñez in a series of papers written soon after the FSLN took power in Nicaragua, is to justify a political strategy that displaces working class control of the revolutionary movement. Instead it suggests that the greater social complexity that today's revolutionaries face in the developing world requires delegating the management of the road to and consolidation of power to a vanguard party.

For Núñez, in fact, direct class struggle is not at the heart of political conflict. The great revolutions of the past, he argues, were between the generalized mass of "people" and the system itself; not between feudal lord and vassals, but between "the total people - liberated by the bourgeoisie" and "the previous feudal tyranny." In the same fashion, revolutionary wars in capitalist societies cannot be expressed simply as an armed struggle between the bourgeoisie and the proletariat without also speaking of the "uprising of the total people (liberated by the proletarian project) against bourgeois and dictatorial domination."[48]

It is "the people" whom the vanguard must organize to seize power. They do so through the establishment of a "proletarian project" but this is not to be confused with the traditional organizations of the working class - trade unions, social democratic, socialist or labor parties, etc. Instead, it is "proletarian ideology" which characterizes the political viewpoint of the vanguard. This must be argued for among the general population. This general mass was perhaps most cogently described by a predecessor to Núñez, Fidel Castro, to whom Núñez defers in his essays on this question:

> When we speak of the people we do not mean the comfortable ones, the conservative elements of the nation who welcome any regime of oppression, any dictatorship, any despotism, prostrating themselves before the master of the moment until they grind their foreheads into the ground. When we speak of struggle, the *people* means the vast unredeemed masses, to whom all make promises and whom all deceive; we mean the people who yearn for a better, more dignified and more just nation; who are moved by ancestral aspirations of justice, for they have suffered injustice and mockery, generation after generation; who long for great and wise changes in all aspects of their life; people, who, to attain these changes, are ready to give even the very last breath of their lives - when they believe in something or someone, especially when they believe in themselves.[49]

Castro, Núñez notes, "goes on to list the sectors of 'the people' which are significant in the struggle: the rural dwellers who barely subsist with no land or work, those who are only seasonally employed, industrial workers whose struggles are continuously betrayed, teachers and professors, small merchants, young professionals, students, artists, journalists, etc."[50]

Núñez gives this general description a more precise definition:

> What was true of Cuba in the 1950's, is true of many imperialized countries today. The third social force is politically significant and plays an important role in the revolutionary process. By third social force, I mean, those sectors that are neither capitalists nor productive wage workers, neither full time peasants nor permanently employed wage earners. In other words, the third social force is constituted primarily by the middle sectors in the towns and cities. Some may be more involved in direct

production, others in providing services. Productive or unproductive, necessary or not, they are the sectors that are created by the process of capitalist development in our countries....The size of the third social force in imperialized countries increases daily with masses of proletarians being created who are *not organically integrated into the centers of productive capital.* They are forced, consequently, to eke out a meager existence on the margins of the sphere of circulation. This is the case in all those imperialized countries where commercial capital and the intermediary state dominate and reproduce capitalism through the creation of an enormous service sector.[51]

I have emphasized Núñez's phrase "not organically integrated into the centers of production" because it describes, in Núñez's view, the fundamental characteristic that the members of the third force share. The third force lacks, he argues, its own means of social expression but has no lack of grievances, hence it makes for rich organizing material for a *new* political movement such as that developed by a vanguard party. Now it is clear why Núñez excludes the traditional classes from this new force. After all, full time industrial workers or the rural proletariat which finds year-round employment or the small landholder may share many of the same grievances as the third force, but they can and do turn more easily to their own organizational forms to raise whatever demands they may wish to express. Workers can form unions and political parties; peasants form cooperatives; rural workers organize land takeovers and unions.

But the members of the third force have no clear political perspective. They are open to a range of struggles that a vanguard party is free to exploit. This is not to say that the vanguard party will ignore the proletariat. But to the extent that it surmises, as was the case in Nicaragua, that the traditional proletariat (defined by them as regularly employed industrial workers) had alternative forms of political and economic organization, the FSLN chose to organize on other fronts. Their earliest recruits came from among students and intellectuals and later from the unemployed. Community or barrio struggles over general social issues (water, electricity, bus service, etc.) were often the locus of these efforts, rather than the shop floor. The moves made in the mid-1970s by one tendency of the Frente to organize workers were weak and of secondary importance to the leading strategy of the movement.

A close reading of Núñez, however, reveals an apparent contradiction. On the one hand, as we have noted here, Núñez argues for a non-proletarian base for the vanguard-led revolution. Yet, at the same time, this vanguard is said to be carrying out "a proletarian project." What is meant by this latter term? Is it consistent with Núñez's argument for a turn to the so-called "third force"?

For Núñez the displacement of the proletariat from a central position in the emergence of a revolutionary situation is paralleled by its displacement from the vanguard party itself. Hence, the party may be made up solely of elements from the "third force." In Núñez's words, "it was not the class background of the combatants that determined the class character of the insurrectionary movement" in Nicaragua.[52] What is important in his view is the "proletarian character" of the revolution's politics. This does not mean simply handing power over to a proletariat, but, rather, the act of creating a genuine proletariat itself - seen by Núñez as the first step to the establishment of a modern industrial nation. What was, prior to the revolution, a tiny minority, should now become the majority - providing the revolution with a key building block for economic modernization.

"Even where the struggle for a transition to socialism starts as one principally against external forces," Núñez wrote, "it requires an internal process of proletarianization, not only of the working class but of society as a whole. Here the concept of proletarianization refers to the very creation of the working class as the historical subject of the revolution and the generation of the economic conditions needed for its development, a process that necessarily begins in the political sphere. I will argue that a proletarian project is indispensable for breaking with capitalism and building an alternative society. The main difference between revolutions in the developed and underdeveloped countries is that in the former, the revolutions can begin under conditions of advanced proletarianization, whereas in the latter the process of proletarianization is still one of the main ideological, political, social, and economic tasks."[53]

This perspective reveals the fundamental *raison d'etre* of the neo-Stalinist movement. It is not to elevate any particular social class to power from which this movement draws its motivation - not even the third force in the form in which it exists during the revolution. The purpose of this kind of revolution is socio-economic development managed from above - force feeding economic development in the manner of Stalin's collectivization drive or Mao's backyard steel mills. The rise to power of a new bureaucratic class emerges from an attempt to develop such a program. Solving the problem of development, in other words, creates the new class - the class does not appear apart from this question (implanted by the KGB, for example), and simply adopt "modernization from above" as its slogan for winning power.

But displacing the proletariat from the road to power does not create a contradiction for Núñez. "Who takes power?" Núñez asks. Here is his answer:

> In the analysis of revolutions the nature of the class that takes power has often been confused. The general belief is that it is the dominated class (i.e., the proletariat) that becomes the new ruling class. But this is a dogmatic view of history. In general, class struggle in all known class systems does not result in the conquering of power by the previously dominated class but rather in the emergence of a third class, which held a secondary position in the previous system. This third class stands out as the class which plays the most revolutionary role after the break with the previous system.

It is "the revolution" which takes state power and "imposes itself on the immediate interests of the dominators and the dominated, and radically transforms them both."[54] In sum, a small vanguard with "proletarian" consciousness can organize in a broad social milieu that can include traditional proletarians but is more likely made up of the disparate elements of the urban poor and disaffected intellectuals - the third force. Out of this organizing pool - a breeding ground for the new class, if you will - grows a movement for state power. It is in the process of taking power, of confronting the development question with a bureaucratic viewpoint, that a new security, administrative and ideological apparatus is built. This becomes the basis of a new social class, a new ruling class, which will, in turn, dramatically reorganize society to cause "the same transformations" which the developed nations of the world underwent during its agricultural and industrial revolutions.[55]

This new class will hold state power and exercise it in a manner analogous to that of the capitalist state. "The state recognizes and develops the interests of a new revolutionary class - its social base - but more importantly it represents the interests of the project as a whole, even if this conflicts with the particular interests of the groups which constitute the revolutionary class it represents. This is how the capitalist state, the most developed of all forms of the state, operates. ... To want to make a political revolution only with the dominated class, or only around the interests of that class, is to lose historical perspective of the struggle."[56] Like the earlier capitalist state, the "proletarian" state will carry out the construction of a new order. "Proletarianization means for us not only the objective process of collectivization," Núñez writes, "but also the spread of socialism to the rest of the population. Proletarianization is analogous to the bourgeoisification that occurred in an earlier era."[57]

Thus, the working class and its independent democratic organizations, such as unions or political parties, are written off the historical stage by the theory of neo-Stalinism. In its place is a new proletariat whipped into place during economic modernization through the various organizational forms described by Núñez with Burbach in the General Theory.

Vilas on Nicaragua: A Special Application of the General Theory

It remains to apply this General Theory to the specific history of the Sandinista Revolution. There is a growing range of scholarship that attempts to analyze the history of the Nicaraguan Revolution from a viewpoint that is more or less sympathetic to what I have called here neo-Stalinist. Most of this work, however, is motivated out of that sympathy, not necessarily out of a conscious advocacy of a neo-Stalinist model. Furthermore this work tends to address specific questions, rather than the overall history of the revolution and the potential theoretical power embodied in that history. However, the Argentinean writer and FSLN advisor Carlos Vilas attempted a general synthesis of this history, using a perspective similar to that of the General Theory of Neo-Stalinism. His argument was first published in 1984 as *Perfiles de la Revolución Sandinista: Liberación nacional y transformaciones sociales en Centroamérica*. It appeared in English in 1986 as *The Sandinista Revolution: National Liberation and Social Transformation in Central America*. I will not review his entire argument here but, instead, pay particular attention to those aspects of it that influence FSLN policy towards the organized working class.

For Vilas a key step in the establishment of power by a national liberation movement is an accurate class analysis of the society to be "liberated." What social classes exist? How can they be organized on the road to power? How can they be managed or reshaped after taking power? He agrees with the argument in the General Theory that the traditional industrial proletariat is tiny in peripheral countries like Nicaragua and that this forced the emergence there of a different approach to revolutionary organization. He is at one with Núñez when he notes that "the Nicaraguan people [are] a complex working mass of artisans, peasants, semi-proletarians, sellers, trades people, people without trades, day workers, students, the poor of the city and the countryside from whose center the proletariat is slowly becoming differentiated; the forge from which emerged the *social subject* of the Sandinista revolution and the popular insurrection."[58]

Together with Núñez he agrees that a revolutionary vanguard

is central to leading this social mass. He refers to Núñez in noting that the vanguard party is like the "the figure of the executor [of a will], who takes care of the inheritance until the inheritor can exercise his rights by himself. The vanguard `will administer' the interests of the proletariat class until the latter, having overcome its ideological backwardness, disorganization, and `mixture' with nonproletarian elements of the labor force, can assume direction of the process." He notes that the same "image is also present in declarations of [FSLN] Comandante Henry Ruíz."[59]

Vilas confirmed that the FSLN avoided organizing within the existing trade union movement where the vanguard would have "had to confront the reticence or opposition to a strategy of revolutionary struggle among trade-union and political leaders of the traditional left and the Social Christian party."[60] As the General Theory would have predicted, the FSLN turned to other locations for recruiting "proletarian" and "third force" elements. "In such conditions of manifest hostility, the approach of the FSLN to the workers, their recruitment into the revolutionary struggle, had to occur more in the barrios - which...appeared as an open camp for Sandinista political work - than in the factories; more in the centers of reproduction than in those of production."[61]

But once in power, the FSLN would emerge with its own trade union policy to make up for the lack of a pre-revolutionary base. Vilas noted that the FSLN not only encouraged unionization, "but also ... a marked change in the conception of what a union is and must be." The implementation of such a view was not without conflict, given the non-FSLN organizations present in the existing unions and the traditional demands of the working class. "This change in the political focus of unionization - *political* in the sense that it is seen from the perspective of constituting a new social order - took place amid intense struggles within the workers' movement and the revolutionary camp, and made up part of the process of consolidation of Sandinista hegemony in this arena." Vilas describes the argument raised by the Frente in their trade union organizing. It is essentially identical to the views of Guevara on "revolutionary trade unionism": In the view of the FSLN, unions are not merely trade-union organizations, but should articulate this activity with the advance of the revolutionary process in all its fronts, and should train the workers in progressively more complex forms of participation. In particular, immediately after the overthrow of the dictatorship, the FSLN demanded of the union movement an active contribution to recovery. To the Frente this implied not only an attentive watch on the business behavior of the bourgeoisie and its administrators, but also a strengthening of *labor discipline* and of the subordination of salary demands to those of reconstruction. This was a blow to the workers' expectations of rapid salary improvements and created a certain initial disorientation.[62]

Vilas argued, "The FSLN generally gives the union the role of transmission belt between the workers and the administration of the enterprise." But he contended that although a tendency to reduce the unions to "a mere state apparatus...exist[ed] in some segments of the state and even of the FSLN; they have been repeatedly denounced by the FSLN National Directorate."[63] Instead, Vilas noted that the active participation of the workers through the unions was considered a central component of raising productivity in the Nicaraguan economy. He described the careful delineation of union and worker activity considered legitimate within the revolutionary process.

Worker participation was encouraged through various committee structures set up at state-run factories and agricultural complexes or through trade union organizing efforts at privately owned facilities. Through worker assemblies and some joint labor-management committees, "the trade union is...assigned a function of *revolutionary vigilance* over the productive process....Worker participation...was fundamentally seen as effective fulfillment of the production goals, political vigilance, and collaboration with state organs in supervising the business conduct of the bourgeoisie and the APP [state property] administrators."[64]

But this structure "did not yet imply incorporating the workers into the elaboration of basic decisions for the enterprises (investments, production goals, organization of the labor process, etc.)"[65] In fact, the key role of these participatory efforts was identical to those laid out by Guevara - raise productivity and impose strict labor discipline. For the FSLN, too, economic productivity was linked to the loyalty of the workers to the revolutionary vanguard. As on FSLN planner noted, "a change in ownership forms is necessary but not sufficient to guarantee more profound transformation of the social economic structure; for that active participation of the workers is necessary in the political, ideological and, of course, economic life of the society."[66]

Hence, the Frente argued that the unions and other mass organizations had the right to a certain level of autonomy, but short of independent actions such as a strike. "The FSLN National Directorate thus outlined the existence of a relative autonomy between the state and the mass organizations," Vilas noted. Vilas cited the comments of Carlos Núñez (no relation to theorist Orlando Núñez), a member of the FLSN National Directorate until his death in 1990, who argued "that the mass organizations, framed within the general line of the revolution, have sufficient right, when these organisms [the offices of state officials] are closed, to recur to internal criticism, to public criticism, to use all means of communication up to mobilization to demand the necessary measures to guarantee that their claims be heard."[67]

Note the limitations imposed: 1) such action had to be "within the general line of the revolution" - that is, the FSLN retained final say; 2) the organizations could go as far as "mobilization," presumably understood as a march or petition, but no adversarial action against the regime, such as a strike or the formation of independent organizations, was permitted; and 3) the FSLN only guarantees that "claims will be heard" not that the organizations could actually make independent decisions.

It came as no surprise to Vilas, therefore, when "toward the end of 1980 the FSLN began to emphasize the necessity of promoting union claims without interrupting the productive process, characterizing stoppages and strikes as a means of last resort."[68] He noted the comments made by FSLN Comandante Tirado López to the First Assembly for Workers' Unity held in Managua on November 15, 1980: "[L]abor conflicts must be resolved without paralyzing production, because it is evident that now strikes not only damage the economy in general, but also the workers in particular. Around these points we must be clear: the salary and right to strike restrictions must be viewed as measures freely, voluntarily, and conscientiously adopted by the workers themselves owing to the situation the country is living through. It is a question of defending the economy by conscientiously assuming the sacrifices and the efforts that this implies."[69] Even the possibility of striking as a last resort was soon proscribed, justly in Vilas' view. At the end of 1981, he noted, the regime calculated that labor stoppages had cost the country $150,000,000 in the first two years of the revolution - equal to 30% of Nicaragua's exports. In Vilas' words, such a move against strikes was "in accord with the necessities and possibilities of the current stage of the revolution."[70]

A key factor in the FSLN's ability to establish hegemony within the labor movement was employment of the vanguard's key dynamic in consolidating its power: the playing off of the proletariat and mass movement against the remaining private sector, and vice versa. This dynamic is one component of the road to power of a neo-Stalinist movement that is not made clear in the General Theory of Burbach and Núñez. As Vilas notes,

This process [of consolidating FSLN hegemony in the workers' movement] was closely tied to the development of the contradictions between the FSLN and the bourgeoisie, whose investment behavior was expected to be a strong impulse to economic revitalization. At the end of December 1979 members of this sector with important posts in the government were replaced in favor of a greater Sandinista cohesion of the revolutionary state. Only the engineer Alfonso Robelo and Mrs. Chamorro temporarily kept their positions in the government and the Frente acted to isolate Robelo from the bourgeoisie and neutralize the pressures coming from Washington. In this strategy, keeping workers' demands within certain limits, strengthening labor discipline, and the like, were essential to avoid excessively alarming the private entrepreneurs. The view of the FSLN toward the worker question seems to have resulted from the relation of forces between the revolution and the bourgeoisie, the limitations imposed by the productive apparatus, and the tensions that arose from the international arena, all framed within a process that defined the worker-peasant alliance as its fundamental base and aimed at profound social transformation.[71]

But this dynamic is a dual-edged sword - useful to contain the mass movement as well as the private sector. "The government ... knows the doubts and inhibitions of the private sector, its internal differences and fears, and takes advantage of them: it combines denunciations, mobilizations, and the actions of the mass organizations with economic incentives, always offering a new opportunity, deferring, for the sake of national unity, the moment of rupture."[72] Hence, Vilas makes an additional contribution to our understanding of neo-Stalinism - describing the social balancing act that the new bureaucratic class undertakes to consolidate its state power.

## Conclusion

With the writings of Carlos Vilas, the discussion of the theoretical and ideological underpinnings of the FSLN's trade union policy is complete. The policy of "Che" Guevara began this discussion. He introduced the concept of "revolutionary development" and the special role that labor unions and their leaders must play in implementing this kind of economic revolution from above. Building on the Cuban and Nicaraguan experience but also from a wider review of third world revolutionary movements, Burbach and Núñez described what I have called here a General Theory of Neo-Stalinism with a concise description of the basic outlook of vanguard parties and the methods they employ to gain and consolidate power. This theory pays particular attention to mass organizations and the system of participatory democracy, in which the pro-revolutionary trade unions play a central role.

Núñez himself provided an analytical framework within which such a revolutionary movement can develop. He replaced traditional class analysis, and with it the traditional centrality of worker-capitalist conflict, with a set of three forces.  These include peasants, workers, and, most importantly, the new third force, made up of disparate elements among the urban poor, intellectuals and those in the petty bourgeoisie estranged from capitalism. Finally, Carlos Vilas examined the Nicaraguan revolution from the same perspective as that outlined by these writers and provided an explanation of important aspects of FSLN trade union policy.  In the process he identified a central dynamic of the exercise of power by neo-Stalinism - the triangular social struggle between the vanguard and its social milieu, made up of both the mass movement and the private sector.

Today, these ideas are alive again in the arguments of Hugo Chavez of Venezuela, in the pronouncements about "market socialism with Chinese characteristics" by the Chinese Communist Party or in the "21st century socialism" of Ecuador's Rafael Correa. Each of these leaders or parties attempts to sustain their legitimacy and thus power by playing off the private sector against the working class.  That triangle of forces remains a critical dynamic in the post cold war global economy.  Thus, the ethereal image of "Che" now spreading around the globe should come as no surprise – he was a key protagonist of such a bureaucratic and authoritarian worldview.  If not a surprise, however, his ubiquitous presence should sound an alarm bell among those who hope for an equitable and democratic alternative to the bureaucratic forms of power, both capitalist and "post-capitalist," that are now taking hold around the world and that are having such a widespread influence on the hearts and minds of millions.

# Chapter Two.

# Killing the Patient: Shock Therapy and Labor in Eastern Europe[1]

The central question facing Eastern Europe and the former Soviet Union today is the tension between economic modernization and the institutionalization of democracy. Can the reform-oriented regimes now in place in much of this part of the world find a way to implement needed economic reforms through democratization or will they be tempted to rely on a new strain of authoritarianism? I should quickly add that a neo-authoritarianism can be found on both sides of the political spectrum. Those who wish to implement "shock" therapy programs, such as Harvard's Jeffrey Sachs, find themselves tempted to authoritarianism every bit as quickly as the old layer of the *nomenklatura*, the heads of the still-extant Stalinist military-industrial complex.

It is difficult to know from the west whether or not this is understood here in the east, or how such an understanding is manifested. It would seem that the waves of strikes and protests throughout the region over the rapidly declining standard of living are genuine evidence that there is concern in the population about an incipient neo-authoritarianism. In what was once Czechoslovakia, it would appear that the divide in approach of each of the two new republics reflects this issue. Slovakians appear to have rejected, or at least stymied, radical market reforms with the outcome of recent elections. The difference in economic structure between the two regions appears to provide a certain logic to this development. The reliance of Slovakia on communist-led heavy industrialization, especially the armaments industry, means that economic restructuring will take an especially heavy toll. Perhaps the dispute over Slovakia's insistence on the construction of the Gabcikovo-Nagymarous hydroelectric power plant on the Danube is symptomatic of this issue. Unemployment is higher in Slovakia and foreign investment lower.[2] The Czech lands are not without problems, of course, as the recent announcement of layoffs of more than 3,000 workers at the Skoda plant indicated. The failure of the state railway company to secure repayment of some 50 million dollars owed to it by the state railway company contributed to the layoffs. Now management is turning to foreign capital markets and investors for a rescue effort. But with that rescue may come a series of restrictions on management and even further workforce reductions.[3]

Similar events could be outlined for both Hungary and Poland. In Hungary, for example, a 1991 loan from the IMF was conditioned on the limitation of the government's budget deficit to 5% of GDP. But shortfalls in tax revenue made reaching this figure impossible and the IMF suspended loan payments. Industrial production was down 20% in 1991 and is expected to fall another 10 to 15% in 1992. Inflation is running at about 20%. A revolving hunger strike helped pressure the government there recently to scale back the impact of economic reforms. Tripartite talks with labor and employer representatives led the Antall government to modify the list of goods affected by a new value added tax and to increases in the minimum wage, pensions, and supplements for families with children 16 years of age or younger.[4] In Poland, the impact of market reforms led to a strike wave culminating in the dismissal of the Olszewski government earlier this year. But the new government soon faced strikes by coal and copper miners and auto and steel workers demanding higher wages and the slowing of economic reforms.

What we might call "Market Authoritarianism" would seem to have had direct and significant social effects. It is possible, as well, that Stalinist remnants have played some role in this unrest – but it is difficult from abroad to discern the role that such elements may be playing. In the west, for example, after the defeat of Nicaragua's neo-Stalinist Sandinista movement, the Sandinista controlled trade unions emerged as lead organizers of opposition to the new Government's efforts to end state controls on the economy. They have effectively exploited genuine concern about economic reforms for their own sectarian organizational ends. A key problem, of course, was that the new government was largely a movement of the middle class and rich. It had little interest in promoting independent democratic institutions among the population, such as economic cooperatives or trade unions, even if it could be shown that these institutions were critical to long term economic growth and stable socio-political development.

Instead, the new regime was far more interested in demonstrating to Washington and the IMF and World Bank that it was willing to rejoin the global economy, on the terms offered by the international marketplace. Hence, although the government could not be called authoritarian in form, its message to the vast majority of Nicaraguan peasants and workers was that they would have little alternative but to buckle down and return to the twelve hour days and six day work weeks common in the dictator Somoza's time. The global market itself, then, has a hidden but genuinely authoritarian effect on such countries and this, in turn, can facilitate the work of socially authoritarian movements like that of the Sandinistas.

If a similar dynamic is underway in this region, is there a way out of its apparent paradoxical impact? Can reform movements come to power supporting democratization and modernization, finally defeating the old Stalinist authoritarianism and, yet, avoid the authoritarianism of the market? Does that market exert such a gravitational pull that a crash program is inevitable? If the crash is inevitable, is the social dislocation that seems to always accompany it also inevitable? Or can the pull of the global market be resisted or shaped differently? Can a deeper democratization take place that allows the new Eastern Europe to move forward in a socially coherent and stable way? Let me suggest that, in fact, only a deep democratization can make such an alternative possible. And, it is this fact that must lie behind any discussion of formal political and legal reform.

Hence, it is almost useless, in my view, to discuss in an abstract way the formal constitutional experience of the West as many legal scholars advocate. It is the social and political history behind the experience that is critical. I think what motivates some of the effort to initiate the more abstract exchanges of information between lawyers and constitutional theorists is that the West and East are engaged in what might be conceived of as a set of protracted negotiations. The East wants to join the world at large, to take part in general global political decision-making, to contribute and benefit from the world market. The question that has yet to be answered is the set of terms upon which the East will rejoin the world. The West is, in essence, presenting a series of demands to the East that must be met prior to your integration with the world at large. These are put to you in a variety of forms, sometimes legal, sometimes economic. The legal form of these demands includes the protection of the right to enter into enforceable contracts, the protection of private property and the establishment of constitutionally backed political institutions.

A succinct summary of this point of view in the Russian context was recently put forward in the *Wall Street Journal*, which argued: "What Russia needs most at this crucial stage of its history is a new constitution that will establish the rule of law and clearly delineate the powers of the president and a new popularly elected Parliament. Only then will Russians and foreign investors have economic rights and sufficient confidence in Russian institutions to begin seriously building a new Russian economy based on the private ownership of land and property and the sanctity of private contracts. A new constitution is the key to ending the political and economic chaos in Russia."[5] What the West, and when I say West I mean it as a metaphor for global capital markets and the economic and political institutions which sustain them, what the West is looking for in constitutional and legal reform in the East is some sort of signal that the East is prepared to integrate on the terms offered by the West.

It seems to me that understanding the period we are in now as a bargaining process is the way to approach the paradox described above. If the newly emerging political leadership of the East sees itself as a middleman between the West and its own population, the role that much of the West hopes it will play, then the paradox between the demands of modernization and democratization will continue to put tremendous pressure on social life here. If, instead, this leadership sees itself as only the voice or agent of the domestic population, a new perspective can emerge. The internal political debate, through institutions that are judged by their transparency and accountability to the population as a whole, can proceed on a different basis. It is only through such genuinely democratic political institutions that the East can clearly voice its own demands at the bargaining table.

By the use of this metaphor, it should also become clear to the population that what the West offers is limited and may have many negative effects on social life. It is instructive to note how quickly calls for a new Marshall Plan for the East have been squelched in the West. It is true that Jeffrey Sachs always appends to his shock therapy programs an appeal for a social safety net and greater aid from the West. But Professor Sachs has no political lobby in the West that can provoke the West to provide such aid. It is possible to imagine, then, a repeat of the old medical joke in a new context: "Yes," the Doctor proclaims, "the operation was a great success. Tragically, however, the patient has not survived!"

The patient in the case of Eastern Europe and the former Soviet Union is society itself. Hence, democratic institutions must not only direct themselves to the demands of the West but to internal demands. That is why I emphasize that the transparency and accountability of these institutions to the general population are the critical yardsticks by which their success should be measured. Quite frankly, I do not think this viewpoint is popular in the West. In financial circles a form of authoritarianism is probably considered a favorable alternative. Hence, President Bush continues to encourage President Yeltsin. Many in the West see only two alternatives to this neo-authoritarianism: either a return to hard-core military and nationalist leaders – the so-called red/brown alliance, or chaos. But in my view, genuine democratic institutions controlled from below by the general population – and these can take various forms – offer an alternative to these drastic choices.

Let me try to reinforce my argument by exploring a recent debate in the United States that I believe has some relevance to Eastern Europe. I raise this example because it demonstrates very vividly the harsh realities of global economic competition that underscore today's political and social developments. The United States, Mexico and Canada recently agreed to establish a North American Free Trade Area. Although the election of the democrat Bill Clinton may slow down the approval process somewhat, the agreement, or NAFTA as it is called in the West, is likely to be put in place sometime next year. The agreement represents a significant defeat for the American trade union movement, a democratic institution once considered a central bulwark of economic and social life in the United States.

NAFTA should be understood as one of the final building blocks of a decade-long process of reintegrating the Mexican economy into the world economy, and, more specifically, into the U.S.-dominated regional economy. The process, now almost complete, represents a model of sorts for what the West would like to see the East be able to do. The process began in the early 1980's with the collapse of Mexico's ability to repay its external debt. Since then, Mexico has taken, or has had forced upon it, a series of steps resulting in greater financial and economic integration with the United States and international institutions. In the upbeat view of the U.S. International Trade Commission: "Mexico's reforms comprise a movement toward a market-oriented, open economy with a disciplined public sector ... These policies allow increasing optimism about Mexico's future."[6]

The primary concern for U.S. business is the growing pressure of worldwide competition from the European community and the Japanese –led East Asian bloc. These regions were built anew in the post World War II era, without the fiscal drag of large military expenditures and with heavily deflated labor costs. They have emerged in the 1980's and 1990's as home to the most productive economies in the world. They have continued to combine a relatively cheaper labor force (shifting to new pools of cheap labor as home country wages rose) with the best technology available, establishing flexible and innovative human resource policies and supplier networks to dominate critical areas of growth. Their success is the ultimate example of the emphasis that Fernando Fajnzylber has so correctly placed on "added intellectual value" in a modern economy.[7] But this should be understood in the widest social sense – including the innovative relationships between the state and industry, the organization of supplier networks, and the just in time and continuous improvements systems of productions.[8]

This is a structure that presents formidable challenges for the American economy. Where American management once found the detailed job descriptions of individual workers in an assembly plant a critical basis of productivity, control and stability, employers now do battle with trade unions which in turn find themselves, somewhat paradoxically, defending the old Taylorist regime.[9] The opportunity to move production into virgin territory, where new relationships can be established on a much lower wage scale and in a less regulated environment is understandably tempting. Employers are anxious to tap into what the Financial Times calls "a rich vein of cheap labour in [the] newly industrializing economies" which is "exert[ing] a gravitational pull on wages in the developed world."[10] Mexico, then, appears as a natural target for U.S. manufacturers. As the Harvard Business Review quipped, "where to find tens of millions of consumers, low-cost workers and a free-market revolution? Right across the Rio Grande."[11]

How did U.S. organized labor respond to the negotiations with Mexico and Canada? They began a battle to hold tenaciously to what little they have left.[12] Though there is very little serious discussion about global developments within labor, every union member knows the telling impact they are having on American life. It is not just a matter of protecting a textile plant here or an auto parts assembly plant there. The globalization of the economy has begun to break down the general fabric of U.S. society. Fewer and fewer Americans are able to be productively integrated into the economy. The most visible signs of this process are seen in the rise of an unproductive service sector, of long-term unemployment, of a steelworkers' union trying to steal members from a union representing supermarket employees, of street people living off of the recycling of aluminum cans.

The less visible reality is also coming to light. A recent Census Bureau study found that the median wealth of the most affluent fifth of all U.S. households rose 14 percent from 1984 to 1988, after adjusting for inflation. But wealth remained unchanged for the remaining four-fifths. The statistics comparing white and non-white Americans are equally disturbing. The median wealth of all households in 1988 was $35,750, but the median for whites was $43,280, while that for blacks was $4,170 and for Hispanics was $5,520.[13]  Robert Reich has pointed to the increasing isolation of that top fifth from the rest of American society. He notes that we now live in a country where there are more private security guards than publicly financed police officers. More and more, the top fifth lives in areas of the country insulated from the world around them – belonging to private health clubs, sending their children to private schools. How far are away is America from the brick walls with glass shards so common in the developing world?[14]

How could democratic institution like labor unions respond adequately to the challenges of the Free Trade debate? A starting point would be to note that there is no such a thing as "free" trade any more than there is a free lunch. In fact, there is now a very intense debate within the business community about how U.S.-Canadian-Mexican economic integration must be "managed" to achieve its full potential. The label "free trade" is little more than a metaphor aimed at limiting the participants in the debate to business interests. This "management" debate takes for granted the need to form elaborate legal and institutional structures to put the agreement into place to regulate its impact once underway. Former United States Trade Representative official Timothy Benett (1991) has outlined twelve different subject areas which must be dealt with in the agreement. Included are discussion of intellectual property rules, changes in Mexico's rules on foreign investment, the cross-border harmonization of product standards and certification, the establishment of a dispute resolution mechanism, and debate about the rules of origin which will ensure that the benefits of cross-border trade are limited to substantial investors in the region.

This "managed trade" position represents what might be called the neutron bomb approach to economic integration. It secures a safe and level playing field for capital, but it ignores the general human and social cost of the agreement. It pays no attention to the unemployed stagnating in the rust belt, it ignores cross-border pollution, and it fails to examine the implications of integrating societies with vastly different standards of living. As an alternative, it could be argued that an agreement must account for the total social cost of the integration process.

Such costs are often labeled "externalities" or "politics" precisely because of the inability of mainstream economic theory to deal with the full impact of economic change and development. But the existence of this wider reality is, in fact, the reason for the establishment in every advanced economy of institutions such as collective bargaining, environmental regulation and minimum standards for labor as well as for products. Only democratic institutions can adequately examine, debate and regulate this integration process. The market alone cannot be relied upon to take account of social and human resources because the horizon of any individual business is inherently narrowed by competitive pressure. Rather than the neutron bomb approach of the so-called free market, the social costs of economic growth and integration should be made central to the debate. Job creation, health care, labor standards, water and air pollution control, migration issues, wages, housing, education, progressive taxation systems and debt relief – these should be the basis of the new global economy.

Some partial efforts in this direction have been made. The AFL-CIO has backed labor and human rights provisions in U.S. trade legislation.[15] These provisions do affect Mexico as well as many of our other trading partners. But these are limited in their impact by broader political conflict and the development needs of the targeted countries. In essence, they raise the cost of development while not necessarily reorganizing economic structures. Another approach is being tried in the Mexican context. A Coalition for Justice in the Maquiladoras, with the backing of the AFL-CIO's Industrial Union Department and church groups, has proposed a Code of Conduct aimed at U.S. firms operating in the already existing export-based free trade zone of northern Mexico.[16] In addition, an attempt to expand the very limited nature of bilateral trade unionism between American and Mexican labor has been made. But only a few meetings have been held at the highest levels of the CTM and the AFL-CIO, with little or no impact on union activity.[17]

Efforts in all three areas – labor rights tied to trade, expanding labor law to cover international investment, and multinational trade unionism – must continue. One of the likely byproducts of any trade negotiation process, even one limited to the current Bush agenda, is that these efforts will be stepped up. International attention to human and labor rights in Mexico can greatly aid the efforts of Mexican workers and their unions.[18] Such pressures will raise the social standards of living in Mexico, while resisting a decline in the living conditions of Americans and Canadians.

One concrete possibility would be to include labor issues as constituent parts of the dispute resolution mechanisms that are integral to trade agreements. American workers, for example, should be able to monitor any plant closings or new investments by American firms. If there is a factual basis for a claim that such investments are aimed not at new markets in Mexico but at taking advantage of cheaper labor costs to re-export to old markets here, then the affected American (and Canadian) workers should be able to bring a charge to a new tri-national social rights agency. Compensation or adjustment spending could be ordered. Or, at the minimum, the agency could order the company to undertake "mandatory" bargaining with the union. This would mean a commitment to negotiate over alternatives to plant closure until an impasse is reached.

Similarly, Mexican workers should have access to this agency to bring claims that foreign investors are refusing to recognize their collective bargaining rights or are not acting as good corporate citizens. The latter concept could cover environmental concerns, plant health and safety issues and taxation. The internal political problems in Mexico point to the need for such an autonomous agency concerned with the social impact of economic integration. This agency could be investor-financed. Those companies that win new markets or higher profits because of integration would be taxed to fund the agency and its essential investigative units.

The advantages of such an agency are many. To modern private investment capital it would provide a policing effort to keep out sweatshop competition. It would mean the establishment of some basic sense of due process and fairness in investment decision-making. It would provide a public forum for argument over the investment process. This would be essential to encouraging Mexican workers to come forward. It would provide an organizing tool for labor movements in all three countries. To bring successful charges forward on behalf of American workers, for example, would require an investigation of investment patterns in Mexico by American unions. This could force American and Mexican workers into greater contact and, eventually, cooperation. It would, at the same time, require a constant assessment of the genuine benefits of the integration process.

I believe this example provides a perspective for Eastern Europe as well. Legal and constitutional forms must be set within the historical context in which they will function. Today that context is one of intense worldwide competition for labor, raw materials and capital investment. Eastern Europe has an opportunity to be "present at the creation" of an alternative approach to economic and social development – where democratic structures can control and regulate what is happening to society's own members. In the words of R.H. MacIver in his forward to Karl Polanyi's classic, *The Great Transformation*:

> Neither a national nor an international system can depend on the automatic regulants [of the market]. Balanced budgets and free enterprise and world commerce and international clearinghouses and currencies maintained at par will not guarantee an international order. Society alone can guarantee it; international society must also be discovered. Here too the *institutional fabric* must maintain and control the economic scheme of things. (Emphasis added)

Only an Eastern Europe willing to set its own terms for the emerging negotiations with the global market will have a chance to contribute in a serious way to the new institutional framework that will, inevitably, emerge in the years ahead.

# Chapter Three.

# Bridging the Divide:  An Alternative Approach to International Labor Rights After the Battle of Seattle[1]

Introduction

      The demonstrations in Seattle against the World Trade Organization ("WTO") in late 1999 tore a major hole in what Gunter Grass recently called the "certificate of infallibility" carried by the global capitalist system since its triumph over Stalinism in the early nineties.[2]  The Seattle protests were followed by similar demonstrations in Davos, Switzerland at meetings of the elite privately-organized World Economic Forum; in Washington, D.C. at the spring 2000 meetings of the International Monetary Fund ("IMF") and World Bank; and in Genoa at the meeting of the G-8. Meanwhile, the summer 2000 trial of French farmers' union activist Jose Bove for his part in the physical destruction of a McDonald's restaurant construction site was greeted by a celebratory rally on its opening day attended by more than fifteen thousand demonstrators in a small town in rural southern France.[3]

      Back in the United States, the protests against the IMF and World Bank were followed by a bitter political battle led by the AFL-CIO, America's central labor body.  The battle targeted the granting of Permanent Normal Trading Relations ("PNTR") by the United States to the People's Republic of China, a crucial step in accession by China to the WTO.  Just as the smoke from this battle cleared, radical consumer activist and trade union supporter Ralph Nader emerged as a candidate for president of the United States as the nominee of the Green Party.  Nader quickly secured the backing of two independent labor unions (the thirty thousand member California Nurses Association and the somewhat larger United Electrical Workers) and the interest of two major affiliates of the AFL-CIO (the United Auto Workers and the International

Brotherhood of Teamsters). Nader had been a major figure in the Seattle events.

These developments are part of an emerging movement against global capitalism or at least against those "globalizing" dimensions of capitalism, with little or no precedent in recent political history.[4] Even the usually staid *Financial Times* paid close attention to these events, noting their resemblance to the early anti-abolitionist movement of the 19th century.[5] At the heart of this new movement is a nascent coalition of forces that includes trade unions, environmental activists, human rights groups, and a range of non-governmental organizations concerned about the impact of international capitalism on developing countries. The movement forced a radical departure from the planned agenda of the governments, multinational corporations, and international institutions assembled in Seattle for what was thought would be the start of a new round of trade negotiations within the new WTO framework. At the center of this alternative agenda has been a push by some for the institutionalization of enforceable labor standards within the evolving WTO administrative apparatus.

In one of the many moments of high drama in Seattle, the evening before his arrival in that city for the WTO meetings, United States President Bill Clinton granted an exclusive interview to the Washington correspondent of the major Seattle newspaper.[6] In that interview, Clinton stated his support for the incorporation of core labor standards into trade agreements tied to potential trade sanctions against violators of the standards.[7] This position was a major step beyond the official position of his administration that had until then supported only the establishment of a WTO Working Group to study the question of labor standards and trade agreements.[8] His comments came at the end of a day of massive civil disobedience actions that had effectively prevented the opening session of the WTO Conference from taking place. Early in the morning that day, some five to ten thousand "direct action" and other demonstrators had physically, though peacefully, blockaded the entrances to the hall where the opening ceremonies had been scheduled to take place. Nearby, the AFL-CIO, joined by trade union representatives from around the world, led a rally and march of some forty thousand workers and students through the streets of Seattle. The confluence of labor and civil disobedience activists made it physically and politically impossible to convene the opening session. The Seattle police, backed by federal agencies and the State of Washington's National Guard, made an initial morning assault on the demonstrators with pepper spray, rubber bullets, and wooden clubs, but they then backed off using nightfall to impose a curfew with a threat to arrest anyone caught on foot in the downtown Seattle area after 7 p.m. Under the circumstances, Clinton's remarks that evening had an electrifying effect, seen by organized labor as an important concession, but by delegates to the WTO as a confusing and frustrating move made for domestic political reasons. At the very least, however, the comments made clear to all observers the significance of labor rights in the ongoing debate over the nature of the new global economy.

Despite the apparent unity of the Seattle demonstrators, however, the question of labor standards and their enforcement is the source of an important divide in the new movement. This divide began to widen in the months after the Seattle events. In the PNTR/China debate, for example, key figures in the Seattle actions broke with the U.S. labor movement over its approach to labor rights issues.[9] In addition, other important activists began to change their approach to the institutionalization of labor rights in the WTO framework. This chapter discusses this emerging divide, attempts to provide an explanation for it, and argues that the original position presented by organized labor in Seattle, while occasionally clouded by the constraints of American labor politics, remains consistent with principles of international law and represents an important contribution to the new movement. Nonetheless, this chapter will suggest that the "international labor rights" ("ILR") strategy of organized labor represents an incomplete response to the emerging stage of global capitalism. The ILR strategy alone will be unable to close the divisions opening up within the emerging movement. Instead, I suggest that the strategy should be broadened to include specific policies aimed at immediately raising the wages, reducing hours and improving the working conditions of workers in developing countries.

Initially, this chapter describes and critiques the emergence of what has become the standard agenda at the heart of the ILR strategy, the narrower set of "core" labor standards built around the efforts of the International Labor Organization and other institutions. Then I explore how these "core" labor standards became the basis of the push by organized labor for the institution of labor rights within the WTO framework. I then examine the divisions that emerged during the Seattle events and after in the debate over China. In conclusion, I argue that the labor movement should break with the "core" consensus behind the ILR strategy and offer an alternative program to workers in the developed and developing world who have expressed growing opposition to the new global economy. It is here that I make the link between immediate improvements in the material conditions of developing country workers and the political problems that are faced within the post-Seattle coalition environment.

## The Current International Labor Rights Framework

### 1. The International Labor Organization ("ILO")

International labor rights have been a secure, if constrained, part of the global state system since the end of World War I. The ILO retains the dubious honor of being the only surviving institution of the League of Nations era that followed World War I. Since that time, the ILO has become an integrated and leading institution within the United Nations system.[10] It relies on a tripartite structure that includes representatives of government, business, and organized labor. Its focus has been on the development of labor standards that become Conventions to be enshrined in the domestic law of ILO members.[11] The juridical impact of this process has been somewhat less salient than its normative effect. A set of so-called "core" labor standards has emerged over decades of research, debate, and both legal and union activism.[12] These standards are now widely recognized to include the right of association (i.e., the right to form and join trade unions), the right to free choice of employment, the right to equal remuneration for work of equal value, and the right to just and

60

favorable conditions of work, including a prohibition against forced labor, discrimination, and the use of child labor.[13]

### 2. The Human Rights Regime

Beyond the ILO, support in international law for labor rights can also be found within the wider human rights regime that is now a recognized part of the global system. For many who are active in efforts to strengthen the international human rights regime, the long and widely recognized experience of the ILO is considered a model to emulate and a base upon which to construct that deeper regime. At an intellectual level, it is widely understood that labor rights must be a constituent part of a society that recognizes human rights. As one analyst has written:

> The basic building blocks of an active and democratic labor movement are the right to organize, the right to bargain collectively, and the right to strike. These rights run parallel to basic political rights found in general social life - the right to assembly, the right to freedom of speech, and the right to petition the government for the redress of grievances.[14]

Thus, no human rights regime is imaginable that does not include basic labor rights; a society that forces its workers to leave their human rights at the door of their employer is not a free and just society.[15] In turn, there is no democratic labor movement that believes that it can fairly represent its members' interests without reliance on basic human rights.[16] Thus, it is no surprise that the major documents of international human rights, such as the Universal Declaration of Human Rights, include references to specific labor rights.[17]

### 3. Regional Trade Initiatives

The emergence of regional inter-state agreements, usually begun as trade agreements, has offered further opportunity to legitimate labor rights within the global system. The most developed of such efforts is, of course, the European Union ("EU") where a fifty-year effort to build a secure place for labor and social protections in the emerging European institutional environment culminated in the 1992 Maastricht Social Chapter that covers a dozen major areas of labor rights. Efforts to place a similar charter into the North America Free Trade Agreement ("NAFTA") between Canada, the United States and Mexico, however, were a near-complete failure.[18] Instead, a so-called "side agreement" to NAFTA included the establishment of a tri-national Commission for Labor Co-operation that monitors a limited range of labor issues.[19] The nature of NAFTA may once again be brought up for public debate in light of the recent election in Mexico of opposition leader Vicente Fox. In the first few days after his election, Fox had already called for reconsideration of NAFTA and the possible development of a European style common market. Despite its current limits, because the provisions stipulated in NAFTA allowed workers organizations in one of the three countries to bring charges on behalf of workers in a second country, a new dynamic was created that allowed some unusual cross-border solidarity efforts to emerge. Thus, among the handful of charges brought since the passage of NAFTA have been those of the International Brotherhood of Teamsters and the United Electrical Workers Union, both American, against Honeywell and General Electric for anti-union efforts in their *maquiladora* plants in northern Mexico. In turn, a Mexican union brought charges against the United States-based operations of Sprint, the long distance telephone company, regarding its treatment of Hispanic workers in its *La Conexion* facility near San Francisco, California.[20] The overall assessment of these efforts, however, is profoundly pessimistic. In the words of one AFL-CIO representative, "We have meetings, we have consultations; but the workers themselves and the redress for their grievances is never really achieved to the point where the workers get something out of this entire process."[21]

The side agreement process may have received a fatal blow in the summer of 2000 when violence erupted at a public seminar on labor rights sponsored by the United States and Mexican Labor Departments held in Tijuana, just across the United States-Mexican border from San Diego, California. The seminar had been organized as a partial remedy on behalf of workers whose rights were violated while attempting to organize an independent union at Han Young, an auto parts supplier to Korean conglomerate Hyundai. The leaders of the union were kicked, beaten, and run out of the Tijuana seminar by supporters of a pro-government union and student group in full view of the representatives of the respective Labor Departments who did nothing to protect the unionists and continued the seminar in their absence.[22]

A series of other United States laws also attempt to link labor rights with the international trade regime. The Caribbean Basin Initiative ("CBI") has been in place since 1983.[23] When considering whether to grant eligible countries duty-free treatment for their exports into the huge United States market, it requires the President of the United States to take into account "the degree to which workers in such country are afforded reasonable workplace conditions and enjoy the right to organize and bargain collectively."[24] The CBI was later amended to make it mandatory for the President to deny a country duty-free status if "such country has not or is not taking steps to afford internationally recognized rights to workers in the country."[25]

A wider application of this approach is found in the United States Generalized System of Preferences ("GSP"). The GSP program sets conditions for the granting of duty-free status for more than three thousand products that are exported to the United States by more than 140 countries.[26] Amendments made to GSP in 1984 prohibit the designation of any country as eligible for GSP benefits if that country is not "taking steps to afford internationally recognized worker rights to its workers (including those in export processing zones)."[27] The recognized international worker rights for both CBI and GSP are nearly identical to the core ILO standards described above: freedom of association; the right to organize and bargain collectively; a prohibition of any form of forced or compulsory labor; the establishment of a minimum age for the employment of children; and acceptable conditions of work with respect to minimum wages, hours of work, and occupational safety and health.[28]

Two other United States initiatives are relevant to the discussion here. In 1988, the United States Congress enacted the

Omnibus Trade Act of 1988 that included a provision that made a multilateral agreement to link worker rights and trade a principal United States negotiating objective in the then current round of GATT multilateral trade negotiations.[29]  Finally, in December 1994, the Congress directed the President in its Implementing Bill for GATT to seek the establishment in GATT and in its successor institution, the WTO, of a working party to:

> (1) explore the linkage between international trade and internationally recognized worker rights ... taking into account differences in the level of development among countries; (2) examine the effects on international trade of the systematic denial of such rights; (3) consider ways to address such effects; and (4) develop methods to co-ordinate the work program of the working party with the International Labor Organization.[30]

These two initiatives explain the statutory basis of the position that the United States took towards the WTO and labor rights in Seattle. Each of these was strongly lobbied for by the American trade union movement and numerous human rights and other non-governmental organizations.  Absent such pressure, given the changing role of collective bargaining and trade unionism in American economic life and the disappearance of the need to push "free" trade unions as an alternative to Communism, it is likely that the official United States position in global trade talks would have been very different.  In addition, the defeat of labor objectives in NAFTA created a deep fissure within the American Democratic Party between its working class base and its New Democrat pro-business wing.[31]  The Clinton Administration needed some way to indicate its support for labor goals, however ineffectual.

### 4. Independent Labor Rights Efforts

In addition to the ILO, the human rights movement, and regional initiatives, a range of other activities to promote international labor standards have gained ground in recent years. These include efforts to obligate multinational companies to adhere to codes of conduct,[32] trade union pressure on the OECD countries to obligate businesses to respect human rights and "contribute" to the elimination of child labor and forced labor,[33] and suits in American courts under the Alien Tort Statute which allows recovery for injuries that are the result of violations of international law.[34] At the January 2000 World Economic Forum in Davos, Switzerland, United Nations Secretary-General Kofi Annan announced a nine-point program to develop a Global Compact among business, labor and government in support of human rights, labor standards, and environmental protection.[35]

Similar efforts are underway at the initiative of labor organizations. In the wake of the Seattle events, the AFL-CIO announced a four point Campaign for Global Fairness that called for an education program among its members on the nature of the new global economy, stronger human rights and labor standards, cross-border organizing to help unions in developing countries, and the adoption of the International Confederation of Free Trade Unions ("ICFTU") Code of Practice by multinational corporations.[36] At the spring, 2000 World Congress of the ICFTU, union leaders from 145 countries passed a unanimous resolution calling for enforceable labor standards in the WTO among a set of measures as part of the launching of an effort to secure fairness in the global economy. Support for the resolution was expressed by trade unionists from Brazil, Malaysia, China, and India. "Guarding workers' rights is not protectionism," stated Amanda Villatoro, Secretary of Politics and Education for the *Organizacion Regional InterAmerican de Trabajadores* in Brazil.[37] "The global economy needs fair rules that protect workers' interests as much as corporate profits. Huge companies constantly call for law to protect intellectual property rights, but are opposed to laws to protect working men and women. That is just wrong."[38]

This effort by the international trade union movement was followed by an attempt to raise similar issues at the meeting of the G-8 in Genoa. Though lost in the haze of tear gas, the Trade Union Advisory Committee ("TUAC") to the Organization of Economic Cooperation and Development ("OECD") presented a statement in conjunction with union representatives from Russia and several developing nations on the question of globalization, debt relief, and labor rights. John Sweeney, President of the AFL-CIO and TUAC, introduced the Global Unions Statement to Italian Prime Minister Silvio Berlusconi. In his opening remarks, Sweeney warned of the "growing crisis of democracy" and of a "global system that remains opaque, remote and unaccountable ... . [A] system increasingly viewed as an illegitimate imposition by powerful private interests that undermines the common good."[39] Calling for reforms he said: "People across the world are calling for a new internationalism, one that protects the common good, not the private interests. One that protects global concerns and holds corporations accountable not one that frees up global corporations and lays waste to the environment."[40] Included in his statement was a call for the promotion of core labor standards.[41]

One of the most promising developments has been the emergence on American university campuses of a movement against sweatshops. These groups have forced dozens of colleges and universities to commit to not marketing products such as college sweatshirts that are made with sweatshop labor. The pressure from students has been so successful that even in the face of the loss of major financial support from multinationals like Nike, universities have been unwilling to back away from commitments to the pro-worker activists.[42] Although each of these efforts may produce modest results on the ground in Third World countries, they are, nonetheless, indicative of the change in the political climate so openly evidenced by the Seattle events. They also indicate the potential outlines of a new broader political perspective on the global economy that could take on greater significance in the near future.

### 5. Constraints

A major stumbling block in the international labor rights framework, however, is the lack of enforceability. In and of themselves, ILO Conventions do not have the force of law.[43] Unless mirrored by Member States in the form of domestic legislation or unless considered to be self-executing, the ILO Conventions do not form the basis of a cause of action in any jurisdiction.[44] The ILO does, however, maintain its own monitoring process which allows both Member States and business or labor organizations to file a complaint or make a representation that a Member State is in violation of a Convention which that State has ratified.[45]  This process can trigger an ILO inquiry that can lead to recommendations or a finding of a violation of the applicable Convention.[46]  The process is a long and complex one, however, with no sanction available, other than moral condemnation, against the violating State.  It is this process that has given rise to the concept of the "Campaign of Shame":  the suggestion that the public scrutiny triggered by an ILO investigation can cause such acute embarrassment to a Member State that it may be forced to comply with the Convention.  As an example, it was with some fanfare in the summer of 2000 that the ILO announced an "unprecedented resolution under the never-before invoked Article 33 of the ILO Constitution" against the dictatorship in Myanmar (Burma).[47]  After years of receiving and investigating complaints of the use of forced labor by the ten-year old military dictatorship in that country, the ILO "called upon Myanmar to 'take concrete action' to implement the recommendations of a 1998 Commission of Inquiry, which found that resort to forced labor in the country was 'widespread and systematic.'"[48]

But what would the Burmese military have to look forward to if it continues its abusive labor practices?  The ILO would review the case at following year's annual International Labor Conference, it would recommend to ILO constituents that they review their relations with Burma and take appropriate measures, etc.[49] And yet:

> This is the first time in the ILO's eighty-one-year history that the Conference has had recourse to measures under Article 33, a procedure that is designed to be invoked only in the event of a country failing to carry out the recommendations of an ILO Commission of Inquiry, which is itself a procedure reserved for grave and persistent violations of international labor standards.[50]

Thus, in the face of this most grave and unprecedented behavior the Member State need only fear yet more reviews, recommendations, and conference talk.[51]   Indeed, a year later the issue was the subject of a Special Sitting at the annual ILO Conference in Geneva, where union representatives pointed out that very little had changed as a result of the Article 33 step.[52]

Nonetheless, this process can, on occasion, lead to substantive change. During the early years of the Sandinista government in Nicaragua, for example, it was ILO pressure, in part, that led to the lifting of restrictions on independent union organization.[53]   Perhaps of greater significance, however, is an understanding of the research and investigative material gathered by the ILO process that underlies its limited legal powers.   This research is substantive, detailed, and objective.   It can be of tremendous value to other actors in situations like Burma. Democracy activists, union organizers, and human rights lawyers can rely on this material for their own forms of intervention.[54]

This is one of the fundamental values of the ILO and one well worth preserving.  The ILO is able to place credible and experienced monitors in conflict-laden environments and produce sober and objective accounts of actual events.[55]  The norms that it applies are the result of years of discussion and analysis by all relevant actors and thus when invoked are rarely subject to attack. This points not only to the ILO's significance as an international body but also to its inherent limitations.  It is not a prosecutorial entity. It has no financial or other incentives at hand to enforce its norms.   But when it acts, its word (and its word is, in the end, its only form of action) has weight, perhaps precisely because of its juridical weakness.

The following comment by Denis MacShane, British Labor MP and former international union official, capture effectively the limitations of the ILO regime:

> But all these instruments that purport to declare international labor rights, and in particular, the ILO group of conventions, cut little ice with employers or unions.  Indeed, they are not known to many workers precisely because they are just that - fine resolutions, helpful benchmarks and useful sources for

moral condemnation. They remain a negation of law because they have no means of enforcement. I have drafted too many complaints to the ILO myself to undervalue the usefulness of having some court to hear labor complaints, nor do I dismiss the cumulative effect on a country's civil servants or leaders of coming under ILO criticism. The arguments of ASEAN (Association of South East Asian Nations) labor ministers for a derogation from ILO standards is an example of how the ILO does stand for something. Anything that is criticized with such passion by anti-labor spokespersons must be useful.[56]

It is this apparent paradox in the ILO process that strengthens the case made by those in favor of using the WTO as a locus for enforcing the core labor standards developed so painstakingly by the ILO and its constituents.

A second major constraint on the existing labor rights regime is in the very notion of a "core" set of labor standards. This core has emerged as an accommodation to the politics of the new global economy. The core standards steer carefully away from promoting substantive improvements in wages, hours, and working conditions. Only the undeniably inhumane practices of forced labor or child labor are sanctioned. However, there is little argument heard for even those minimal standards that are taken for granted within the developed economies of Europe and North America. Thus, there is no active push to add a reduction in working hours or a genuinely adequate minimum wage to the core, though these concepts have been a part of developed country industrial relations for many decades. In fact, many developing countries do have statutes that require a minimum wage and maximum hours. Alas, these are largely paper standards with little or no respect for their actual enforcement. Third world political actors used the alleged pressures of "industrial catch-up" in those regimes to justify the repression of efforts by independent unions to enforce those laws that do exist. Where an argument about the "demands" of national development fails, batons, tear gas, prison, and bullets are not far behind.[57]

In fact, as is contended below, there is a credible argument that the push for significant improvements in wages, hours and working conditions, which can only be done effectively by independent and democratic trade unions, can be a crucial variable in progressive economic development. The separation of the core standards from substantive standards does have a logic that is related to the achievement of substantive gains.[58] It is also consistent with traditional arguments in law about the importance of process as a check on the abuse of power. The compromise that organized labor has been willing to live with in the emerging debate about labor rights in the global economy rests on this distinction. It suggests that a kind of two step evolution can take place, whereby nations can first allow the right to organize and engage in collective bargaining, and then allow those processes to produce the substantive result appropriate for each nation's stage of development. It was on this basis, for example, that one legal scholar criticized the relatively weak side agreements to NAFTA, yet advocated labor's participation in that process.[59] However, it is increasingly clear that this approach does not work. In fact, in the new global economy, generating the confidence and skills for organizing among the unorganized, whether in the Mexican *maquila* zone, or the Export Processing Zones of Asia, or among the huge numbers of low paid and abused workers in the United States who are without union representation, requires substantive argument about material economic and social progress.

## From Berlin to Seattle: The Emergence of the International Labor Rights Strategy

The patchwork structure and normative orientation of existing labor rights provisions led advocates of an international labor rights regime to shift their attention in the 1990's to the newly established WTO. These activists took seriously the comments of the first Director-General of the WTO, Renato Ruggiero, when he suggested that the WTO was "writing the economic constitution of a single global economy."[60] If that were literally true, it was thought, then social protections should be, to borrow the words of one of the architects of the post-World War II global system, "present at the creation."[61] Although there was some nominal support by the

United States for labor rights as part of GATT in the Bush Administration, it was only with the election of Bill Clinton in 1992 that the issue took on genuine salience.

Clinton represented the so-called New Democrat wing of the Democratic Party and, as such, would ordinarily have been expected to move the party away from its traditional base in organized labor. That, in fact, was the overall direction of the Clinton presidency. Clinton won office by campaigning against a Republican Administration that had been unable, despite foreign policy successes, to push the economy forward. A decade or more of debt built up from the efforts of the Reagan Administration to outspend the Soviet bloc in new weapons systems proved to be a serious drag on the economic recovery from the crisis of the late 1970s and early 1980s. Only Wall Street prospered in a binge of leveraged buy-outs and junk bond offerings. Thus, President Bush could take partial credit for overseeing the collapse of the Berlin Wall, but could do nothing about the 1992 Clinton campaign's successful attempt to portray domestic economic problems as, in part, the result of that very same foreign policy. Clinton adviser James Carville famously crowed, "It's the economy, stupid!" and that mantra helped sweep Clinton and Gore into office.[62] Under those circumstances, Clinton understood that he had won office on an appeal to American workers, yet he fully intended to press ahead with support for measures to enhance the global operations of American corporations, even if it meant an open battle with organized labor.[63]

What emerged was a particular sleight of hand. In international forums, Clinton was more than happy to have his Trade Representative or Labor Secretary call for the linkage of labor rights to trade agreements at this or that international conference, but when it mattered these calls amounted to little more than empty promises. The trade deals would get done, with or without labor rights, mostly without, of course. Hence NAFTA and the Uruguay Round of GATT that gave birth to the WTO, each were concluded with only nominal consideration of labor rights concerns. American labor leaders found themselves in an increasingly difficult situation. They had helped elect Clinton - some forty percent of the delegates to the quadrennial convention of the American Democratic Party are labor union representatives. Organized labor was pleased when Clinton nominated Robert Reich, a long-time personal friend and advisor, as his Labor Secretary. However, Reich's efforts to push a moderately pro-worker agenda in the Clinton Administration were quickly killed in the face of the pro-Wall Street advice of the far more powerful economic advisor and later Treasury Secretary, Robert Rubin. Reich was effectively silent during the NAFTA campaign.[64] A continuing decline in union membership hampered the ability of the AFL-CIO to put serious pressure on the Clinton Administration. When Reich left the Administration in 1996, Clinton replaced him with a figure with as many ties to business as to labor, despite the objections of the AFL-CIO and pro-labor congressional representatives.[65]

The end of the Cold War had also meant that the traditional role for labor in United States foreign policy had disappeared overnight. For nearly fifty years, American trade unions had been considered a constituent part of American foreign affairs. The labor movement was seen as a crucial counterweight to the emergence of more radical alternatives in Europe and the developing world. This was, in a sense, a continuation of the original purposes behind the ILO.[66] Thus, the international promotion of the "benefits" of American-style collective bargaining became an accepted norm of United States foreign policy. Labor officers were placed in American embassies around the world, ready and willing to aid non-Communist labor organizations.[67] This effort was very much a mixed bag, with a great deal of evidence that these organizations often served as front groups for covert CIA activity, and much more often providing political cover for moderate groups that would favor pro-American political efforts in the subject country.[68] At home, labor very much felt that it had a "seat at the table" of the major decision-making institutions of the country. The fall of the Berlin Wall signaled the definitive end of this era. In the words of one left-wing critic of American labor:

> With the breakup of the Soviet bloc, and the consequent unraveling of its international labor arm...the U.S. labor institutes [government financed arms of the AFL-CIO that

operate abroad] are facing an evaporating enemy. The concept of promoting "free" (i.e. anticommunist and pro-U.S.) unions is rapidly becoming outdated and irrelevant.[69]

America now unabashedly stood for globalization, portrayed as the inevitable spread of the Anglo-American capitalist model with an emphasis on shareholder value, a market for corporate control, and efficient markets for capital as the centerpieces of economic development.[70] There would appear to be no place in that framework for a vigorous labor movement.[71] In this new era, the Cold War legacy of the AFL-CIO has come back to haunt them. Third world governments adroitly exploit the explicit alliance between American labor and United States foreign policy, even though there is now far more to divide these two forces than to unite them. As the AFL-CIO's international economist Thea Lee stated:

> Why is there so much resistance among the developing countries to this issue [of linking trade and labor rights]? There are some good reasons. The first is that the U.S. Government and the U.S. labor movement have not, in the past decades, covered themselves with glory when it comes to trade *vis-a-vis* our southern partners. I think that the U.S. labor movement ... certainly has a history of virulent anti-Communist interventions in the south, which has not always made us friends.[72]

The AFL-CIO's Secretary-Treasurer Richard Trumka echoes these views: "For too many years, ideology has been the chief export of the AFL-CIO when it comes to international affairs. We've changed that and now the chief export and import of the department [of International Affairs] will be a far more precious and relevant commodity, one called 'international solidarity.'"[73]

It is in this context that the "international labor rights" strategy to link such rights with the trade regime emerged. It has met great resistance from developing nations at the WTO.[74] The initial agreement that established the WTO as the successor to GATT was silent on labor issues. A joint United States-European push for the establishment of a formal Working Party on the issue was successfully rebuffed when the signing ceremony took place in Marrakech, Morocco, in April 1994.[75] This occurred in the face of threats from the United States to refuse to sign the agreement.[76] As noted above, the President was under a statutory mandate to lobby for a Working Party but lobbying pressure continued, despite opposition from the developing world, and American Congressional Republicans and business groups. In December 1996, the first Ministerial Conference of the new WTO took place in Singapore.[77] There, despite aggressive opposition from the ASEAN alliance, including New Zealand and Australia,[78] the final Ministerial Declaration did secure a "Commitment" from WTO members "to the observance of internationally recognized core labor standards."[79] The ILO was recognized as "the competent body to set and deal with these standards." The commitment does "affirm [the Member States] support for its work in promoting them." However, it offers two important "outs": "We reject the use of labor standards for protectionist purposes, and agree that the comparative advantage of countries, particularly low-wage developing countries, must in no way be put into question." Thus, we have a highly contradictory statement that leaves little resolved.[80]

These final "outs" are direct attacks on the effort to achieve a globally recognized international labor rights regime. "Protectionist purposes" are nowhere defined, though they are obviously aimed, in part, at the kinds of efforts undertaken by organized labor to protect their members' jobs. This would seem to contradict the longstanding principle in American labor law that unions must "fairly represent" the interests of their members.[81] In fact, the whole edifice of American collective bargaining is built upon an adversarial argument between labor and management. Thus, no self-respecting union leader in the American garment, auto, or steel industry, much less one who intends to remain a union leader, has any alternative but to "protect" his or her members' interests, arguably in any arena in which those interests are at stake.

Perhaps more significantly for the development of consistent principles in international law, it seems contradictory to attempt to exempt the use of low wages as a "comparative advantage," when it is the very reverse principle that undergirded the founding of the ILO.[82] There is perhaps one saving grace in the Commitment: in theory, the concept of labor rights, other than that related to some kind of global minimum wage, has now been legitimized within one of the world's leading international economic institutions by every Member State. Thus, the arguments of free trade economists against such linkage should be silenced once and for all. All that should be left is the question of the appropriate institutional means of enforcement. In the words of the ICFTU, "the challenge before the international trading community now is to devise procedures to pressure the minority of countries which violate core labor standards to live up to their commitment."[83]

## The "Battle of Seattle" and Beyond

Under these ambiguous legal circumstances, it should not have been a huge surprise that conflict would rein in Seattle. In fact, in the weeks leading up to the planned Ministerial Conference, the press was filled with reports not only of the planned demonstrations but also of the inability of Member States to even fix an agenda for the conference. Of course, none of the participants, including Member States, NGOs or the trade union movement, could have anticipated the unusual events that actually unfolded. Certainly the Member States were quite unprepared to deal with the independent actions launched outside the official meeting rooms, in both the streets but also in a myriad of seminars, conferences, rallies, and debates that turned downtown Seattle into a massive week-long teach-in on the international economy.

Since the breakdown in late 1999, however, it has become clear that among those demonstrators concerned about the labor rights issue were two distinct camps with very different agendas. Each had its own reasons for criticizing the WTO. For the AFL-CIO and its supporters among students and intellectuals, Seattle represented an opportunity to express growing frustration with the pace and structure of the international labor rights regime. Their official call was for the implementation of the well-established United States position in favor of a Working Party on Worker

Rights. They were backed in this effort by the ICFTU, which scheduled its annual Executive Board meeting in Seattle at the same time as the WTO in order to press the case. Thus, the AFL-CIO could legitimately argue that its demands had the backing of labor leaders from more than one hundred countries. Many of these leaders came from developing countries and some appeared as speakers at the huge public rally the AFL-CIO organized on Tuesday, November 30.

The AFL-CIO was also openly angry with the Clinton Administration for its surprise announcement just weeks before Seattle that it had reached agreement with the People's Republic of China on its accession to the WTO. This came as a shock to labor. The AFL-CIO thought that the question of China's entry into the WTO was "off the table" until after the 2000 presidential elections and, as a result, felt relatively confident in its decision to endorse Vice-President Al Gore in his campaign to succeed Clinton.[84] China made clear, however, that labor rights were a "deal breaker" for them. In addition, because the WTO operates by consensus, it was certain that unless the AFL-CIO could defeat China's bid through domestic political action in the United States, the ILR strategy would have reached a dead end.

Many of the thousands of rank and file trade unionists from across North America and the world who paid their own way to Seattle might have thought that among the many other thousands of anti-WTO activists they met *en route* and in the streets, they would find unqualified support in their efforts to secure the core labor standards that had been at the heart of the international system for nearly a century. In fact, the two major forces within the non-labor protest groups were firmly anti-globalization but also either anti-labor rights or quite ambiguous about the labor rights strategy.

The unambiguously anti-ILR protest groups were largely part of the United States-based International Forum on Globalization ("IFG"). The IFG includes a wide array of NGOs from both the developed and developing world, but no representatives from trade unions. The inner workings of the privately run IFG are not known to the outside world, but the positions of many of its affiliates can be readily discerned.[85] One of the most active is the Third World Network ("TWN"), led by Martin Khor, and based in Malaysia, an authoritarian regime where unions face significant constraints in representing their members and organizing unorganized workers.[86] Malaysia, for example, not only has not ratified the ILO Conventions on Forced Labor it has, along with its sister authoritarian state of Singapore, affirmatively denounced them.[87] Both Singapore and Malaysia have come to the defense of the Burmese military dictatorship in international forums. Yet it is from Malaysia, that the TWN publishes its magazine *Third World Resurgence*, in which one can find a kind of glee that the Seattle WTO meetings fell apart, not because of what that meant for the advancement of human rights, but because it meant that the push for labor and environmental protections coming from the "North" had been *defeated*. Thus, Chakravarthi Raghavan writes in a post-Seattle issue of the magazine:

> The Seattle meeting ended in failure when [among other factors] developing nations *refused to be cowed* - by some of the street protests and by the U.S. administration - and said "no" to labor and environmental standards being linked to trade rights and obligations and open to "sanctions."[88] (Italics added; quote marks in original)

Raghavan goes on to suggest, absurdly, that the AFL-CIO rally and march were actually stage managed by the Clinton Administration:

> U.S. media reports indicated that the Clinton White House had given support to a controlled "street protest" by organized labor and some of the "environment" groups in order to "persuade" the conference to accept U.S. "demands" for labor and environment standards at the WTO, but lost control when other movements of civil society staged their own protests, and delegates refused to yield. (Quote marks in original)

In fact, the Clinton statement to the Seattle press in favor of enforceable labor rights apparently took even his senior staff by complete surprise and threw them into great confusion. This kind of politics has led another well-known intellectual in this camp, Walden Bello, to call for an attempt by nations of the "South" to revive the powers of UNCTAD, precisely because UNCTAD can be controlled by Third World governments and is already on record against a linkage between labor standards and trade.[89]

It may not be a major surprise to see a revival of neo-Third Worldism among longstanding advocates of exhausted national liberation strategies like Khor and Bello, but their apparent influence through the IFG on debate in the United States did cause what even these activists will surely come to realize was an "unintended consequence." The AFL-CIO stood almost alone in the effort to prevent the granting of PNTR to China. This was not because of a racist or nationalist prejudice against China or Chinese citizens, though in the heat of debate, there were mild echoes of this viewpoint among a small minority in organized labor. Rather American labor had no illusions about the Clinton-Gore globalization strategy and the crucial role that China plays in that strategy. That was why they had fought so hard earlier in 1999 to prevent an accession agreement with China. The AFL-CIO understood that the surest route to an established labor rights regime in the WTO was to win that regime prior to China's accession and then condition China's accession on acceptance of that regime. However, instead of joining in this campaign, several key American-based NGOs moved in a different direction, towards the neo-Third Worldism of the IFG, Khor, and Bello.

A key defector, for example, was the Global Trade Watch group affiliated with the Ralph Nader-founded organization, Public Citizen. Its well-known leader is trade activist and lawyer, Lori Wallach. Wallach had been a crucial player in previous campaigns to defeat the Multilateral Agreement on Investments and United States Presidential "fast track" authority that vests significant power in the executive branch of the government on trade legislation. But soon after Seattle, Wallach began a campaign to win support for a statement on the WTO that made an explicit commitment to pursue labor rights protection *outside* of the WTO. An open letter, "'WTO - Shrink or Sink!' The Turn Around Agenda," was placed on the Public Citizen website with a call for signatories.[90]   Among those to sign?   Third World Network from Malaysia.   Publicly, Global Trade Watch opposed PNTR, and Joan Claybrook, the head of its parent entity, Public Citizen, spoke at an AFL-CIO rally on Capitol Hill.   But nowhere was there to be seen the kind of vigorous campaign that had earned Wallach a cover photo in the very establishment journal *Foreign Policy* immediately after the Seattle events.[91]

The approach of Public Citizen and Global Trade Watch soon became the norm in the NGO milieu during the China debate.   The San Francisco-based Global Exchange, for example, a key force in the organization of the civil disobedience actions in Seattle, debated entering the anti-PNTR campaign internally and then decided against it.   However, they, too, made a facial effort to oppose PNTR on their website.   When their cofounder Kevin Danaher was asked why they had not entered the campaign, he stated that he was opposed to the very existence of the WTO and therefore did not want to oppose or support the membership of a particular state.[92] He could not explain, however, how he expected to dismantle the WTO unless he entered such campaigns.   Finally, as one more example, the left-leaning Institute for Policy Studies in Washington, D.C. issued a highly qualified statement in opposition to PNTR, noting that the communist regime in China deserved credit for its many social and economic achievements over the past several decades that are now under attack by the WTO and globalization.[93] The statement did not mention the massacre of democracy activists on Tiananmen Square in 1989 nor the strike wave among Chinese workers that has taken place in recent months.[94]

## Conclusion: Moving Beyond the Core

Despite a fierce effort by the American labor movement, the campaign against PNTR for China went down to defeat.   Had they won, however, the WTO would have been under significant pressure to take a sizeable step towards the creation of an enforceable labor rights regime.   What many of the NGO and pro-Third World activists did not appear to understand was that had the AFL-CIO succeeded, labor rights would have been taken out of the hand of an individual state, the United States, and placed firmly within the hands of a multilateral organization. Thus, if the developing world governments and their sympathizers like Bello and Khor wish to throw the charge of "protectionism" at the labor movement, they must explain how such an institutional arrangement would be consistent with that charge. Certainly they could argue that given the "consensus" nature of decision-making at the WTO the large powers would still be in a position to dominate implementation of such a regime. However, the labor movement is itself sympathetic to calls to reform the decision-making process and make that process more democratic, transparent and publicly accountable.

The labor movement has often had to go it alone in battles for basic civil liberties. If that is now the case in the battle for an international labor rights regime which, alone, can give workers in the developing *and* developed countries the weapons they need to establish genuinely democratic and equitable societies, it will mean that labor must itself acquire an understanding of the new economic and political forces that have done so much damage to its members over the last twenty years.[95] A crucial misstep, in my view, in the PNTR debate was to not meet the argument made by proponents in the Clinton Administration and their allies in business, and softly echoed by some NGOs, that China's entry into the WTO would help its democratic evolution and economic development. That would require the articulation of an alternative argument about economic development and a discussion about the internal dynamic of Chinese politics.[96] The raw material for such a discussion existed. There is a nascent independent labor movement underway in China.

Perhaps just as importantly, there is a serious economic argument to be made about the relationship between labor rights and progressive economic change in the developing world. In the literature of the neo-Third Worldists one often finds only a parroting of the arguments made by the Lee Kuan Yews and Mahathirs of the world that developing countries cannot afford labor rights. These analysts seem to think that becoming an export platform for the already developed North is a viable economic strategy. They do not seem to have explored very carefully the crucial role that a battle for increased wages and an eight-hour day played in pushing development *forward* in both Europe and North America. By capturing a larger piece of the economic pie, organized labor not only pushed capital to improve productivity, but higher wage rates and the creation of leisure time enabled the creation of a mass market. One may quarrel with the qualitative value of this achievement from a variety of standpoints, but its power in undermining the neo-Third Worldist strategy of moving forward by taking industrial work out of the American rust belt or the decaying North of England or the German Ruhr Valley and shifting it to the sweatshop zones of Asia seems straightforward.

In fact, it is often argued in trade debates that "free trade" is essential to prevent the return of the so-called "beggar-thy-neighbor" policies that led to the Great Depression. Of course, the validity of that historical reference is highly questionable.[97] However, it is important to realize that the global economic program that lies behind today's "free trade" drive is very much built on a similar dynamic:

> Developing countries that wish to improve working and living conditions are the most vulnerable to being undercut in world markets by countries whose governments suppress workers rights. Often the victims are young and unorganized female workers in export processing zones that advertise the absence of trade union rights as incentives to investors. Universal adherence to core labor standards would prevent extreme forms of cut-throat competition and exploitation....[98]

This is how the ICFTU put the case in advance of the Seattle meetings and the subsequent granting of PNTR to China. The race to the top by developing country elites is to be accomplished by pushing their workers and peasants to the bottom. As against the draconian and authoritarian forms of state-imposed development underway in east Asia and China, a labor rights-based approach that places significant improvements in wages, hours, and working conditions front and center as part of a global development plan would find a ready and wide audience among Asian workers generally. It would also have helped undermine the "siren song" of "constructive engagement" played here in the United States by Clinton and Gore, so effectively, it seems, that even many of labor's erstwhile allies in Seattle fell for it.

Given the deeply divided opinions among the major actors, the potential for success with the current ILR strategy is terribly limited. A shift in political direction to the central question of economic development - income - opens up the possibility of a strong link between the concerns of workers in the advanced economies and those in the developing economies. If conditioned upon significant debt relief and the imposition of controls on capital mobility, a demand for substantial improvement in the material well being of developing country workers could break through the political logjam built up by developing country elites and their allies in the international institutions and advanced economies. Concrete proposals for a living wage and reasonable hours and working conditions point to the potential in globalization for equity and stability, rather than the vast inequalities in wealth and opportunity that persist and grow larger every day.[99]

Such an approach is consistent with the actual impact of WTO policy today. The WTO is not, and has never really been, just a trade body.[100] Its policies directly affect economic development. A "wages, hours and working conditions" program should be part of a campaign to reorganize the WTO as a "World Trade and Development Organization." Within such a body the ILR strategy could be used on the ground by labor organizations and the legal system to push for and then enforce wages and working conditions sufficient to provide a reasonable standard of living for workers in developing and developed countries alike. Enforceable monetary and criminal sanctions against both governments and corporations should result from violations of these new norms. The Seattle events and those that have occurred since put the *means* - respect for labor rights enforced by the world's key economic body - for progressive change in the global economy on the table. However, the proponents of such a view must also make the *end* - a better life for the world's billions - just as clear if the potential of Seattle is to become reality.

# Chapter Four.

# The "Race to the Bottom" Returns: China's Challenge to the International Labor Movement[1]

Introduction

In the early morning of March 3, 2003, two young women, Yao Dan and Xiao Yu, were sitting in a Beijing hotel room when 20 officers of the Chinese Public Security Bureau burst in and detained them. Their crime? They were in Beijing to attempt to meet with the defense lawyer representing Xiao Yu's father, Xiao Yunliang. Xiao Yunliang had been tried several weeks earlier along with Yao Dan's father, Yao Fuxin, for allegedly "subverting the political power of the [Chinese] state." Both men were arrested in connection with their participation in a labor protest that had occurred a year earlier in the industrial town of Liaoyang in northeast China.[2] But that was not the reason given to the women for their detention, according to the independent and widely respected *China Labour Bulletin* of Hong Kong.[3] They were told, absurdly, that the hotel they were staying in was "too shabby," and that they would be taken to another hotel and allowed to meet with Xiao's lawyer. Instead they were taken to yet another location in the city where they were held while their possessions were searched. They were then driven back to Liaoyang in a police van accompanied by eight police officers, held separately in a government office and questioned for several hours. Before their release, the police requested they sign a doctored transcript of the interrogation including a statement that the purpose of their visit to Beijing had been "to talk to foreign news media." Three months later the Intermediate People's Court of Liaoyang Municipality duly announced that the fathers of both women had been convicted of their "crime" and sentenced Yao to seven years, and Xiao to four years, in prison with an additional two-year period for each in which their "political rights" are to be suspended.[4]

As it turned out, the women were probably mostly guilty of bad timing. Their visit to Beijing happened to come just before the opening of the Chinese National People's Congress and the National People's Political Consultative Conference, which were both engaged in sensitive discussions and negotiations about the transfer of power to a new generation of Chinese leaders.[5] But why would that cause the police to be so concerned about the attempt of these women to meet with the lawyer representing one of their fathers? Was Beijing attempting to send a signal about the right of counsel in the new China? No. It appears far more likely that this event signals the fear and sense of fragility that grips the Chinese leadership. The fathers of these two women had been active in one of the most important worker protests among many thousands of such protests that have swept through China in the last few years. When originally arrested the two men were threatened with the death penalty. Only an international campaign of solidarity and further protest by fellow workers succeeded in getting the Chinese regime to reduce the sentence. The convictions of these worker activists for engaging in what much of the rest of the world would consider mild social protest, together with the harassment of their families for attempting to engage legal counsel, highlight the true state of labor relations and of the law in modern China.

Unfortunately this is no longer a phenomenon that can be viewed from a distance. China is now, and increasingly, an integral player in the global economy and in international relations. The detention and harassment of Yao Dan and Xiao Yu indicate what is at stake: economic and political restructuring in China today is affecting the lives of millions, yet only a small number of top bureaucrats and wealthy regime-backed entrepreneurs are making the basic decisions about the outcome of this process. This bureaucratic and entrepreneurial class resists fiercely any serious attempt to build independent and democratic institutions such as trade unions. If this means exposing the regime as hypocritical about its commitment to the rule of law in China, they seem willing to take the political heat. The globalization process that has done so much to integrate the Chinese economy into the world economy has only encouraged the regime. Japanese, Korean, Taiwanese, European and American corporations are fighting tooth and nail to take advantage of the changes underway in China. They see China as offering the world a vast pool of relatively cheap labor that comes not a moment too soon as declining profitability has hit returns to investors in the advanced economies. According to official government statistics, China's urban population has more than quadrupled since the early 1950s, whereas its rural population has only increased from 503 to 866 million.[6] This massive population shift is contributing to a significant unemployment problem. And that, in turn, is the cause of widespread social unrest. The Chinese Communist regime views this unrest as subversive of their entrenched power. Thus, rather than being concerned that the violation of universally recognized civil liberties such as the right of access to legal counsel and the freedom of association is the source of increased tension with the outside world, the regime views these violations as the solution to a significant problem facing the global economy. The international labor movement has struggled for more than a century to establish basic human rights, including labor rights, as an inviolable floor beneath which the world could not sink. Unless the labor movement and the world community as a whole confronts China directly with an alternative path of economic and political development, the integration of China into the global economy puts that century-long achievement at great risk.

The emerging Chinese model - a "socialist market economy" according to the regime itself - represents a new stage in the evolution of post Cold War global capitalism. The core principle of this model is the so-called "race to the bottom" where global multinational corporations ally with repressive developing country governments to combine high productivity manufacturing and services with cheap labor at the expense of unionized workers in developed economies. Free market advocates typically attempt to reduce the idea of a "race to the bottom" in global labor conditions to a caricature. If there really were a race to the bottom, they ask, then why are there so few multinationals operating in central Africa or countries like Haiti, where wages are indeed the lowest in the world? It is certainly true that capital is reluctant to invest in countries like Haiti or Rwanda, though such countries have long been the source of vital natural resources and agricultural products for global multinationals. It is also true that an examination of cross-border trade and investment flows demonstrates that the vast majority of such flows are between developed economies, not between the developed and developing world.[7]

But that misstates the problem. The "race to the bottom" defines a different and new issue: the ability of sophisticated multinational corporate capital to combine high-productivity technology with labor that is paid substantially less than that found in the developed world. Developing this dynamic is not as simple as finding the worst paid and most repressed workers in the world. What one finds, in fact, in countries like Haiti or Rwanda are not workers in the classic sense who are ready and available to be part of the disciplined structure of a modern capitalist firm. In large part the populations of those countries are at a near-feudal level of development, with the "workforce" resembling displaced peasants, not modern workers. The difference in China or Mexico or Indonesia is that decades of rule there by modernizing authoritarian states has produced a new kind of workforce that is akin in skill level and discipline to that found in Europe or the United States, but available at an artificially low wage level far below that of the advanced economies and without the independent political power that characterizes countries with strong labor movements.

The "race to the bottom" is, in fact, what Harley Shaiken calls "high productivity poverty."[8] This "isn't the poverty of Haiti or Bangladesh," Shaiken argues, "where industry is antiquated and the societies and people are poor.... The problem isn't developing countries attracting advanced manufacturing, but rather that wages aren't simply low; they are artificially depressed. The law or the club - or both - are used to prevent workers from sharing the gains.... The historic link between workers producing more and earning more is tragically reversed - workers produce more and earn less."[9] Financial analyst Richard Duncan confirms this trend:

Almost any labor-intensive product that can be made in the United States, Western Europe or Japan can be made at considerably less cost in China or a dozen other low-wage nations. Impediments once thrown up by transportation problems or capital shortages have long since been overcome by technological developments and the removal of capital controls. Today, the most capital-intensive manufacturing processes can be financed and built in any number of developing countries, so that the most advanced facilities can be combined with the lowest-cost labor.[10]

This break in the link between productivity and wages is the key to understanding the phenomenon known widely as the "race to the bottom." The creation of that link was the result of decades of effort by the international trade union movement. In the late 1920s and 1930s it led economists to speak of a new development: wage rigidity. This was the reflection in economic theory of the power of trade unions in a business downturn. It caused John Maynard Keynes to conclude that the normal process of wages falling to a market-clearing price, often referred to as "Say's Law" as Keynes understood it, no longer functioned.[11]

But today China's entrance into the world economy represents the attempted integration of nearly a billion new workers into the global labor market at wages far below those found in the advanced economies. This signals the return of a world that operates according to Say's Law because the constraints on free markets, such as "wage rigidity" and the union power reflected in an effective international labor rights regime, may dissolve. As one leading Wall Street economist told his clients:

China's labor force is bigger than that in all of the OECD countries combined. Its rapid development has caused dramatic shifts in relative factor prices in a short period of time. Some of the changes will be permanent even with China's maturity. The most important one is that the value of labor will be permanently devalued against scarce resources. This is likely to have far-reaching consequences to the distribution of income in the world. The speed comes from the fact that the labor productivity gap between China and the mature economies is far less than the wealth gap between them.... China's reintegration into the global economy, therefore, presents a major discontinuity. The gaps between China and developed economies for productivity and for wealth are expressing themselves through rapid capital reallocation from mature economies to China and the consequent rapid growth of China's exports. The key driver is China's low wages resulting from its vast surplus labor and low level of wealth.[12]

Far from being an anomaly, then, the arrest and conviction of Chinese labor activists, the harassment of their families for attempting to meet with legal counsel, and the violent suppression of democratic institutions such as free trade unions and independent political parties, represent a stark, if not dark, future for the global system. In fact, the effort to move the world in this direction has been given significant support by attempts to change the basic structure and purpose of central international institutions such as the International Labor Organization ("ILO") and the World Trade Organization ("WTO").

Such a conclusion runs counter to the arguments made about the nature of political and economic reform in China today. For the most part, supporters of the Chinese restructuring process argue that the market reforms underway there today will naturally create an opening for political pluralism and, eventually, a genuine rule of law and democratization.[13] This viewpoint is reflected inside the international labor movement itself by those who argue that the trade union movement should begin a process of "constructive engagement" with the government-controlled All-China Federation of Trade Unions ("ACFTU").[14] The view held by some westerners that China will evolve towards democracy simply because it undertakes market reforms and the subset of this view held by some within the western labor movement that China's state-controlled labor organization, the ACFTU, will begin to, or already does, behave like a genuine trade union and thus helps reinforce the alleged evolution towards democracy, is viewed as naive by longtime specialists in Chinese politics and labor issues.[15] Such views may, in fact, reflect changing attitudes towards democracy and labor rights in the West as much as they do a genuine assessment of the current situation in China.

This chapter takes its lead from the actions of the Chinese regime itself. The regime's fear that the mere presence of two young women in Beijing trying to meet with a lawyer representing their labor activist fathers suggests that there are two major issues of concern to the Chinese regime: law and labor. Thus, at the level of law, the focus will be on the changes that have taken place in the WTO and the ILO that are reinforcing the emerging Chinese model. China entered the WTO after a bitter political battle between the American trade union movement, on the one hand, and nearly the entire U.S. political and business establishment, on the other. But this could only be accomplished by the codification of a certain new approach to international labor rights in both the WTO and the ILO. This chapter will argue that this new approach has actually created a legal pathology that only postpones resolution of the real problems associated with the Chinese model. It is an unstable compromise that conflicts with other principles at work in the international legal environment.[16]

These international legal developments are being met domestically within China by an attempt to impose a new regime on the Chinese working class. This new regime relies on the same heavy-handed authoritarian measures that have long been constituent elements of modern Chinese politics. In the past the Chinese Communists justified such measures by the alleged need to resist the encroachment of capitalism, while now the Party defends the same authoritarian approach as necessary to succeed in the capitalist world. These developments feed each other. As accommodations are made to undemocratic approaches to human rights in international institutions, those elements in countries like China that see a shortcut to wealth and power through authoritarianism are encouraged to continue to suppress democratic movements. In addition, there is an unhealthy feedback into the advanced economies as the "race to the bottom" undermines the ability of those economies to provide better wages, hours and working conditions in industries that compete with

Chinese authoritarianism. Thus, the international labor movement may have the most to lose among an array of democratic institutions. Even commentators reluctant to embrace the idea of a "race to the bottom" in the global market pause when they consider the overwhelming impact of China.[17] An example from just one industrial sector - textile, clothing and footwear - illustrates the problem. While throughout the 1990s the number of people working in this industry remained stable at 30 million, Cynthia Williams has noted, "there has been a dramatic shift in the distribution of those jobs towards Asia," with that region now accounting for 72 percent of world employment in the sector and China alone 20 percent. Meanwhile, employment in Europe and the United States in that sector "fell steadily throughout 1990-1998." Williams refers to an ILO study that notes that the average hourly wage rate in the industry ranges from a high of $10 an hour in Europe to a low of $0.45 an hour in China.[18]

But if labor loses so does democracy. The trade union is a central force for democratization, transparency and social responsibility in a modern industrial economy. Without the ability to form effective trade unions, workers cannot be said to enjoy fundamental human rights such as the freedom of association or the freedom of speech or the right to have grievances heard and redressed. Without an effective labor movement there is no counterweight to the power of business interests or volatile market forces in society or to the state itself. The power of the market to force new forms of brutal competition can easily take hold, generating deep political conflict and social unrest. Equally possible is the emergence of a Leviathan state that suppresses human freedom. In fact, as this chapter should demonstrate, this is precisely why exploring the process of economic reform in China is so important. The economic changes underway there are creating huge new inequities and imbalances. This is now leaking into the international arena as China's cheap labor export-led model of growth has generated a massive trade imbalance between China and the United States. As the presidential elections approach this is becoming an increasingly important problem in domestic U.S. politics. Thus, this chapter will argue, there is a need to articulate an alternative model that restores the role of democratic institutions as a counterweight to Say's "law of markets."

To explore these issues, this chapter will consider four areas of concern. First, the structural changes underway in the Chinese economy are creating both domestic and international imbalances that exacerbate inequalities among Chinese workers and create new inequities in the global labor market. Second, the Chinese regime's approach to labor rights remains rigidly authoritarian and, as a result, it is triggering ever more dramatic confrontations between workers and the Chinese state, despite the regime's nominal commitment to "socialism." Third, these developments are being reinforced by a pathological evolution in the principles that govern key international institutions such as the WTO and the ILO. A conflict has emerged within the international legal arena between the founding principles of these institutions and their current approach to labor and human rights issues. Fourth, within the international labor movement itself a small current is emerging which views an accommodation with the Chinese regime as a feasible alternative to the long-standing support of the international labor movement for independent and free trade unionism in China. This approach threatens the credibility of the labor movement's opposition to the most damaging aspects of the globalization process, a major commitment of organized labor at least since the "Battle of Seattle" that took place at the failed ministerial conference of the WTO in November 1999.[19]

These four developments militate in favor of the need to reassert core principles of labor solidarity but these must not just be mindlessly repeated. These developments signal a new form of global capitalism that increasingly sees authoritarianism as having a natural role in a modern economy. The unquestioned acceptance of the outcomes of the "law of markets," no matter how volatile, uneven, or unjust, now appears to be the norm as social movements and democratic institutions are rendered a nearly mute Greek chorus. Thus critics must take into account the new forms of capitalism and the power of its norms as it devises alternatives. Restoring the validity of questioning outcomes and thus of the value of social input and control of those outcomes must lie at the heart of these alternatives. This means that support, for example, for labor rights in China must go beyond the typical anti-Stalinist rhetoric that labor has used in the past. While the Chinese regime may fear the emergence of a Polish Solidarity-style movement, the labor movement must also learn from the mistakes and limits of the Solidarity experience.

## China's Economy at a Turning Point

It is hard to overstate the magnitude of the changes underway in China today. While still only accounting for 5 percent of global manufactured exports in 2002, according to Morgan Stanley chief economist Stephen Roach, China nonetheless accounted for 29 percent of that year's growth in that sector.[20] This remarkable development is the result of twenty years of economic policy change in China. In the early 1980's, the regime partially freed up prices in the agricultural sector and allowed farmers to retain a portion of their profits. This, in turn, unleashed pent-up demand for consumer goods, and so the regime went one step further, endorsing the new light industry and consumer goods businesses that began to emerge in the rural townships and villages. What one observer called an "extraordinarily virtuous economic circle" emerged whereby higher prices for food stimulated demand for basic consumer products like bicycles, televisions, and refrigerators and, increasingly, for light industrial goods such as tractors.[21] This process sustained growth rates averaging 9 percent for most of the 1980s.[22] Non-farm employment tripled from thirty million to ninety-three million people in that decade alone, with some sixteen million new rural businesses established.[23]

These new entities are seen by western Sinophiles as evidence of the emergence of a new private entrepreneurial class in China allowing the country, in the words of mainstream economist Barry Naughton, to "grow out of the Plan."[24] But many of these new firms were formed with local state and party official endorsement and participation. They have become a new competing power center in Chinese society, absorbing scarce financial resources. They are also the source of huge new income inequalities. Although the country has indeed registered huge gains in national income during the last twenty years, the gains have not been equally reflected in the personal income of ordinary Chinese households. In an articulate and thorough study entitled *Inequality and Poverty in China*, economists Azizur Khan and Carl Riskin take careful aim at the impact of market reforms and find the results disturbing.[25] Communist Party reformer Deng Xiaoping had declared "let some get rich first" and the lucky few have done so with a vengeance. Khan and Riskin note, "between 1988 and 1995 inequality in the distribution of income in China increased sharply [as] China [became] one of the more unequal of the Asian developing countries." Thus, despite the impressive macro-level gains of the 1980s, as the 1990s unfolded there was, this study concluded, "an unusually rapid widening of income inequality ... a much retarded rate of poverty reduction in the countryside ... and a significant increase in absolute poverty in the towns and cities." In rural China, the Township and Village Enterprises ("TVE's") have actually worsened income inequality as the enterprises offer higher wages but to only a small portion of the newly available workforce of former peasants, who are mostly forced to survive at or below the poverty line on whatever their backyard plots of land can produce.

Nonetheless, despite its apparent growth, the new so-called private sector does not have anywhere near the resources to meet the huge industrial needs of Chinese society. The single largest fully private entity in China has annual revenues of $600 million, half the sales of the very last company on the Fortune 1000 list.[26] Even today the private sector contributes only one-eighth of the nation's gross domestic product and employs less than twenty million workers in a nation of 1.2 billion people. In any case, the apparent economic miracle began to slow precipitously after the initial boost in the 1980's. In the early 1990's, it was discovered that the TVE's "had overstated production by more than 40 percent" wiping out $100 billion from the country's national income accounts.[27] Much of the actual gain in GNP has been created by the regime's continued reliance on heavy capital investment, thus only exacerbating inequality and poverty. Khan and Riskin identify what is called "investment hunger," especially among local governments that are now less constrained by Beijing as the early stages of the reform process loosened the grip of national power.[28] "The state allowed an expansion of credit to pump up accumulation and drive a wedge between growth of GDP and that of personal income."[29]

Despite the pace of reform, China's state-owned enterprises, or SOE's, still control the "commanding heights" of the economy in industries like steel, oil, and automobile assembly. In contrast to the still-tiny private sector, China's two state-owned oil companies together have revenues of more than $80 billion and are comfortably placed on Fortune magazine's Asia's Top 50 list.[30] In the state sector, one finds that instead of the massive privatization that took place in the former Soviet Union with such disastrous effect, the regime has tried only partial privatizations, while continuing to feed these enterprises massive amounts of credit, recycling the savings of China's billion people into outdated and poor-performing industrial behemoths. China, in fact, actually seems committed more than ever to state control of key economic sectors.[31]

Many of these enterprises are truly out of a different age - the age of Soviet-influenced heavy industry or the American variant, the massive auto complex at Ford's River Rouge. These plants were, like their Soviet, American or Eastern European counterparts, impressive achievements - fifty years ago. But in the context of industry today, they are bankrupt. The regime thus finds itself in a trap of its own making. Having created this heavy industrial base, it has also created a massive industrial working class - or rather its new post-revolution working class created this massive industrial base, subject to the most brutal forms of forced labor in the 1950's and 1960's.[32] But to restructure now in a fashion that would allow these companies to be globally competitive would require huge layoffs and huge new capital investment. In the spring of 2000, for example, the regime restructured its large state oil industry and attempted an initial public offering ("IPO") of shares in the newly formed PetroChina to global investors, including a listing on the New York Stock Exchange. To make the PetroChina IPO even barely credible to global capital markets required the layoff of hundreds of thousands and a promise to push billions in debt back to the state through PetroChina's parent company, China National Petroleum (CNPC), which remained entirely in state hands.[33]

The only way that the regime believes it can preserve its own power in this process is to "muddle through," in the words of economics writer and China specialist Joe Studwell.[34]   Thus, the regime allows foreign companies to set up assembly plants in the special economic zones in coastal areas and, in the niches not already occupied by the state sector, encourages a limited domestic private sector to evolve from below.   But it cannot allow the resulting inequalities and poverty this process causes to become so extreme that workers revolt.   The regime fears a social explosion, called by the Chinese *da luan* or "total chaos," a fear made real by the labor insurgency that took place in the spring of 2002 in the oilfields run by PetroChina and in the industrial zone of Liaoyang.[35] The pall of Hungary in 1956, Czechoslovakia in 1968 and Poland in 1980 continue to hang over the Chinese Communists.

Meanwhile, the regime continues feeding enough credit to the SOE's to keep them alive; conditioning the credit on hoped-for restructuring, but not so much credit that inflation is unleashed. Inflation has been a continuing concern, causing the regime to punctuate the growth of the last two decades with binges of harsh austerity.   What many in the West view as a struggle between hard and soft-liners, or between a "Maoist" left and a "market socialist" right, is really a reflection of managing a business cycle with "Chinese characteristics." This is a risky business for the regime. The price controls of the late 1980's certainly tamed an inflation rate that reached 50 percent in 1988, but that austerity was considered a key factor in triggering the 1989 social revolt centered in Beijing's Tiananmen Square.[36] The protests received widespread popular support with marches of a million workers or more in several major cities.   The regime could only kill the movement by relying on the brutal efficiency of crack troops from the People's Liberation Army.   After that event controlling wages was much less of a problem for several years.[37]

Thus, "muddling through" may not be sufficient.   The credit that sustains the growth process must come from somewhere.   The free trade zones on the Chinese coast are fed by foreign direct investment. But the SOE's and the domestic private sector rely on the recycling of the huge savings of ordinary Chinese people. Since the banking system is state-owned and, in theory, the renminbi is not convertible into foreign currencies, Chinese workers, peasants and small businesses are forced to finance the continued capital accumulation drive of the Communist regime. The whole game depends on the regime's continuing top-down control of that financial system. Thus, promises of convertibility of the currency as early as 1993 are now put off well into the future.[38]

Of course, if the renminbi were freely tradable on the world markets and if ordinary Chinese savers could freely hold their savings in foreign banks or invest them in the equities of European or American companies as their counterparts do in the West and much of Asia, there would most likely be a massive "run on the bank" as the value of Chinese assets would be forced to come into line with global values. The pressure on domestic values is so great that Studwell argues that even without convertibility or an opening of the financial sector a bank run is still a possibility: "everything comes down to psychology... the psychology of the ordinary Chinese people," he notes.[39] From this vantage point, events like the 1989 Tiananmen revolt take on new meaning. China may be in the grips of an investment bubble that, once it bursts, will cause a social and economic crisis that dwarfs that which afflicted most of Asia in the late 1990's. In the case of China, the "hot money" that sparked the Asian financial crisis is actually represented by the domestic savings of ordinary Chinese, fueled by the bulging domestic reserves linked to Chinese exports. A "flood of credit [in the 1990's] allowed an over-investment binge that caused the ratio of private investment to personal consumption to peak at 83 percent in 1993 and to remain above 70 percent thereafter."[40] The regime's credibility, and therefore its power, depends on maintaining the credibility of its economic policy. It is not just that the regime fears a Solidarity-like protest movement rising up in reaction to political repression or unemployment; it also fears a tearing away of the veil that covers up the country's financial fragility. This could, in turn, cause the population to lose their faith in the regime and, in turn, trigger a massive political upheaval.

What are the escape routes for the regime? A massive debt-for-equity swap is one. Since the debt the state has accumulated using domestic savings must eventually be repaid and in the meantime the state must pay interest, the debt can get very expensive. The state-owned banks now hold massive amounts in non-performing loans made to the SOE's and the TVE's. On top of that, the government has huge under-funded pension liabilities. When these massive liabilities are added together, Studwell estimates a debt-to-equity ratio of nearly 500 percent for the state sector - outstripping even South Korea on the verge of its economic collapse in 1997.[41] So by creating stock markets, the regime has tried to encourage Chinese savers to invest instead in equity issued by these same state companies. The regime even dreams of large mutual funds rescuing them from the pension trap they face, hoping they can convince Chinese workers to trade the "iron" rice bowl guarantees of an earlier era for the volatile world of publicly traded equities. But equity holders expect capital gains over time and hope that inside managers will pay out regular dividends, and neither is legally mandated. And in China, senior corporate insiders, for the most part still members of the ruling Communist Party, have the additional advantage that they need not fear the disciplinary effect of a potential takeover by competitors or financial players since there is, as of yet, no competitive market for corporate control in China.[42] This shift to equity finance explains the stock market mania that hit China in the 1990s. The regime engaged, it appears, in a massive "pump and dump" scheme touting share ownership in companies that by any stretch of the imagination were actually worthless. In the first half of 1992 the Shanghai stock market index registered an unsustainable gain of 1200 percent.[43]

A second strategy has been to turn to foreign stock markets, first in Hong Kong, but more recently to the London and New York Stock Exchanges. There Chinese companies have been notably less successful. The pump-and-dump has not fooled quite as many investors. Where Chinese companies trade their stock both at home and on the Hong Kong exchange, the shares sold in Hong Kong trade at a substantial discount, as much as 85 percent, giving the outside world some idea of the discount factor that one might have to apply to the entire Chinese economy if its assets were freely tradable.[44] Finally, the regime has encouraged the establishment of foreign investment in the so-called Special Economic Zones. But even the explosive growth of the Zones makes a relatively small dent in this massive country. More importantly, their potential future growth is limited. Most of these plants are only final assembly points in a global assembly line so that the value added by Chinese workers is a small percentage of top-line revenue. The sector shipped $ 150 billion worth of goods in 2000, but less than 25 percent of that was value added in the free trade areas in China.[45] The state sector cannot compete yet in quality and reliability with the foreign suppliers that feed parts into the assembly plants. In addition, the companies are heavily dependent on the infrastructure provided by coastal proximity to Hong Kong and Taiwan. Interestingly, as Khan and Riskin note, despite what free trade theory might predict, the industrialization in this and the TVE sectors "so far ... has been quite employment-hostile" with increases in employment declining "drastically" even as output spurted ahead.[46]

The social and political effects of this process are equally striking. As a result of this reform process there are estimates that as many as 20 million people a year are leaving the rural areas of China for the cities in search of work.[47] To put this in perspective, a single year's inflow of new urban workers in China is equivalent to the entire manufacturing employment base of the United States. In fact, because of the recent downturn in the U.S. economy some 2 million jobs have been lost and manufacturing employment in the U.S. has now dropped to a twenty-year low of 16 million jobs. This has now made the U.S.-China trade balance a politically sensitive issue inside the United States.[48] China's trade surplus with the United States is now the world's largest, reaching $ 83 billion in 2001, while the balance with Mexico was in surplus only to the tune of $ 30 billion.[49] Even Japan, America's most feared competitor in the 1980s, had a surplus of only $ 69 billion that year.[50] This has led to pressure by the U.S. government on China to revalue its currency, currently pegged to the dollar at a rate of roughly 8 to 1, thus making U.S. exports relatively more expensive.[51] Meanwhile, as discussed below, domestically China is experiencing an unprecedented wave of worker unrest. Thus, the reform process is creating internal and external imbalances that are increasingly the stimulus for domestic social conflict and global tension.


## Chinese Trade Unionism

A central feature of China's approach to economic policy is to maintain tight control over its workforce even as it opens up the economy. Thus the country's policy towards trade unionism is crucial to understanding the relationship of China to the world economy today. As is widely accepted in political theory and history, trade unions provide a counterweight to the power of government and business interests in a modern industrial society. The aggressive spread of neo-liberal policies through globalization has undermined the ability of unions to play this role in the post-Cold War world. But the need for trade unions has only increased. The political impact of trade unions is widely recognized. The effort to organize a union requires certain political liberties, such as free speech, the right of assembly and the right to have grievances redressed. These broader political liberties run parallel to core labor standards like the right to join the union of one's own choice and the rights to organize, to bargain, and, if necessary, to strike. A country with a strong union movement is also likely, therefore, to be a country with a vibrant democracy and respect for the rule of law.

These rights are still largely absent in China and this is reflected in the status of the labor movement there. The ACFTU is simply a creature of the Chinese state and the Communist Party. It is obligated by its own rules and law to act as a transmission belt for party and state policy. As labor unrest has spread across China in the last few years, the ACFTU has sat on the sidelines, emerging on occasion only to condemn these rank-and-file efforts to secure jobs, pensions and other basic economic benefits. In the wake of the mass protests in the spring of 2002 by workers in the metal industry of Liaoyang that led to the imprisonment of Xiao Yunliang and Yao Fuxin,[52] the ACFTU publicly condemned the two worker leaders at the annual conference of the ILO in Geneva for "illegally demonstrating" and charging them with having "burned cars and destroying public property" although the latter charge was never brought forward in court.[53]   Later, in a reply to the ILO's own investigation of the Liaoyang events, the Chinese government accused the leaders of "terrorism and sabotage,"[54] though these charges also were never brought against the activists in the eventual court case discussed above.[55]   During the same time period workers in the oil industry in Daqing in northern China organized demonstrations against cuts in severance benefits.  Their actions were condemned as "unacceptable and illegal" by the ACFTU.[56]   This is a pattern that is all too familiar to students of societies in transition from Stalinism to modern capitalism.  There is little hope that China will avoid this pattern.  And thus the international labor movement has generally given its support to efforts to form genuine, independent unions in China as part of the support for the development of the rule of law and respect for human rights.[57]

Independent trade unions are outlawed in China.[58]   The ACFTU maintains what the International Confederation of Free Trade Unions ("ICFTU"), the leading global labor umbrella organization, calls a "trade union monopoly."[59]  The right to strike does not exist.[60]   An effort to establish a Workers Autonomous Federation (WAF) as part of the wider Democracy Movement of 1989 was met with particularly harsh repression.  Many affiliates of that Federation are still in prison or labor camps.   Amnesty International details numerous ongoing abuses of workers for their organizing and other activity.[61]   Arrests and arbitrary detentions were made throughout 1999 as labor unrest increased due to the worsening economic situation.  Here are some of the examples they report:

> Li Qingxi, a laid-off worker from the Datong coalmine in Shanxi province, was arrested in January when he posted publicly a statement calling for independent trade unions. He was sentenced in March without charge or trial to one year of "re-education through labor," reportedly to be served "at home." Zhang Shanuang, a labor rights activist from Hunan province, was detained in July after trying to set up a

group to help laid-off workers. He was sentenced in December to 10 years' imprisonment, accused of having "illegally provided information to overseas hostile organizations and individuals," reportedly for speaking about farmers' protests in his province in a Radio Free Asia interview.[62]

The widely respected China Labour Bulletin, based in Hong Kong, confirms that the process of "economic restructuring has led to huge pressures on the Chinese labour market ... many workers laid off from SOE's have expressed dissatisfaction with the long working hours, short-term contracts and miserly benefits that more than not await them in the private sector."[63] Linked to this dissatisfaction is a rise in labor disputes, despite the frightening risk that such voicing of grievances to official bodies entails. Even the state-controlled Labor Disputes and Arbitration Committees reported a 58 percent increase in cases heard in the first six months of 1999. Of course, the vast majority of such disputes are reported only as "solved" with few details available on the facts. There are serious procedural obstacles to bringing such disputes to the dispute resolution bodies, so it is unknown how many on the job grievances go unreported.[64] In fact, the worst fears of critics of the PetroChina IPO and restructuring process came true in the spring of 2002 when massive demonstrations by laid-off workers took place in the Daqing oilfields owned by CNPC and PetroChina.[65] These were soon followed by large protests by unemployed workers in several parts of China, including an unusual demonstration by workers in Beijing itself. Arrests of protest leaders such as the fathers of Yao Dan and Xiao Yu were paired with modest economic concessions by the regime thus ending this particular wave of unrest.[66] However, one sociologist calls these demonstrations evidence of a "labor insurgency" underway in China.[67]

All of China's industrial workers are members of the only "trade union" body allowed to exist - the ACFTU. The ACFTU is a constituent body of the Chinese State and thus is controlled by Communist Party cadre. As in the former Soviet Union and its Eastern European satellites, this is a "trade union" in name only. It is, in fact, in the Chinese regime's own words, "a mass organization of the working class" and it serves as a transmission belt for the party and state leadership. The Communist Party appoints all of its officials. As the ACFTU itself stated in 1990: "the administration of union cadres by the Party is an unchangeable principle. The ACFTU should work together with the Organization Department of the Central Committee of the Chinese Communist Party in laying down regulations concerning cadre management and in monitoring the nomination, investigation, election, approval and allocation of union leaders." The same document goes on to state that:

> [T]rade unions must resolutely oppose any organization or individual expressing political views countering those of the Party ... On discovering the formation of workers' organizations which oppose the Four Cardinal Principles[68] and endanger the national regime, the trade union must immediately report to same-level party committees and senior-level unions, and must resolutely expose and dissolve them. When necessary, the union should demand the dissolution of such organizations by the government in accordance with the law. Concerning organizations initiated by workers out of their specific economic interests, the union should advise them to dissolve and terminate their activities through persuasion and counseling.[69]

Thus, the ACFTU serves as the "eyes and ears" of the state inside every workplace. Far from supporting democratic and free trade unionism, the ACFTU's central purpose is to carry out State and Party directives and to do everything it can to insure that all workers fall into line as well.

It is no surprise to find out, therefore, that the ACFTU is viewed by the state as a vehicle for encouraging worker support for the very economic reform process that is devastating the social conditions of tens of millions of workers. Dan Gallin, then General Secretary of the International Union of Food, Agricultural, Hotel, Restaurant, Catering, Tobacco and Allied Workers Associations ("IUF"), noted after a mission to Hong Kong in December, 1997, that earlier that month at a meeting of the Executive Committee of the All-China Federation of Trade Unions Hu Jintao (then a senior member of the Chinese Communist Party and now President of China) urged trade union leaders to "arouse workers' enthusiasm about reforms in [the state-owned enterprises], especially about turning losses into profits and to complete the tasks set forth during the recent 15th party congress." Hu Jintao added that trade unions should "encourage workers to contribute to the development of new products and technological improvements," that they should provide more job opportunities and professional training for laid-off workers, and encourage them to change their old ideas and find new jobs themselves."[70] Those who do not conform to the new economic order are subject to ACFTU "mobilizations." The Chinese political police (Public Security Bureau or "PSB") have issued "guidelines" that state that "the unions must ... co-ordinate with the PSB, organize 'public order and prevention teams' to protect the internal security and order of the enterprises, as well as social order. Staff and workers should be mobilized to struggle against all forms of criminal and illegal behavior. The union must also assist the relevant authorities to deal adequately with the education and employment of dismissed employees, workers who have committed errors and those have completed sentences and been released."[71] This kind of directive can only be characterized as chilling.

Far from encouraging progressive change, as China has integrated itself into the world economy, its approach to trade unions has remained rigidly closed. A 2001 revision to the Trade Union Law, last revised in 1992, only confirmed this. A new version of Article 4 of the Law, for example, confirms the obligation of the ACFTU to: "... take economic construction as the centre, adhere to the socialist road, uphold the people's democratic dictatorship, abide by the leadership of the Chinese Communist Party, adhere to Marxism-Leninism Mao Zedong Thought and Deng Xiaoping Theory."[72] The Law also mandates that the ACFTU role in the face of a strike is to "... assist the enterprise or institution in making proper preparations for resuming work and restoring work order as soon as possible."[73] The China Labour Bulletin concludes that such provisions:

> Reaffirm ... the ACFTU's subordinate relationship to both the government and the party at three levels: the union must

abide by the Party's guiding principles; the union must subordinate its organization to the Party machinery; and the union must perform the function of carrying out the wishes of the Party in its intervention in labour disputes at local or enterprise level.[74]

In addition to the dramatic human rights picture and the suppression of basic trade union freedoms, the general situation of workers presents additional problems. Unemployment and forced migration have already been mentioned. Other problems include the widespread use of underemployment, short-term work, and contract labor, the continued control of labor mobility by the state and massive violations of basic health and safety precautions. Official statistics report nearly seven million unemployed urban workers, but the China Labour Bulletin estimates that the total is closer to 21 million.[75] And even official statistics admit to 30 million "more than needed" workers in the urban areas. These are now supplemented by some 80 to 100 million "floating people" who have left their villages looking for work in other areas of the country.[76]

Despite the need for a massive shift in employment to new entities, the state fears that uncontrolled mobility could open the door to organized opposition to the regime. Thus, it has largely kept in place a decades-old system of labor registration - the hukou system.[77] Under hukou every Chinese citizen is required to "have a registration with the hukou authority or hukou police at birth." In theory no Chinese may work or live outside of the area where they were registered at birth. To accommodate some economic pressures, the regime has instituted a system for providing workers with temporary residence permits. Punishment of both employers and employees is meted out if workers are hired without a permit.[78]

Nonetheless, in the face of the officially backed repression of genuine trade unionism, workers have consistently attempted to organize independent movements throughout the history of post-1949 Communist China.[79] Far from passively accepting the ideological claim of the regime to be a "workers' state," Chinese workers have defied the mythology of the regime in successive waves of unrest. Interestingly, in the first few years of Communist rule the newly established ACFTU was independent and militant - somewhat like the trade unions in the first few years of Castro's rule. But as in Cuba the state soon stepped in and deposed the independent ACFTU leaders, turning the organization into a party-run transmission belt organization after the classic Stalinist model. Worker restiveness did not take long to reemerge, however, with a strike wave in 1956-57 that was apparently directly influenced by the Hungarian uprising of that same year. Repression followed but so did periodic worker unrest, particularly during the Cultural Revolution and in the wake of the death of Chou En Lai in the 1970's. In each case, the state cracked down. In the early 1980's the Democracy Wall movement emerged and included specific references to Poland's Solidarity. Sociologist Ching Kwan Lee notes, "the ascendance of the Polish Solidarity Movement emboldened Chinese workers ... to take action."[80]

As economic reform under Deng gathered steam, worker unrest resurfaced. The spring 1989 movement led to the most important period of independent worker organizing in recent years. The activists of the newly established Beijing WAF, which sparked numerous WAF's all over the country, initially met with some hostility from the student demonstrators, who restricted the workers' presence in Tiananmen to a corner of the square.[81] The China Labour Bulletin describes what happened:

> As the numbers of students directly participating in the Democracy Movement slowly began to dwindle, the WAFs became stronger. Links between WAFs all over China were being forged and some activists traveled to Beijing for discussions. Correspondingly the position of the ACFTU hardened towards the WAFs and on June 2, 1989 the official Workers Daily called for the banning of the WAFs as illegal organisations. The call was perhaps premature. Two days later government troops fought their way into the Square and made straight for the BWAF tents. In the repression that followed, thousands of workers suspected of taking part in WAF organisations were rounded up and shot or sent to prison.[82]

According to Ching Kwan Lee, "in May and June 1989, workers in Beijing, Shanghai and other cities left the confines of factory gates and their collective action took the forms of public protests, independent unionism and political mobilization."[83] She notes that workers detained in the 1989 crackdown "received the heaviest [prison] sentences."[84] Thus, the burgeoning workers' movement was central to the dynamic of the 1989 events. Sporadic efforts to organize independent unions and even political parties continued through the 1990s, but with leaders almost invariably ending up in prison.

In the late 1990's, however, widespread unrest began to reemerge among workers responding to massive shutdowns of state industries. In many instances these companies were being restructured with the crown jewels of what remained being appropriated by party insiders. Most of these protests were small (a few dozen or a few hundred at most). But there have been some important exceptions. Chinese coal miners face some of the most horrendous working conditions to be found in China and have been heavily victimized by mine closures. The Labour Bulletin report noted, "in 1999, the PLA was employed to put down a three-day protest by 20,000 miners in Liaoning province where miners were reported to have taken over a town."[85] There were also steady reports in the same time period of other "large-scale clashes between miners and armed police over closures and wage arrears."[86]

In the spring of 2002, as noted earlier, this unrest hit the famed Daqing oil fields, where PetroChina had begun a massive downsizing project after its IPO in 2000.[87] Tens of thousands of workers took to the streets there to protest an attempt by the regime to cut back on promised severance benefits. The part the ACFTU played in these events demonstrates its true role. Its representatives called the Daqing oil workers protest "illegal and unacceptable" because according to the ACFTU constitution new unions could only be established by existing unions from above and not by workers themselves. It said that it had "no role to play" in the battle by these workers for their pensions because of official

106

instructions they had received from the Communist Party committee in the oil industry that their role was only to "understand" the situation, not to advocate the workers' interests. In the words of the ACFTU representative in Daqing: "under the union system in China, the organizational relation of a union is defined by the party. ... The trade union has a subordinate relationship to the Party, and a trade union must be set up according to an organizational structure of leadership that runs from top to bottom."

Tiananmen Square veteran union activist Han Dongfang issued a statement condemning the role played by the ACFTU in the Daqing protest and urged the ACFTU to recognize the right of the workers to organize their own union. For such efforts in the past Han Dongfang has been condemned at the ILO's annual conference by China's representatives as a "criminal." Ching Kwan Lee's research confirms the "ambiguous and conciliatory role played by the local ACFTU."[88] Even in the foreign investor-controlled Special Economic Zones, where some western union advocates of a rapprochement with the ACFTU feel it could act to genuinely defend worker interests, "union officials were ... helpless in defending workers during strikes in foreign-owned enterprises when public security personnel were often called into the [company] compounds by management to intimidate strikers."[89] Indeed, Lee notes that the widespread reports of high-density unionization rates in the foreign enterprise sector largely reflect "ACFTU-approved unions [that] were led and staffed by management personnel who were mainly responsible for collecting union fees, organizing birthday parties and recreational events. These union leaders were also salaried shop floor supervisors or section heads in the factory administration."[90]

A central theme of the state's behavior in the current period is to try to placate pure economic demands (over issues such as severance pay) while clamping down when the actions move to the formation of some kind of independent workers' organization. Since repression of potential unrest is so crucial, it is no surprise that until very recently the head of the ACFTU, Wei Jianxing, was the same government official who as a member of the Standing

Committee of the Chinese Communist Party's seven member elite Politburo had been in charge of the regime's anti-crime "Strike Hard" campaign. This campaign was aimed at suppressing alleged corruption and led to widespread arrests and use of the death penalty against thousands of party officials and businessmen.[91] Wei's approach to independent unions could not be clearer. He views them as "an attempt to 'westernize' and 'pluralize' us" by "our enemies, at home and abroad" who "seek to overturn the leadership of the Party and subvert the socialist system."[92]  The Labour Bulletin concluded its report by noting that:

> Where the state has definitely not adopted a "soft" approach has been when labour organisers have attempted to take advantage of the situation and set up labour organisations. These are rarely actually in workplaces. Unemployment has been such a major feature of recent economic trends that many of the angry workers involved are protesting because they have no workplaces to go to. The case of Hunan-based independent trade unionist Zhang Shanguang is an example of how brutal the regime can be in dealing with labour organisers. While Zhang's association for laid off workers was largely apolitical, the attempt to register the organisation legally - on the back of China's signing of the International Covenant on Economic Social and Cultural Rights and the International Covenant on Civil and Political Rights - was a profoundly political act. Zhang Shanguang was locked up for trying to organise the Shu Pu County Association for the Rights of Laid Off Workers. Zhang has a history of labour organising and in 1989 was sentenced for his involvement in the Hunan Workers Autonomous Federation (HWAF). On his release, he was blacklisted by employers and denied work. In the more recent arrest, the police handed Zhang's wife an official "Notice of Detention," which stated that Zhang was a threat to national security and was being detained under Article 61 of the Criminal Procedures Bill. After a secret hearing lasting two hours, he was sentenced to 10 years.[93]

As in most authoritarian regimes the real fear is of independent organization. A real trade union would rob the official state labor organization of its legitimacy and thus would open the door to deeper political change. A real trade union movement in China could also have an important economic, as well as political, effect. Economists have noted three major macro-level imbalances in China today: limited domestic demand, deflationary pressures and regional unevenness in the pattern of development. A trade union movement would, through genuine adversarial bargaining, force the regime to be more transparent and balanced in its economic decision-making. Wages would increase, thus stimulating domestic demand and price levels. This could lead to a more balanced domestic development pattern but also weaken global tensions with countries that already recognize trade unions. Financial analyst Richard Duncan, for example, has recently called for the establishment of a global minimum wage for workers in export industries as a means to restore balance to the global economy, particularly because of the impact of cheap labor in China:[94]

> Increasing wages in the developing world would augment global aggregate demand. It would succeed in putting more money in people's pockets, something that traditional monetary policy is incapable of doing in [the] post-bubble environment [the world is now experiencing.] ... As consumption expanded in the newly industrializing countries, so would demand for imported goods, an important development that would help restore balanced trade in the world.[95]

But to make this argument about the impact of a genuine labor movement in China is to point to a post-Communist China that is no longer wed to the "race to the bottom" export-led model of growth and that is precisely why the regime must resist in every conceivable forum such a movement.

## The International Legal Arena

This concern for the wider political and economic impact of a real trade union movement leads to the third area of concern: the role that international legal institutions are playing in the process. Unfortunately, rather than serve as a reminder of the importance of balance, equity and accountability in a major socio-economic experiment like that occurring in China today, these institutions are actually pushing the regime forward. There are many explicit examples of this process when, for example, the World Bank provides technical advice on the downsizing and privatization of key industries. But just as problematic are those steps taken at the WTO and the ILO that undermine the ability of independent unions to emerge as counterweights to the muted form of shock therapy now underway in China. The story of the granting of Permanent Normal Trade Relations with China by the United States is relatively well known.[96] In doing so, the United States gave up one of its most important levers of influence over the progress of labor rights and human rights in China. Less well known, however, is the groundwork that was laid for China's entry into the global economy at the ILO and the WTO.

One of the important achievements of the international labor rights movement over the last decade has been its promotion of the concept of "core labor standards" that comprise those rights seen as essential to the development of an effective trade union movement. This campaign has given labor activists in many arenas the ability to push for a coherent global agenda. Recognition of the core standards has now been made in a variety of environments, though the precise content of the standards varies slightly across institutional settings. In 1998 the ILO's International Labour Conference, its central body made up of all the member states together with worker and employer representatives, issued a Declaration on Fundamental Principles and Rights at Work. The Declaration stated that there are four fundamental rights which its members had "an obligation ... to respect, to promote and to realize," including: "freedom of association and the effective recognition of the right to collective bargaining; the elimination of all forms of forced or compulsory labour; the effective abolition of child labour; and the elimination of discrimination in respect of employment and occupation."[97] Respect for these same principles is now found in the emerging markets investment strategy of the California Public Employees Retirement System ("CalPERS"), the world's most important institutional investor, and in the Generalized System of Preferences in the global trade regime.[98] Even the WTO recognized its members' obligation to foster respect for Core Labor Standards at its Ministerial Conference in Singapore in 1996.[99]

But there is a catch. The ILO and the WTO each carved out an exception to the core standards that flatly contradicts the central principle of international labor solidarity that has guided the international labor rights movement since the founding of the ILO in 1919. Paragraph 5 of the ILO's Fundamental Declaration states that:

> The International Labour Conference... Stresses that labour standards should not be used for protectionist trade purposes, and that nothing in this Declaration and its follow-up shall be invoked or otherwise used for such purposes; in addition, the comparative advantage of any country should in no way be called into question by this Declaration and its follow-up.

Yet labor standards are promulgated precisely *because* they are protectionist: protective of the relatively advanced conditions won by workers in economies with established trade unions. Many of these protections were won only after bitter battles with employers and governments alike. Thus, the Preamble to the ILO's Constitution, drafted at the ILO's opening conference in 1919, states that "the failure of any nation to adopt humane conditions of labour is an obstacle in the way of other nations which desire to improve the conditions in their own countries."[100] This concept of labor standards as a protective floor beneath which the world should not fall was reaffirmed at the Philadelphia Convention that restarted the ILO in the post-World War II world. Thus, it was precisely the need to avoid the allegedly non-existent "race to the bottom" in global labor standards that explains the very origin of the ILO.

As former National Labor Relations Board Chair and leading labor law scholar William B. Gould IV has pointed out, this principle of international labor solidarity has a firm basis in domestic U.S. law.

> The idea of unfair competition ... is also reflected in portions of the National Labor Relations Act's own preamble, enacted to promote freedom of association and collective bargaining in the Untied States shortly after the United States joined the ILO.... Interestingly, in enacting the NLRA, Congress announced that a primary purpose of this policy was to remove the downward pressure on wages that a failure to protect collective bargaining produces.[101]

It was no surprise, therefore, that the proposed carve-out language that aimed to protect the cheap labor export model of growth found in developing countries was the cause of bitter debate in the ILO during its 1998 Conference. The United States representative (from the Clinton Administration) and the delegates representing the trade union movement bitterly opposed the language, while many developing countries, including China, pushed hard for it. If the leading United Nations agency responsible for promoting global labor standards was unable, or unwilling, to stand up to the pressures of globalization - tossing aside an 80-year-old core principle in favor of cheap labor and the return of sweatshops - is it any surprise that the international labor movement finds itself in such a challenging position?

As if to add insult to injury, in the summer of 2002, the ILO elevated the representative of China's ACFTU to an alternate seat on the ILO's Governing Body.[102] Apparently some ILO delegates attempted to justify the vote, which meant that Israel's Histadrut would lose its seat, as a fair protest of Ariel Sharon's policies towards the Palestinian people. The China Labour Bulletin called this a "ploy" and stated that those who fell for it "are guilty of confusion, at best, and [of] a serious lack of principle at worst." Unfortunately, this move seemed to echo the attempt of some in the international labor movement who have advocated a process of "constructive engagement" with the ACFTU.[103] An argument that these same activists dismissed with derision in the anti-apartheid movement is now welcomed despite the lack of any evidence that such "engagement" helps Chinese workers. The China Labour Bulletin condemns this approach as "the creeping legitimation" of the ACFTU.


Global Labor's Approach to China

As might be expected, the international labor movement has largely been very supportive of efforts to establish genuine, independent trade unions in China. The ICFTU has been a strong supporter of workers' rights in China, backing efforts to bring charges against the regime for violation of such rights at bodies like the ILO and providing resources to groups like the China Labour Bulletin and the Global Unions Liaison Office, both in Hong Kong.[104] While the ICFTU's official "China Policy" statement of November 2002 recognizes that there are different views on how to approach China within the international labor movement, it notes that "China violates human, religious and workers rights on a massive scale, including the central enabling rights of freedom of association and collective bargaining."[105] Further, in the face of these differences, the ICFTU concluded that the ACFTU "is not an independent trade union organization and, therefore, cannot be regarded as an authentic voice of Chinese workers." It thus "reaffirmed its request to all affiliates and Global Union Federations having contact with the Chinese authorities, including the ACFTU, to engage in critical dialogue ... including raising violations of fundamental workers' and trade union rights in any such meetings, especially concerning detentions of trade union and labour rights activists."[106] Such a position of "critical" dialogue appears to lie somewhere in the middle of the range of relationships now found within international labor, which include everything from "no contacts" to "constructive dialogue." The ICFTU defines "critical" dialogue as including "raising violations of fundamental workers' and trade union rights in any such meetings, especially concerning detention of trade union and labour rights activists."[107]

Somewhat surprisingly, however, some within the American labor movement, where a "no contacts" viewpoint has largely driven labor policy towards China, are now making an argument for a so-called constructive dialogue with the ACFTU that is precisely the kind of effort that so concerns the China Labour Bulletin about the possible "creeping legitimation" of that state body.  Kent Wong, an American labor lawyer and former official of the Service Employees International Union and currently director of the UCLA Center for Labor Research and Education, Elaine Bernard, Executive Director of the Harvard University Trade Union Program and Gregory Mantsios of the Worker Education Center at Queens College of the City University of New York, have all recently advocated that the AFL-CIO should recognize the ACFTU.[108]

In the spring of 2002, Mantsios led a trip of U.S. academics and labor educators to China to meet with the ACFTU.  He later issued a report calling for its recognition.[109]  Despite the evidence presented consistently over the last decade by Han Dongfang and other human rights organizations like Amnesty International and Human Rights Watch, Mantsios argued that the "ACFTU is an important advocate on behalf of [Chinese] workers."[110]  A review of the report indicates that this delegation may have violated the ICFTU's official policy of critical dialogue with the ACFTU if and when such contact does take place, though admittedly that policy was only put in place after this particular trip.  The Mantsios trip was undertaken "at the invitation" of the ACFTU and the delegation was "escorted throughout [their] trip" by the Deputy Head of the ACFTU's international department.[111]  Thus, there should be some initial concern that the information presented to the delegation was filtered to favor the Chinese government and that delegation members were not free to engage in an open dialogue with any Chinese workers they may have encountered.  Indeed, Mantsios admits that "because the delegation was visiting China at the invitation of the ACFTU, we did not meet with independent trade unionists, nor did we request to do so." The delegation "tried to compensate" for this deficit "by reviewing material written by independent activists." Of course, such material is widely available from organizations like the China Labour Bulletin, Amnesty International and Human Rights Watch and would hardly justify a trip to China.

Clearly the delegation had another goal. As Mantsios reports, "our purpose ... was twofold: 1) to improve mutual understanding of our respective labor movements, and 2) to explore ways in which relations between the Chinese and U.S. labor unions could be improved." Thus, from the outset, before the delegation even left the United States, it had already concluded that the ACFTU constitutes a genuine labor movement. The trip, then, had a political goal, not a legitimate research or educational aim, despite having been organized by the university-based director of a worker education program and including in the delegation Kent Wong of UCLA, Elaine Bernard of Harvard, and Ruth Milkman, a UCLA sociology professor and Director of the newly established Institute of Labor and Employment at the University of California.

The Mantsios Report ignores, sidesteps or outright contradicts what is widely known about the status of worker rights and the role of the ACFTU in China today. At one point, for example, it states "China's international agreements as well as its domestic labor and trade union laws provide important rights and protections. Workers in China have the right to join a union, to elect and remove union leaders democratically, and to strike against an employer."[112] The only source for these almost laughable conclusions is a reference to the recent ratification by China of the International Covenant on Economic, Social and Cultural Rights and a note that "other union rights are embedded in China's Trade Union Law, revised in 2001."[113]

What do these laws actually indicate? Since the ACFTU exists to defend the interests of the state it cannot, of course, be called a genuine trade union and that is the conclusion reached by the ICFTU in its China Policy Statement promulgated in late 2002. By law, the ACFTU enjoys a legal monopoly;[114] there are no legally protected union alternatives for Chinese workers. Efforts to form alternatives to the ACFTU have been met consistently with the full force of state power. The Trade Union Law, instead of protecting the freedom of association, establishes a strict organizational hierarchy that requires each level of union organization in the country to submit to the will of the next higher level of organization, culminating in the ACFTU, "which shall be established as the unified national organization."[115]

In fact, all of the sections of the Chinese labor organization are mandated to follow "the principle of democratic centralism," a hallmark of undemocratic Stalinist regimes.[116]  While the Law states that worker assemblies "shall have the right to remove or recall"[117] union representatives, the "trade union organization at a higher level shall exercise leadership over a trade union organization at a lower level."[118]  Further, new local unions can only be established with the "approval" of "the trade union organization at the next higher level."[119]  Finally, union financial resources are controlled jointly by the ACFTU and the Chinese state.[120]  Thus, the China Labour Bulletin concluded "independent trade unionists in China will find nothing to celebrate in [the new] legislation that guarantees the finances of an official trade union with a legal monopoly on organising."[121]

The Trade Union Law does not contain any mention of the right to strike, and the explicit affirmation of this right once found in the Chinese constitution was deleted in 1982.  As the ICFTU concluded in its 2003 Annual Survey of Violations of Trade Union Rights, "the right to strike was removed from China's Constitution in 1982 on the grounds that the political system in place had 'eradicated problems between the proletariat and enterprise owners.'"[122]  In fact, according to one leading scholar of the Chinese labor movement, the elimination of the right to strike was a reaction by the regime to a wildcat strike wave that hit China in the wake of the emergence of Polish Solidarity in 1980 and 1981.[123]  Instead, China's Labor Law only provides that "where a labour dispute ... takes place, the parties concerned may apply for mediation or arbitration or take legal proceedings according to law, or may seek for a settlement through arbitration."[124]

It is true that the ICESCR does recognize both the right of individuals "to form trade unions and join the trade union of his choice ... [and] the right to strike."[125]  China ratified the ICESCR in 2001.  However, the right to strike in the ICESCR is limited by a proviso that states that the right exists "provided that it is exercised in conformity with the laws of the particular country." Given the severe constraint on the right to strike in China in law and practice it seems unlikely that any worker can hope to take refuge in the ICESCR.  Even if one could read the ICESCR to override the absence of the right to strike inside China, it is not a self-executing agreement and thus does not automatically become law inside China upon ratification but explicitly requires China "to take steps ... including particularly the adoption of legislative measures ... with a view to achieving progressively the full realization of the rights recognized in the present Covenant."[126]  Far from taking such steps, China appears to have moved away from its apparent commitment to genuine trade union freedom.  Mantsios' sweeping conclusion that the right to strike actually exists in China by virtue of the ICESCR and the Trade Union Law is thus unwarranted. Further, upon joining the ICESCR, China issued a specific reservation, as it is allowed to do under international law, that "the application of Article 8.1 (a) [the right of workers to form trade unions and join unions of their own choice] of the Covenant to the People's Republic of China shall be consistent with the relevant provisions of the Constitution of the People's Republic of China, Trade Union Law of the People's Republic of China and Labor Law of the People's Republic of China."[127]  Thus, the monopoly of the ACFTU has been explicitly preserved.

In the fall of 2002, following the release of the Mantsios Report, UCLA's Kent Wong also led a trip to China, bringing with him, among others, Andy Stern, the President of the Service Employees International Union, and Tom Rankin, President of the California Labor Federation.  This group met only with ACFTU representatives, not with independent union activists. A report on the visit appeared in the *South China Morning Post* in which Kent Wong called for a "dialogue" with the ACFTU and argued that "reopening lines of communication" would "better serve the interests of U.S. companies" investing in China.[128]  These

117

statements received a quick and sharp rebuke from Barbara Shailor, the director of the AFL-CIO's Department of International Affairs, who wrote a letter to the editor of the Morning Post stating that the Wong-led group was not an official AFL-CIO delegation and that the AFL-CIO shares the official view of the international labor movement that "the ACFTU is not an independent trade union but rather part of the Chinese government and party structure."[129]

The viewpoint of Wong, Bernard and Mantsios has yet to gain wider traction in the American labor movement but it is symbolic of the intellectual problem that the current situation poses. A detailed analysis of the pitfalls of "constructive engagement" by organized labor with authoritarian regimes was undertaken by the International Union of Foodworkers, the official international body representing union organizations in the food industry, in 1997. An IUF Mission to Hong Kong and China, which did meet with many independent Chinese unionists, reached very different conclusions than these individuals. Consistent with the analysis presented here, which indeed relies in part on the work of the IUF Mission, the Mission noted that, first, "the ACFTU remains a subordinate organisation under tight party control, with no autonomy whatsoever"[130] and therefore a "dialogue between the ICFTU (or any other democratic trade union organization, also at national level) and the ACFTU is not a dialogue between two trade union organisations but between a trade union organisation on the one hand and a state organization on the other."[131] Furthermore, the IUF Mission concluded "all informed observers concur that there is no possibility of the ACFTU evolving into an independent organisation by itself.... There would have to be serious division in the party and the emergence of a strong reformist-progressive tendency prevailing over the party conservatives ... it is certainly not visiting foreign trade unionists who will influence the outcome of such political struggles."[132] Given this likely stasis in the character of the ACFTU, the "China issue is too important and it [is] too complex to be handled by persons unprepared for the task. Participants in delegations have to take the time to be briefed in depth.... Chinese democratic trade unionists [including the Hong Kong Confederation of Trade Unions and Han Dongfang of the China Labour Bulletin] as well as NGOs with specific relevant expertise, should be involved in preparing any dialogue and in the discussions themselves."[133]  Finally, the Mission concluded "full support, politically and financially, should be extended to Han Dongfang and other Chinese democratic trade unionists, by the ICFTU, ITSs (International Trade Union Secretariats) and national trade union organisations in a position to do so."[134]

Unfortunately, these core conclusions of a major international labor body appear to have been either readily ignored or violated by both the Mantsios and Wong delegations.  In the face of widespread evidence they argued that the ACFTU is a genuine trade union and brushed aside the political situation in China today.  They ignored Han Dongfang and consciously chose not to meet with dissident labor activists, while shaking the hands of those very individuals who are responsible for the repression of a genuine labor movement in China today.  In light of the vigorous efforts of many thousands, if not millions, of Chinese workers such as Xiao Yunliang and Yao Fuxin to express their basic human rights to freedom of speech and association, it seems tragic that those in a position most capable of providing them support and encouragement at this crucial turning point in Chinese history willfully ignore them and, instead, present a distorted picture of Chinese reality to the outside world.  An alternative view must be articulated if Chinese and western workers are to join together to reverse the "race to the bottom."

# Chapter Five.

# The PetroChina Syndrome: Regulating Capital Markets in the Anti-Globalization Era[1]

<u>Introduction</u>

As one of her last acts as Acting Chairman of the Securities and Exchange Commission, in the spring of 2001, Laura Unger threw what the Financial Times called a "bombshell" into the global capital markets.[2] Responding to pressure from Congress and an emerging independent political campaign, Chairman Unger issued a letter that acknowledged that the human rights violations by issuers of securities can be considered "material" to investors, and, therefore, foreign issuers of securities in the United States will now be required to provide disclosure of the risks associated with any investments by these issuers in countries where the United States has imposed sanctions for human rights or other legal violations.[3] The Unger Letter followed the unprecedented effort over the previous year by a range of labor, religious, human rights, and anti-slavery groups to change American securities law in part by attempting to derail the initial public offering ("IPO") of common stock by PetroChina Company Ltd. ("PetroChina"), a large oil-producing company controlled by the government of the People's Republic of China ("PRC").

For decades, the U.S. capital markets have been considered relatively free of the risk and uncertainty of political interventions that are common in many other jurisdictions. Thus, issuers have been thought to benefit from a lower cost of capital and greater transparency and predictability about regulatory action. Because of these apparent advantages, it is argued that, in recent years, a larger number of foreign issuers have tapped into the deep and liquid U.S. capital markets by listing their securities on a U.S.

exchange. In the words of Federal Reserve Chairman Alan Greenspan, "The openness and the lack of political pressures within the [American financial] system ... has made it such an effective component of our economy and, indeed, has drawn foreigners generally to the American markets for financing as being the most efficient place in many cases where they can raise funds."[4]

Thus, the Unger Letter on the U.S. capital markets represents a significant break with the hands-off tradition in the United States. Indeed, perhaps not surprisingly, its impact was felt almost immediately. Soon after the release of the Unger Letter, Lukoil, a large Russian oil company that was considered a crown jewel in that country's privatization and economic reform process, announced that it would withdraw a planned listing of its common stock on the New York Stock Exchange in order to list its shares instead on the United Kingdom's London Stock Exchange. In a brief statement, Lukoil said that it wanted to avoid what it called the "political risk" now associated with a U.S. listing.[5] This followed a decision some weeks before by the PRC to withdraw a planned sovereign debt offering in the United States.[6] These were precisely the kinds of developments that critics of the approach taken by Unger had feared.[7] Nonetheless, this reaction to the Unger Letter did not stop those who argue that the capital markets are now an appropriate, and indeed, crucial arena for advocacy of certain political goals. The AFL-CIO, for example, the thirteen million-member umbrella body for America's trade union movement that had played a key role in the protests about PetroChina's IPO, followed that effort with a campaign to block the proposed tender offer by integrated oil giant Amerada Hess (AHC) for the publicly traded shares of the exploration and production specialist Triton Oil (Triton).[8] AHC had a twenty-five percent stake in the British oil company Premier, one of the last major multinational companies to maintain an active investment in Burma, or Myanmar, a country laboring under a brutal military dictatorship.[9] In addition, Triton has operations in Equatorial Guinea, on the west coast of Africa, and in Colombia. Both countries have severe internal political strife and are the locale of concerns about human rights violations. The AFL-CIO has also been conducting an aggressive shareholder campaign to force Unocal, the California oil producer, to change its investment policy in Burma in light of accusations that the company, among other allegations of human rights violations, engaged military forces there to use forced labor to help build a natural gas pipeline.[10]

This unprecedented development in the capital markets, I will argue, can only be understood in the context of the broader debate about globalization[11] that has emerged over the last several years.  A problem is emerging in the global economy that may indeed prove to be fatal for Anglo-American capitalism[12] as we now know it.  This model of capitalism has evolved and survived for some two hundred years or more in significant part because of its ability to generate legitimacy, understood as a sense inculcated in the general population that the system is not only the best that can be achieved under the circumstances, no matter how unjust or unequal actual social outcomes, but that these outcomes are reached in a manner that reflects the needs or desires of a substantial majority of the population.[13]  The ability of capitalism to generate this legitimacy depends crucially on certain compromises crafted with the general population through ideology, institutions, and mass organizations.  This was true, for example, throughout the four decades of the Cold War, for both contending parties.  The bureaucratic regimes of the east justified their existence by appealing to the alleged material improvements they provided for the bulk of their populations.  This apparent achievement helped those regimes generate an attractive ideological agenda that appealed to hundreds of millions of desperately poor people around the world, and thus posed a serious political challenge to the traditional capitalist regimes of the West.  Stalinism made (and, in the case of a handful of countries like Cuba, China, and North Korea, continues to make) this appeal not just through the exercise of mindless propaganda, but also through the active efforts of mass organizations controlled rigidly from above by the government or a Communist party.[14]

A variation of this legitimation process was also found in the West in tripartite and corporatist institutions that, for example, brokered wage and productivity deals between workers, employers, and the government.  In the West, of course, the strength of the system's legitimacy was not found largely in arguments about the material conditions of the working class, though such arguments were certainly made, but rather in the argument that basic civil liberties guaranteed freedom for all its citizens. The existence of process acting as a check on the arbitrary exercise of power, through institutions like free trade unions and collective bargaining, helped western capitalism win the hearts and minds of its working class.[15]

The result, in both East and West, was the widespread social acceptance, at least for several decades, of what can be thought of as a social variation of Pareto optimality: the working class would not revolt no matter how much better off the wealthiest or politically connected became, as long as the participatory institutions available to the working class generated steady improvement in their welfare.[16] With the collapse of the Soviet Union and its subsidiary regimes in Eastern Europe, the Stalinist variation of the legitimation process disappeared. No ideology has since emerged which attempts to justify its existence on the basis of widespread material improvement of the population. In fact, to the extent that coherent ideologies advertising a general explanation of the world's ills have emerged, such as Islamic fundamentalism or racialist nationalism, they actually aim to take the world back to a pre-capitalist, if not primitive, era.[17] While the absence on the world stage of the Stalinist approach has been widely remarked upon, particularly in the West during the heady triumphalist period of the 1990s, what has been less well understood is the change in the kind of appeal that that same western, or Anglo-American, capitalism now makes, whether consciously or not, to the billions of the world's desperate, poor, and hungry. Western capitalism has, in fact, also broken with its approach to legitimacy, thus opening up an ideological and institutional vacuum in the global economy.

While the Cold War forced both East and West to legitimate their respective systems, now that a more aggressively neo-liberal form of capitalism has emerged from that period, its advocates no longer feel the same social or political pressure to craft the institutions that were once relied upon to generate legitimacy. Thus, in the new global, post-Cold War environment, Western capital has joined hands with a new post-Communist elite to forge new corporations, markets, and, indeed, entire countries. This process is taking place largely from above with less and less consideration of its impact on the general population. At the same time, however, an independent response is being crafted from below through new social movements and also through variations in activity by those older institutions, such as trade unions, that once participated actively, if not always willingly or enthusiastically, in the legitimation process of the Cold War era.[18] A new kind of global fracture is emerging, not on a geographical basis, not between east and west, as in the Cold War, but on a social basis, between those, on the one hand, who control dominant institutions from above and, on the other hand, from below by those who are impacted by these institutions.[19] This fracture signals the emergence of a legitimation deficit created by the globalization process. The anti-globalization protests against the World Trade Organization in Seattle in November 1999 are the most visible evidence of this phenomenon.[20]

To explore this new social fracture and its challenge to the legitimacy of Anglo-American capitalism, this chapter presents a case study of the attempt by the Chinese government and major Wall Street investment banks to complete an initial public offering by a major Chinese corporation. Their efforts represented a classic example of the effort to build a new global capitalist order from above without significant concern for the legitimation question. And, as we shall see, the effort was met from below with a vigorous social response. Thus, I suggest that a kind of syndrome, the PetroChina Syndrome if you will, is emerging that reflects the failure to resolve new conflicts caused by the globalization process. Part II of the chapter examines the PetroChina IPO itself, explaining the reasons why the stock offering occasioned such controversy and demonstrating the unwillingness of the Chinese regime, the company and its advisors to consider its associated social and political problems. Part III discusses the unprecedented campaign against the IPO itself so that the political forces generating the PetroChina Syndrome are better understood. Part IV describes the key features of the resulting Unger Letter.[21] Part V reviews conventional explanations and arguments that help, in part, to explain the Unger Letter and the PetroChina Campaign, including traditional securities law concerns, a change in the political climate represented by the anti-globalization movement and structural changes in the global capital markets. Part VI begins the discussion of the emergence of the legitimation deficit by exploring the work of economic historian Massimo De Angelis. De Angelis' innovative reconsideration of the work of two archetypal economists of the twentieth century - John Maynard Keynes and Milton Friedman - helps us come to a deeper understanding of the issues raised by what can be called the PetroChina Syndrome. I will argue, in Part VII, that this understanding is incomplete without a deeper exploration of the role of process in generating legitimacy in the modern industrial era. Without that concern for process, the PetroChina Syndrome cannot be correctly diagnosed. The legitimation deficit this Syndrome signals can only be filled by the design of new institutions that respond constructively to the problems of the new era.

## The PetroChina Offering

In early 2000, an international consortium of investment banks, law firms, consulting groups, and accounting firms, led by the American investment bank Goldman Sachs launched an initial public offering of the common stock of the newly-formed mainland Chinese oil company PetroChina Company Limited, popularly known as "PetroChina."[22] When plans for the IPO first surfaced, the company and its advisors hoped that it would mark the largest ever public offering of stock in a Chinese state-owned enterprise (SOE) and represent a watershed event for pro-free market reform elements currently in power in China. But the transaction also meant potential devastation for the workforce of the Chinese oil industry, as more than one million workers at the restructured company were to be dismissed as "redundant" with only minimal social protections and, at best, uncertain prospects for alternative employment.[23]

In accord with longstanding plans, the PetroChina IPO was to be the first of several that the Chinese government planned to bring to the global capital markets in the following year. In each case, the workforces of major industrial companies would face unemployment as downsizing and restructuring were forced upon them. These transactions were not to be subjected to the widely accepted checks and balances found in the developed world. China remains without the basic democratic institutions that investors and the wider public outside of China take for granted. There are no legislatively established, transparent, and accountable regulatory agencies to oversee the social impact of major economic changes. There is no independent trade union movement or a collective bargaining process to provide some form of representation for the tens of millions of workers whose lives are being severely impacted by economic reform.[24] In addition, there are no open, efficient, and regulated capital markets to provide investors and companies with a viable pricing mechanism for their assets. Further, investors in the proposed IPOs were to be sold only minority stakes and serve as junior partners of the Chinese state that planned to retain for itself majority control and effective influence over the future of these entities.[25] This first section explores each of these key areas in greater depth, including the new corporate structure at PetroChina, the changing Chinese economic context in which the IPO took place, the human rights concerns raised by the offering and an assessment of the offering from the standpoint of traditional investor concerns about corporate governance.

## A. The New Structure

PetroChina was formed in November of 1999 as a result of months, perhaps years, of planning by the government of the People's Republic of China (PRC).[26] PetroChina was initially established as a wholly owned subsidiary of its parent company - China National Petroleum Corporation (CNPC). CNPC is one of several Chinese state-owned oil companies. The three largest of these are CNPC, the China Petrochemical Corporation (Sinopec), and the Chinese National Offshore Oil Corporation (CNOOC). CNPC and Sinopec divide among themselves the assets of all of China's domestic oil extraction, refining, and distribution. Roughly, CNPC operates in northern and western China, and Sinopec in the eastern and coastal regions of the country.[27] Meanwhile, CNOOC, as its name suggests, is responsible for offshore production and distribution, including the strategically important oil reserves in the South China Sea.[28]

PetroChina emerged from within the much larger CNPC as an attempt to create a business that could attract foreign capital. PetroChina is viewed by the Chinese and its foreign advisors as holding the "crown jewels" of the assets of CNPC, including the key Daqing oil fields and the pipelines that move eighty-four percent of China's natural gas. It has five business units: oil and gas exploration and production, oil refining and petrochemical production, oil sales and pipeline operations, foreign joint ventures, and research and development. It controls more than two-thirds of China's oil and gas production and ranks among the world's largest oil companies.[29] It contributes a substantial portion of the total profits earned by China's largest SOE's. PetroChina took with it from CNPC close to 500,000 of the total 1.5 million workers employed by CNPC. The 1 million who remain are considered largely redundant and are now in the process of being dismissed with minimal severance payments.[30] With government plans to lay-off tens of millions of workers throughout China in the next several years as restructuring of other SOE's moves forward, Chinese oil workers are unlikely to find alternative employment easily. Industry analysts even argue that the 500,000 workers that will go to work for PetroChina are far more than necessary. Exxon employs only one-fourth as many people.[31] The oil industry generally considers China's oil companies to be "grossly overstaffed, even by the bloated standards of other national oil companies."[32]

A small army consisting of more than two thousand investment bankers, consultants, accountants, and lawyers, designed the new PetroChina structure. The lead manager of the IPO was the American investment bank, Goldman Sachs. The key co-manager was the China International Capital Corp., a joint venture of the PRC's China Construction Bank and Morgan Stanley Dean Witter. PricewaterhouseCoopers (accounting), McKinsey & Co. (consultancy), and seven foreign law firms rounded out the foreign team advising the Chinese company.[33]

The new company attempted to lure several key business leaders in the oil industry and elsewhere to serve as outside directors. Of the three names that surfaced during the marketing of the deal, only two accepted: Chee-chen Tung, the brother of the Chief Executive of Hong Kong, and Wu Jinglian, a leading PRC economist and an advisor to Premier Zhu Rongji.[34] Another senior government economist, Liu Hongru, who received his academic training at the University of Moscow in 1959, replaced Wu Jinglian in late 2002.[35] Franco Bernabe, former head of the Italian oil conglomerate ENI, initially turned down the opportunity but later became the sole non-Chinese member of the Board.[36] The two "outside" Chinese directors were likely, in fact, to act as proxies for the Beijing regime given their close ties to the government.[37] To appear more like companies familiar to the international investment community, several Board committees were established as well, including an audit committee; a health, safety and environmental protection committee; an examination and salary committee; and an investment and development committee.[38] However, without a competitive market for corporate control or an independent judiciary, there were no clear guarantees that these bodies would operate in a manner comparable to their counterparts in developed market economies.

Initially, it was reported that PetroChina hoped to raise as much as US $ 10 billion in the IPO. This figure was then scaled back several times as bankers ran into severe political and financial headwinds.[39] When the dust settled, the company was only able to raise US $ 2.9 billion, and much of that was provided at the very last minute by friendly Hong Kong investors and BP, the large UK oil company, in side deals negotiated by the underwriters. All told, this represented an approximate ten percent stake in PetroChina. The parent company, CNPC, retained majority control of PetroChina as owners of the remaining ninety percent of the common stock. In addition, PetroChina put in place a dividend distribution policy that obligated the company to share half of its future earnings with CNPC. One leading oil industry source stated: "CNPC remains in total control of the new entity."[40]

As state-owned enterprises, CNPC, Sinopec, and CNOOC are controlled, in turn, by the government of the People's Republic and, hence, by the Chinese Communist Party. Corporate officers of the SOE's are appointed by the government and serve at its whim. In fact, at one point during the IPO process, Dow Jones reported that the President of Sinopec, Li Yizhong, had been reassigned to become "governor or the communist party secretary" of the Gansu province in northwest China.[41] Replacing Li at Sinopec would be the current President and Chairman of CNPC, Ma Fucai. Ma Fucai had been slated to serve as Chairman of PetroChina and, hence, lead the planned "road show" to Hong Kong, London, and New York - a crucial corporate step in the effort to sell an IPO to major institutional investors. The new President of CNPC, replacing Ma Fucai, was to be Yan Sanzhong, a former deputy director of the government agency that oversees the oil and petrochemical industry. He did not have extensive experience, however, in the oil extraction operations that are key to PetroChina and he had only been a vice president of CNPC for six months.

This move was very unpopular with potential investors and was eventually reversed. "Analysts doubt if Ma and Yan are qualified for their new positions," Dow Jones reported. "The managerial overhaul sends a confusing signal to the oil industry as it comes just before the two companies launch their initial public offerings."[42] The motivation for these changes appeared to be domestic political considerations. They were "seen as part of the government's strategy to accelerate the development of northwestern China."[43]

To impose such a significant change in corporate leadership in the middle of an IPO would be considered a disaster in the United States or Europe. In fact, it would be unthinkable because no government diktat could force a company to move its CEO around in such a manner. Although many state-owned companies in Western Europe have been privatized through public share offerings in the last decade, this kind of move has never been made. It was no surprise that this change was cancelled, but the mere reporting of such a possibility made potential investors very nervous about the governance structure in place at the new entity.

Evidence of the political connection between the company and the regime has continued since the IPO. In early 2002, PetroChina announced it was conducting exploratory discussions with Husky Energy, a Canadian oil company controlled by Hong Kong-based billionaire Li Ka Shing. However, when the discussions fell apart, the public announcement by PetroChina that it was withdrawing from the negotiations was made by the PRC's State Development Planning Commission vice-minister Zhang Guobao, with PetroChina Chairman Ma Fucai sitting silently beside him.[44] Commenting on the nature of the announcement, a writer in the South China Morning Post noted that "what this PetroChina cameo illustrates is that Beijing has yet to recognise the sanctity of listed private companies ... shareholders have to add on a new level of risk if politicians, with their different set of priorities, can waltz in and turn things upside down."[45] Serving time in the senior management at PetroChina also remains a conduit for political power. Ma Fucai was recently appointed as an alternate member of the Central Committee of the Communist Party.[46] And the former head of PetroChina parent CNPC was recently named head of the Ministry of Public Security, which controls China's police forces. This Ministry has been responsible for the crushing of the Falun Gong religious movement in China.[47]

### B. The Chinese Context

#### 1. Economic Reform

The PetroChina IPO must be viewed in the context of the dramatic economic changes that have been taking place in China for several years. As far back as the early 1980s, the Chinese Communist Party began to search for alternative economic forms that would allow it to maintain its political control, while at the same time improving economic growth and worker productivity. Reaction to the excesses of the Maoist era led to the emergence of a concept called "market socialism," where the regime would establish a variety of new structures that made room for a private sector and foreign investment. Initially, these were limited to the freeing up of prices for the agricultural sector, the encouragement of a small-scale private sector in consumer and light industrial goods, and the establishment of Special Economic Zones, particularly in coastal regions. The latter were able to take advantage of their proximity to the regional economic powerhouses like Japan and the so-called "tigers" of East Asia, including South Korea, Hong Kong, Malaysia, and Singapore.[48]

Slowly the reform process expanded to the point where the core assets of the state-owned economy were to be restructured and privatized. In theory, the regime's goal is to privatize the great majority of SOE's.[49] Many of these have already carried out a form of homegrown privatization built around "debt for equity" swaps, where a company's workforce is forced to buy shares in their own debt-laden and unproductive firms or else face dismissal. Alternatively, worker pension funds are expropriated by current management and invested as operating capital in the money-losing ventures "so workers become "shareholders' by default without any say in the management of the enterprise and, in addition, risk losing their share when the company is sold."[50] Often, despite their reorganization as joint-stock companies, management remains the same and local government officials continue to control the entities.[51]

This process is linked intimately to efforts to cut costs and slash work forces. The economically active population of China consists of about 890 million people, with some 600 million in rural areas and 280 million in urban areas. The state sector employs approximately 100 million people, and it is thought that as many as one-third of these are slated for dismissal. In addition, 100 million rural workers are said to be surplus labor and are now being encouraged to move to urban areas, despite the dim prospects that await them there. Some 82,000 rural migrants to Beijing, for example, earn their living as scavengers of the city's trash dumps, sharing their workspace with rats and flies.[52]

The risk that the regime faces in this restructuring effort is the possibility that it may spark social turmoil that it cannot control. Thus, "modernization" of some sort becomes crucial, both to provide new jobs and to earn income to provide some minimal social safety net. The unanswered question for Chinese society is the final outcome of this important transition. The IPO of PetroChina was viewed by the regime as "a propeller for the mainland's painful state-sector restructuring," which Premier Zhu hoped would win the "heart and soul" of international investors back to China after the East Asian financial crisis of 1997-1998.[53] In 1999, an attempted IPO by CNOOC, the offshore oil company, failed to attract serious investor interest and was shelved.[54] Capital markets also reacted weakly to an offering of stock in the Beijing Capital International Airport entity.[55] These events highlight the risks that a privatization and capital market strategy entails for the state. In one view, the attempt to tap foreign capital markets is a way to provide a bridge to a new era of renewed growth and economic development. However, this strategy can also be viewed as an attempt by a dying bureaucratic regime, one that has outlived its social and economic relevance, to preserve its privileges.

Prior to his recent retirement, Premier Zhu was the leader of a faction within the Chinese Communist Party that is known as the "Shanghai mafia" or the "Shanghai gang." He is a former mayor of Shanghai as was his predecessor, Jiang Zemin. The last Shanghai mayor was said by U.S. businessmen to spend more time in Beijing than in Shanghai and was once thought of as a potential successor to Zhu. Many appointees to the top leadership positions in China are considered members of this faction.[56] Because of its long history as a port and industrial city, Shanghai has been the center of efforts to develop alternative economic forms in China. The Shanghai-headquartered Baoshan Steel Group was slated to become the next IPO for the regime once the PetroChina IPO was completed.[57] (Though, as we will see below, those plans had to be altered once the PetroChina IPO ran into serious trouble.).

Although the Shanghai gang's "market socialist" ideology now predominates in the Communist Party, Maoist views favoring a strong state still receive a hearing. Events like the bombing of the Chinese embassy in Serbia, or the entry of China into the World Trade Organization, are used by the anti-reform elements to assert their views.[58] Thus, the leadership must navigate between the so-called "left," on the one hand, and, on the other, elements within the reform groups that want to push reform faster, or that have personal stakes in the success of their particular industry or party faction. The decision, for example, to make PetroChina the first IPO in the planned pipeline was apparently made only after an intense internal battle in the regime. The other domestic oil entity, Sinopec, hoped to go first, but top executives in PetroChina parent CNPC threatened a kind of "shock therapy" to win the day.[59] They asserted that they were so in need of foreign investment, without it they would be forced to lay off up to one million workers overnight, thus threatening the regime with widespread social unrest. It is no surprise, therefore, to find that there was speculation that Premier Zhu played a personal role in the offering process.[60]

Behind the PetroChina IPO is the fear of the Chinese state bureaucracy that as China opens up to the outside world, it risks a collapse of key industries that can no longer compete on a global basis. The choice for the regime can be viewed as a fork in the road, with one road leading to Singapore and the other to Moscow. If the regime gets to Singapore, it will have established a modern industrial country without major social unrest and yet have maintained its authoritarian power over Chinese society. The road to Moscow demonstrates the alternative: the regime could try the imposition of "shock therapy" in an effort to "catch up" with the West overnight, but it may face the unintended collapse of the older SOE's which cannot match the superior competitive power of foreign capital.

Clearly, the regime wants to get to Singapore but fears it may wake up and find itself in Moscow. Thus, the modernization of its "crown jewels" in the energy sector serves a dual purpose: provide the increased resources necessary for continued economic expansion, and defend the ability of its oil industry to compete, or at least hold its own, with foreign capital. PetroChina is optimistic about its ability to lead this effort. In the view of company spokesman Zhang Xin: "We believe PetroChina has the strength, given the wide range of CNPC reforms in recent months to become one of the world's top hydrocarbons majors."[61] Industry experts, however, think this goal is more than a decade away.[62] Premier Zhu's goal was to find a way to build a competitive oil sector without using state assets. He is viewed as the "architect" of the policy of tapping international equity markets to find the needed cash.[63]

### 2. A Changing Oil Industry

With economic growth comes an increase in energy use.[64] China is no exception. China experienced double-digit growth in the early 1990s and the economy was still growing at a pace of 8 to 9% at the end of the decade. Total primary energy use, a Rice University study indicates, rose from 665 million tons of "oil equivalent" (mtoe) in 1990 to 935 mtoe in 1996. This figure could double by 2010. The relative decline in the importance of oil to the advanced economies is a process that, China is not yet able to benefit from. In fact, the rate of oil use could accelerate as the economy develops - transportation needs alone could drive this process.

Inevitably, China has in recent years become an oil importer after decades of being able to rely solely on its own land-based and offshore reserves. Domestically, China can rely on proven reserves of some nineteen billion barrels - less than half that of Russia and far below the reserves of the leading OPEC members.[65] China must now import between 500,000 and 700,000 barrels of oil a day (b/d) but this is expected to climb to as much as 3.5 million b/d by 2010. Imports in 1999 alone jumped 43%.[66]

China has attempted to secure additional reserves internationally. To date, its efforts consist largely of various joint venture projects such as those by CNPC in Kazakhstan, Peru, Venezuela, and Sudan.[67] China also had plans to invest in Iraq once the U.N. sanctions were lifted. Industry experts believe, however, that these efforts have a natural limit - unless China can modernize its refinery assets, it cannot process large amounts of the type of oil available from many of these sources. Its efforts to secure offshore sources of oil in the South China Sea - through CNOOC - have borne fruit but are now reaching a limit. Crude oil production from offshore sources dropped in 1999 after a five-year plateau in growth rates. New fields are to be brought on line in joint ventures with foreign companies. But until recently, China's offshore production was largely earmarked for export (mainly to Australia) to earn much-needed foreign exchange. This has changed. In 2000, for example, exports were down two-thirds from the previous year. The oil is now needed domestically to compensate for reduced output driven by cost cutting coupled with growing domestic demand. Thus foreign investors see three major opportunities: reliance on high sulfur Middle East oil requires expensive upgrades to China's refineries; the breakup of the domestic oil industry gives foreign capital new opportunities to compete; and the pace of economic growth has led to a permanent shift in the source of China's oil supply.

The planned IPOs then, led by PetroChina, represent a last ditch attempt to protect key state assets from the inevitable onslaught of the global market. It is thought that one of the arguments used by the domestic oil industry managers in discussions with the top Beijing leadership rested on what was being called "the last free lunch" - an argument which said, in effect, the state owes us this one last favor (support for access to capital markets) before the state carries out its intention to join the World Trade Organization (WTO). Once in the WTO, China will face increasing pressure to open up key sectors of the economy to direct competition and greater foreign ownership, and this could well spell the end of the days of privileged SOE's.[68] "The Chinese oil companies have to act now, before it is too late, to improve their efficiencies," in the words of one oil industry source.[69]

A variation on this theme suggests that it is the Government itself, not the oil potentates of CNPC, that want to retain control of the oil industry. Proponents of this view point to the desire of the PRC to appear to be competing while retaining actual control of the publicly traded firms. "PetroChina management will not be able to prevent the looting of its resources on the instructions of its parent or even the government, which many fear may happen if crisis situations, especially of a financial nature, develop making dipping into PetroChina's pockets irresistible," a leading oil industry source argued.[70] The parent company, CNPC, retains majority ownership and is a privileged recipient of earnings distributions.[71] In turn, the Chinese government retains control of CNPC.

Thus, it is plausible to suggest that the division of assets between Sinopec and CNPC is intended to create a permanent duopoly rather than spark domestic competition. As one leading oil industry source put it, "the purpose of the CNPC-Sinopec monopolies was to strengthen resistance to foreign petroleum company penetration of the business, which would take place at some non-negotiable defined stage, after China was admitted to the WTO."[72] This suggests that the restructuring strategy devised by the CNPC, the Chinese government, and the Goldman Sachs-led team of advisers, in fact, relies on the lack of domestic competition. Together with an extended phase-in period of the WTO-forced opening of the energy sector, this would give the Chinese oil giants "several years to strengthen their fortresses, making it very difficult and certainly costly for any foreign firms to take them on in their own respective backyards."[73] As one thorough study of the restructuring put it:

> CNPC [PetroChina's parent entity] has been groomed to be at the forefront of China's strategy to enter the global top 500 transnational corporate league. The Chinese party-state has, over many years, selectively favored its petroleum monopoly corporation, with many policy decisions designed to make it bigger, stronger, more profitable, and better able to compete, both within China and around the world, with the major oil corporations which are household names to anyone in the western world who owns a car.[74]

The key move was to find a way to offer up the best of the assets available without the "dead weight" of the aging state monopoly. This need was reinforced by the failure of the CNOOC offering in 1999 and led to the so-called "Plan B": PetroChina was set up with only the best operational assets of CNPC, very few of the debts, and none of the overhead associated with retaining a million redundant workers and their families.[75] According to Hart's Asian Petroleum News:

> The fundamental policy being put in place confirms that CNPC and Sinopec will put into practice their domestic market

muscles aimed at keeping foreign intruders at arms length. The use of foreign money, through minority stock sales will continue to be pursued, on the theme that "their money' will be sought and used, but control will always be in the PRC hands.[76]

### C. Human Rights

Just as the PetroChina IPO was ready to launch, reports were reaching the West that the Chinese regime had undertaken yet another crackdown on alleged affiliates of the spiritual movement, the Falun Gong.[77]  A Hong Kong-based human rights group reported that Chinese security forces detained approximately 2,000 members of the movement during February of 2000.  The group estimated that 5,000 members had been sent to prison labor camps for "re-education" and another 300 sent to jail since the crackdown started last year.[78]  This crackdown began to reach even those Chinese who might have been thought, in the Chinese context at any rate, to be above the law:  a Chinese civil court judge was detained for three months and "given daily injections of a drug that made him sleepy and muddled...."[79]

Membership in Falun Gong is illegal in China, though the threat to public safety that might justify such a law is unknown to outsiders.  The regime believes that any form of independent organization is a threat to its legitimacy and power.  This untimely crackdown was apparently sparked by a demonstration by Falun Gong members on Chinese New Year's Eve, the fourth of February. Demonstrators assembled in Tiananmen Square in Beijing and attempted to unfurl banners.  One hundred people were arrested, and the arrests then spread to more than forty cities throughout China.

This fear of independent activity by the population serves well as a general theme for assessing the approach of the PRC to human rights in general and labor rights in particular.  Thus, in a statement to senior party figures in early 2000,[80] PRC President Jiang Zemin "warned that the Falun Gong sect poses as much of a threat to the Communist Party as the Solidarity movement did to the communists in Poland in the 1980s."[81]  Of course, to deal with

Polish Solidarity, the Polish government imposed martial law for a decade, arresting thousands, and setting back the democratic reform process in Eastern Europe for years. Jiang suggested that the sect members, together with "unemployed farmers and workers and splittists among ethnic minorities [are] the most destabilizing factors in society."[82] Jiang "expressed concern that the jobless in rural and urban areas might "join hands' to pose a challenge to the leadership."[83] As the International Union of Foodworkers put it in a 1997 report following a research mission to Hong Kong: "There is no dispute about the nature of the regime in China: it is a one-party state where the CPC bureaucracy constitutes a ruling class exercising a monopoly of power enforced by extensive police control and by the repression of dissident opinion and activity."[84]

The Falun Gong crackdown is only the latest example of the approach that the Chinese Communist regime has long taken to basic civil liberties and human rights. Amnesty International summarized the human rights picture in China at the end of 1999 on the eve of the PetroChina IPO:

> Hundreds, possibly thousands, of activists and suspected opponents of the government were detained during the year. Thousands of political prisoners jailed in previous years remained imprisoned, many of them prisoners of conscience. Some had been sentenced after unfair trials, others were still held without charge or trial. Political trials continued to fall short of international fair trial standards. Torture and ill-treatment remained endemic, in some cases resulting in death. The death penalty continued to be used extensively.[85]

Despite suggestions by some that limited reform is leading China to the "rule of law," it is very clear that the country remains under the arbitrary "rule of men." China signed the International Covenant on Civil and Political Rights in October of 1999 and allowed the UN High Commissioner for Human Rights, Mary Robinson, to visit the country, but, according to Amnesty International, "repression of dissent continued, culminated in December in the trial of high profile dissidents" and the introduction of new regulations controlling "social groups" and publishing.[86] Amnesty concluded that these were signs of "increasing restrictions on freedom of expression and association."[87]

Those minimal legal protections that do exist are often abused. "Political trials continued to fall far short of international fair trial standards," Amnesty concluded, "with verdicts and sentences usually decided by the authorities before trial, and appeal hearings usually a formality."[88] Amnesty reports that a series of trials of pro-democracy activists took place in several provinces where defendants were not provided adequate time or resources to mount effective defenses. One veteran pro-democracy activist and bookseller from Qingdao in the Shenzung province, Chen Zengxiang, was "reportedly tried in secret [in October 1999] and sentenced to seven years' imprisonment for "seeking to subvert the State power."[89] He had been held in jail without access to a lawyer since May of 1999.[90]

One legal scholar who attempted to put an optimistic face on recent legal reforms in China nonetheless admitted, "re-education through labor continues to be imposed on dissidents...."[91] He noted that this penalty could be used to incarcerate individuals without a charge or trial. He describes several instances of torture of those held in the re-education camps.[92] The PRC Ministry of Justice itself admits that 200,000 people are living in prison labor camps.[93] The Laogai system forces prisoners "to plant, harvest, engineer, manufacture and process all types of products for sale in the domestic and international markets."[94] Ironically, perhaps tragically, Dun & Bradstreet actually publishes statistics that assess the output of these prisons. In a 1998 report, they indicated that ninety-nine of these camps produced more than $ 800 million in revenue for the state.[95] The camp list included the Nanbao Salt Works, where famed Chinese dissidents Wei Jingsheng and Wang Dan were once held.[96] Here is how Wei described Nanbao, "At Nanbao, political criminals and other criminals labor as slaves - with no income, no job safety - and make this enterprise one of the largest salt chemical factories in Asia. Every year, millions of yuan in profit from this industry contribute to the Chinese government's efforts to oppress its own people."[97] The Dun & Bradstreet report includes a wide range of industrial companies encompassing cement, rubber, machine tools, motorcycle engines, aluminum products, diesel engines, a paper mill, a fertilizer factory, and a silk plant.

Given China's continued abuse of the civil liberties and human rights of its general population, it should come as no surprise that it brutally suppresses any effort to establish a free trade union movement and the labor rights that are generally associated with such a movement. Independent trade unions are outlawed in China. The right to strike is forbidden. An effort to establish an Autonomous Workers Federation as part of the wider Democracy Movement of 1989 was met with particularly harsh repression. Many affiliates of that Federation are still in prison or labor camps. Amnesty details numerous ongoing abuses of workers for their organizing and other activity.[98] Arrests and arbitrary detentions were made throughout 1999, as labor unrest increased due to the worsening economic situation. Here are some of the examples they report:

> Li Qingxi, a laid-off worker from the Datong coal mine in Shanxi province, was arrested in January when he posted publicly a statement calling for independent trade unions. He was sentenced in March without charge or trial to one year of "re-education through labour," reportedly to be served "at home." Zhang Shanuang, a labour rights activist from Hunan province, was detained in July after trying to set up a group to help laid-off workers. He was sentenced in December to 10 years' imprisonment, accused of having "illegally provided information to overseas hostile organizations and individuals," reportedly for speaking about farmers' protests in his province in a Radio Free Asia interview.[99]

The widely respected China Labour Bulletin, based in Hong Kong, confirms that the process of "economic restructuring has led to huge pressures on the Chinese labour market ... many workers laid off from SOE's have expressed ... dissatisfaction with the long working hours, short-term contracts and miserly benefits that more than not await them in the private sector."[100] Linked to this dissatisfaction is a rise in labor disputes, despite the frightening risk that such voicing of grievances to official bodies entails. According to Tim Pringle, a longtime and very close follower of Chinese labor conditions based in Hong Kong,

> The [Chinese Government's] Ministry of Labour and Social Security [reports that] there were increases in labour disputes in all types of enterprises in 2000. Of the 327,152 that officially occurred, 24.2 percent [were] in SOEs, 20 percent in so-called collectively-owned enterprises, 15.5 percent in foreign-invested enterprises and 14 percent in private Chinese-owned companies. These statistics represent the continuation of a spectacular increase in disputes that began in the early 1990s.[101]

Of course, the vast majority of such disputes are reported only as "solved" with few details available on the facts. There are serious procedural obstacles to bringing these conflicts before the dispute resolution bodies, so it is unknown how many on the job grievances go unreported.[102] In fact, the worst fears of critics of the PetroChina IPO and restructuring process came true in the spring of 2002, when massive demonstrations by laid off workers took place in the Daqing oilfields owned by CNPC and PetroChina.[103] These were soon followed by large protests by unemployed workers in several parts of China, including an unusual demonstration by workers in Beijing itself. Arrests of protest leaders, two of whom were charged with "sedition" and were initially charged with the death penalty in a secret trial, were paired with modest economic concessions by the regime, thus ending this particular wave of unrest.[104] However, one sociologist calls these demonstrations evidence of a "veritable labor insurgency" underway in China.[105]

All of China's industrial workers are members of the only "trade union" body allowed to exist - the All-China Federation of Trade Unions (ACFTU). The ACFTU is a constituent body of the Chinese State and thus is controlled by Communist Party cadre. As in the former Soviet Union and its Eastern European satellites, this is a "trade union" in name only. It is, in fact, in the Chinese regime's own words, "a mass organization of the working class" and it serves as a transmission belt for the party and state leadership. The Communist Party appoints all of its officials. As the ACFTU itself stated in 1990, "The administration of union cadres by the Party is an unchangeable principle. The ACFTU should work together with the Organisation Department of the Central Committee of the [Chinese Communist Party] in laying down regulations concerning cadre management and in monitoring the nomination, investigation, election, approval and allocation of union leaders."[106] The same document goes on to state that:

> Trade unions must resolutely oppose any organisation or individual expressing political views countering those of the Party ... On discovering the formation of workers' organizations which oppose the Four Cardinal Principles[107] and endanger the national regime, the trade union must immediately report to same-level party committees and senior-level unions, and must resolutely expose and dissolve them. When necessary, the union should demand the dissolution of such organisations by the government in accordance with the law. Concerning organisations initiated by workers out of their specific economic interests, the union should advise them to dissolve and terminate their activities through persuasion and counseling.[108]

Thus, the ACFTU serves as the "eyes and ears" of the state inside every workplace. Far from supporting democratic and free trade unionism, the ACFTU's central purpose is to carry out State and Party directives and to do everything it can to insure that all workers fall into line as well. It is no surprise to find out, therefore, that the ACFTU is viewed by the State as a vehicle for encouraging worker support for the very economic reform process that is devastating the social conditions of tens of millions of workers. Those who do not conform to the new economic order are subject to ACFTU "mobilizations." The Chinese political police (Public Security Bureau or "PSB") have issued "guidelines" that state that:

> The unions must ... co-ordinate with the PSB, organise "public order and prevention teams" to protect the internal security and order of the enterprises, as well as social order.

Staff and workers should be mobilized to struggle against all forms of criminal and illegal behaviour. The union must also assist the relevant authorities to deal adequately with the education and employment of dismissed employees, workers who have committed errors and those have completed sentences and been released.[109]

This kind of directive can only be characterized as chilling.

In addition to the dramatic human rights picture and the suppression of basic trade union freedoms, the general situation of workers present particular problems. Unemployment and forced migration have already been mentioned. Further problems include the widespread use of under-employment, short-term work and contract labor, the continued control of labor mobility by the State, and massive violations of basic health and safety precautions. Official statistics report nearly 7 million unemployed urban workers, but the China Labour Bulletin estimates that the total is closer to 21 million.[110] And even official statistics admit to 30 million "more [workers] than needed" in the urban areas. These are now supplemented by some 80 to 100 million "floating people" who have left their villages looking for work in other areas of the country.[111]

Despite the need for a massive shift in employment to new entities, the State fears that uncontrolled mobility could open the door to organized opposition to the regime. Thus, it has largely kept in place a decades-old system of labor registration - the hukou system.[112] Under hukou every Chinese citizen is required to "have a registration with the hukou authority or hukou police at birth."[113] In theory, no Chinese may work or live outside of the area where they were registered at birth. To accommodate some economic pressures, the regime has instituted a system for providing workers with temporary residence permits. Punishment of both employers and employees is meted out if workers are hired without a permit.

The PetroChina IPO emerged within this matrix of workforce issues. It was seen by the regime as part of a long-range plan of the State to dismiss the one million or so workers of CNPC. The precise plans were, and remain, unclear. The sketchy offering documents provided to investors indicated that the new entity would send a portion of the proceeds from the IPO up to the parent CNPC to make severance payments to the laid off workers.[114] Severance varies from region to region in China, but was expected to be one year's average salary, or $ 1200 per worker. PetroChina and CNPC tried to reassure investors that these obligations would not absorb the lion's share of the new entity's profits, but doubts persisted.[115] Further, any such reassurances meant appearing to leave the problem of severance unsolved. In fact, the Daqing protests in 2002 were in reaction to an attempt to cut back on the severance package awarded to dismissed CNPC and PetroChina workers.[116] Since collective bargaining does not exist in China, the CNPC workforce has no voice in any of the discussions about these issues now underway among CNPC executives, State and Communist Party representatives, and the legions of foreign investment bankers, lawyers, accountants, and consultants periodically employed to advise the company and regime. Thus, foreign investors - many of them institutions like pension funds, university endowments, and mutual funds that now are at the core of global capital markets - were being asked to participate in a large socio-economic experiment masked as just another IPO. It was this unusual situation that would help give rise to the unprecedented PetroChina Campaign.

### D. Corporate Governance

As is widely understood among the fund managers responsible for the assets of large institutional investors, the concept of "fiduciary duty" must guide all investment decisions. This is a judicially created doctrine that obligates the fiduciary "to act for someone else's benefit, while subordinating one's personal interests to that of the other person."[117] It is considered the "highest standard of duty implied by law."[118] In the memorable words of Justice Cardozo:

> Many forms of conduct permissible in a workaday world for those acting at arm's length, are forbidden to those bound by fiduciary ties. A trustee is held to something stricter than

the morals of the market place. Not honesty alone, but the punctilio of an honor the most sensitive, is then the standard of behavior. As to this there has developed a tradition that is unbending and inveterate. Uncompromising rigidity has been the attitude of courts of equity when petitioned to undermine the rule of undivided loyalty by the "disintegrating erosion" of particular exceptions .... Only thus has the level of conduct for fiduciaries been kept at a level higher than that trodden by the crowd. It will not consciously be lowered by any judgment of this court.[119]

In a financial context, such a duty requires the fiduciary to manage the assets under his or her control as a prudent person would manage his or her own property. In the context of a decision to purchase equity in an unprecedented structure and in a foreign country that has little or no experience with private enterprise and capital markets, it can only be considered prudent for an investment manager or trustee to consider a wide range of issues that in an American or European context can be taken for granted. Whereas in the United States, for example, it is at least plausible to rely on the price and volatility of the stock markets to provide investors with sufficient information to make investment decisions. This was simply impossible in the case of the PetroChina offering.[120]

The PetroChina IPO raised a wide range of additional concerns. These included the risks associated with the outmoded physical assets of the Chinese oil industry, the potential for continuing state interference in the new entity's management, the influence of the regime's broader policy concerns on the future direction of the entity, and the human and labor rights concerns that massive layoffs raise. However, an additional set of issues that are traditional areas of interest for investment managers were of particular concern in the offering. These formed the backdrop for the eventual success of the campaign against the IPO. In turn, these issues, together with the labor and human rights concerns, have become a significant part of the content of changes to the capital markets that are being raised in a variety of settings in the wake of the campaign, including the issuance of the Unger Letter.[121] These fiduciary-related questions, all of which are the subject of disclosure requirements under U.S. securities laws, included concerns about the size and price of the offering, the use of proceeds from the offering, the potential difficulties for the new entity in an intensely competitive global market, the lack of modern forms of corporate governance in China, the absence of a market for corporate control to enforce discipline on management, and several other risk factors.

### 1. The Size and Price of the Deal

Throughout the offering process, the deal team appeared to be uncertain about its direction. Early reports indicated that PetroChina would sell as much as $ 10 billion worth of common stock.[122] That was then scaled back to as little as $ 5 billion in some reports, though the consensus figure was thought to be about $ 7 billion. This was then publicly scaled back by the deal team to $ 5 billion - with a suggestion that that had been their goal all along. However, when the $ 10 billion amount surfaced in the business press, the team made no apparent effort to dissuade investors that that was their goal. As indicated, the final amount was scaled back again to the end result of $ 2.9 billion. Only a last-minute injection of cash from BP[123] and several Beijing friendly Hong Kong financiers saved the offering.[124]

Deal size often fluctuates prior to the pricing of a deal, but rarely in such large volumes. In addition, the fluctuations appeared to reflect great uncertainty about the potential success of the offering, in light of the failure of the October 1999 effort by CNOOC and the weakness of the Beijing Airport offering. This offering was part of a larger plan to bring through several additional deals in the oil sector and other major industrial sectors. All told, China probably hoped to raise almost US $ 20 billion in the year following this IPO. Even at US $ 7 billion there was some doubt that the capital markets would be willing to absorb the issue. "Oil and gas is not exactly a hot spot for IPOs right now," one portfolio manager said.[125] "Technology has been and continues to be the place to be." While a leading oil industry source noted that "it was clear that demand was weak for the IPO when lead underwriter Goldman Sachs slashed the size of the offering in mid-March."[126] In addition to cutting back on the deal size, the underwriters aimed for a conservative price of 5.5 times 1999 EBITDA,[127] below the 7.5x multiple that contributed to the CNOOC disaster. But this priced PetroChina well below the 8-10x generally found in the oil industry. Thus, the Wall Street Journal concluded, "investors are likely to get their low price because reformers believe that the listing must succeed. But as an executive close to the company says: "It's a story that takes some explanation."[128] Once again, the larger political context of the offering is crucial to understanding its dynamic.

### 2. The Use of Proceeds from the Offering

There was serious dispute about the proposed use of proceeds. The public controversy centered on the investment by CNPC in an oil exploration venture in the Sudan. Feeling the political heat, PetroChina and its underwriter Goldman Sachs altered the text of its first draft of the preliminary prospectus and alleged in an amendment that the Sudan project would stay at the parent level and not be managed by PetroChina.[129] Potential investors also expressed concern about suggestions that PetroChina had agreed to dividend earnings up to CNPC for the retirement of corporate debt and to make severance payments to laid-off workers. Such payments would consume half the proceeds of the offering, leaving investors wondering what they were really buying: social protection for the threatened management of an obsolete company or the shining "crown jewels" of a new global player in the energy business? The remaining proceeds were not felt to be "enough to invest in exploration or infrastructure projects, let alone expanding its petrochemical and retail network of petrol stations.... What CNPC is saying is: "We are big and we are lousy but we will get better with your money," said one banker. That is not the way to enter the international markets. Investors are not a bunch of simpletons."[130]

### 3. Competitiveness of the New Entity

It is unclear whether or not PetroChina would be a profitable firm if it were truly to stand on its own and compete with foreign oil companies. CNPC remained the beneficiary of substantial government protection. Much of the Chinese oil sector receives price protection on the domestic market and benefits from restrictions on imported product. The Financial Times reported that CNPC "must persuade investors it can compete in the absence of government protection. Its profits ... have been virtually guaranteed by the state."[131] When this concern was placed next to the issue of repaying CNPC's remaining indebtedness, approximately US $ 14 billion at the time the offering was announced,[132] investors clearly had reason to worry about where their money would be going. PetroChina would take over the key productive assets of CNPC and the parent was to be left with one million redundant workers. How would those debts be repaid and the pension obligations for the redundant workers be met? The need to fend off social unrest with a severance package is apparently the motivation behind a requirement that half of PetroChina's earnings be earmarked as dividends for CNPC. Yet this has clearly not worked.[133] Since CNPC remains in control of eighty-five percent of the company's stock, enforcing that requirement will not be a problem - but any expectation that outside shareholders will share equally in the rewards is called into question.

### 4. Parent and Party Control

CNPC, of course, controls both the board of directors and shareholders' meetings. Some smaller CNPC subsidiaries had shares listed in Hong Kong in the past and in no instance have outside shareholders been given any management or board-level role in the company. This past history led one oil industry analysis to suggest that "by offering corporate shares without allowing any participation in the corporate management, the Chinese state oil companies will have to prove to the potential foreign investors that their business operations are competitive, transparent and well-managed."[134] Of course, it should also be asked precisely how an investor is to exercise "shareholder democracy" - which lies at the heart of capitalism's investment philosophy - in a country where the most basic democratic rights are violated on a daily basis. Will shareholders be free to speak at shareholder meetings? Will they be granted the right of assembly, free speech, and the ability to present grievances to management that are denied PetroChina's own workers? For that matter, can the new management team at PetroChina - to be compensated via an unprecedented incentive scheme tied to company performance[135] - be counted on to speak freely about the company's problems?

Chinese law makes it illegal for the shares held directly by the state or state-owned enterprises in an SOE to be traded on a secondary market.[136] Thus, mergers and acquisitions are practically impossible. PetroChina management will be free of one of the basic sources of competitive pressure on the modern corporation: the fear that poor performance will result in the sale of the company and the dismissal of current management. In the words of one observer,

> even after converting a state enterprise into a joint stock company under the Company Law and publicly offering its stocks for trading under the securities laws, the pressure on the state enterprise's manager to perform well remains minimal. The state still maintains effective public ownership, and private investors have very limited influence on management.[137]

As noted above, all top Company officers are cadre of the Chinese Communist Party and thus never face the prospect of real unemployment.

While share offerings by Chinese companies are the exception, some prior experience is available. A review of the risks that these companies face, taken from their filings with the SEC, indicate the following common concerns: the value of China's currency, the renminbi, is subject to change based on government policy and should be considered potentially volatile; the Chinese government controls the convertibility of the renminbi into foreign exchange and this could be used to hinder payouts to shareholders; companies may not be able to secure sufficient foreign exchange to carry out restructuring; China's legal system is not complete and, therefore, enforcement of existing laws or contracts based on existing law may be uncertain and sporadic, and it may be difficult to obtain timely and equitable enforcement of those contracts and laws.[138] All of these issues have a common root: the continued role of an undemocratic regime in its nation's core economic entities. These would all fuel the concerns that led to the PetroChina Campaign.


## The PetroChina Campaign

As word of the proposed initial public offering of PetroChina began to spread in late 1999, a loosely formed coalition of groups emerged to oppose it. This was an exceptional event in the capital markets. Boycotts of economic activity have been used by political groups for many years, most notably the divestment campaign aimed at breaking the apartheid regime of South Africa.[139] Opposition to a particular offering by a specific company, however, was then and remains exceptional.[140] In the end, though, it was the structure and then the success of this coalition that was the true exception. It was this exceptional quality, I will argue below, that signaled the larger political, social, and legal significance of the Campaign.

Opposition emerged, initially, from anti-slavery, religious, and conservative national security groups who focused on the operations of PetroChina parent CNPC in the oil-rich African nation of Sudan. The Sudanese-based Greater Nile Oil Project, a joint venture in which CNPC held a minority position, was accused of human rights violations including the use of forced labor.[141] In fact, the Chinese originally intended to bring CNPC itself public directly but backed off when it realized that the parent company's role in the Sudan would trigger political opposition. The decision was then made to set up PetroChina as a subsidiary of CNPC, leaving the Sudanese operations at the parent level. In its prospectus prepared for investors with the assistance of Goldman Sachs, PetroChina explained that it received "most of the assets, liabilities and interests of CNPC relating to CNPC's domestic exploration and production, refining and marketing, chemicals and natural gas businesses," while "CNPC retained ... assets and liabilities relating to international crude oil and natural gas exploration and production and refining and pipeline operations."[142] In addition, CNPC and PetroChina pledged to "establish separate accounts into which their respective proceeds" from the IPO would be deposited. CNPC asserted that it would use its income from the sale of its shares in the IPO only to repay debt and fund employee retraining and severance, and not for its Sudanese joint venture.[143]

This structural arrangement, known in financial circles, perhaps regrettably, as a "Chinese Wall," was insufficient to quell these early critics. A largely, though not exclusively, conservative group of some 200 people led by former Republican Secretary of the Treasury William E. Simon and former Nicaraguan contra backer and Assistant Secretary of State Elliott Abrams signed an open letter to President Clinton on December 9, 1999, soon after the first draft of the PetroChina registration statement had been filed with the SEC. They argued that:

> CNPC and its investment banker, Goldman Sachs, will shortly seek to avoid the Executive Order[144] [blocking U.S. funds from the Sudan] and public censure by a "restructuring" scheme purporting to withhold IPO funds from CNPC's commitments in Sudan, Iraq and other terrorist states. The fungibility of money and the scale of CNPC's activities in Sudan thoroughly undermine the credibility of the contrivance. No such arrangement would have been permitted to evade America's successful assault on South African apartheid, and it must not be permitted to do so in the service of Sudanese genocide.[145]

These objections began to register politically. President Clinton's Treasury Department expanded the list of prohibited companies in the Sudan to include the Greater Nile Petroleum Operating Co., Ltd.[146] A group of largely conservative religious leaders sent a similar letter to large institutional investors, including major pension funds.[147]

Nonetheless, PetroChina and Goldman Sachs continued to plunge ahead with their preparations for the offering. An upbeat account of the proposed new offering appeared in Business Week in late January 2000, with only scant reference to the Sudanese connection.[148] Even this was swatted away with nary a second thought by Goldman's leading international spokesman, Robert Hormats: Sudan is "not an issue because of the extraordinary steps the company is taking to ensure IPO proceeds are only used domestically," he argued.[149] At this point it was not clear that the emerging PetroChina coalition would have the weight to stop the offering. The largest and most politically-sensitive pension funds, the giant college teacher based TIAA-Cref and the California Public Employees Retirement System (CalPERS), together managing more than $400 billion in assets, refused to commit one way or the other.[150]

At this point, the new coalition received an exceptional boost. The AFL-CIO publicly announced its opposition to the IPO with the publication of a detailed report echoing the concerns of the religious, human rights, and anti-slavery groups but also discussing the kinds of corporate governance, legal, and labor concerns described in Part I of this chapter.[151] Pointedly, the AFL-CIO report ignored the national security concerns raised by the conservative elements in the informal coalition. The labor federation held a conference call with Wall Street investment managers to announce the release of the report and it was widely reported in the financial press.[152] The federation's new Office of Investment, headed by experienced shareholder and labor activist William Patterson, began a systematic effort to discuss the problems with the offering with fund managers and pension fund trustees.

The AFL-CIO was able to bring considerable weight to the discussions. The labor federation has thirteen million members in the United States. Labor union trustees sit on the boards of union-sponsored pension funds that manage approximately $ 400 billion in financial assets. They also sit on the boards of major public pension funds that manage an additional $ 1 trillion in assets. These funds, in turn, hire fund managers that were part of the same investment banks conducting the PetroChina IPO and planning several other Chinese IPO's. With tens of millions of dollars of fees at stake, there was little doubt that Wall Street would be forced to listen to this new voice in the capital markets. Within a few days of the AFL-CIO intervention, both TIAA-Cref and CalPERS announced their intention not to purchase shares in the IPO.[153] Over the next several weeks the Campaign snowballed as more funds agreed not to purchase shares in the offering.

Some on Wall Street seemed to get the message. Mark Melcher, a leading analyst at Prudential Securities, and his colleague Stephen Soukup, issued a report assessing the impact of the Campaign. Responding to some who called the IPO's opponents "economic Luddites" who would have a "temporary" impact, they said that such a view was:

> Dead wrong...this is, as the song goes, the start of something big.... When the dust settles on this dispute, the gurus of international investment banking will find that their jobs have been made permanently more difficult by the appearance of a new social investment category that has been declared taboo by some of their largest customers, and by the addition of a new and highly complicated variable to their already crowded due-diligence agendas.[154]

The high point of this Campaign, or perhaps the low point from the perspective of PetroChina and Goldman Sachs, was a near physical confrontation between the bankers and their oil company clients, on the one hand, and, on the other, the protestors at the St. Regis Hotel in New York City in late March 2000. As part of its "road show," a standard means of bringing company executives together with potential investors in advance of a securities offering, Goldman had scheduled a luncheon at the hotel for potential investors in the IPO. The AFL-CIO scheduled what it called a "counter road show" in the same hotel. Richard Trumka, as its Secretary-Treasurer the number two leader of the labor federation, and a former head of the militant United Mine Workers Union, led the union delegation. The trade unionists brought with them a Tibetan monk to talk about the oil company's impact in Tibet and Harry Wu, the well-known survivor of the Laogai, China's prison labor camps. The morning of the road show Goldman Sachs decided to avoid the confrontation and cancelled their luncheon at the St. Regis, setting up shop instead a few blocks away at the Four Seasons.[155] The labor-led force, meanwhile, held their very visible press conference at the St. Regis.

A week after the near confrontation in New York, a Congressional group including Republican Spencer Bachus, Democrat Dennis Kucinich, and Socialist Bernard Sanders, addressed a letter to President Clinton echoing the Campaign's concern that the company would use proceeds from the IPO to support environmentally-damaging projects in Tibet and the joint venture in Sudan.[156] These events took their toll. The company and its bankers were forced to rethink the deal. The launch date was pushed back and, as reports of investor disinterest or opposition came in, they scaled back the size of the offering, from an initial goal of raising $ 10 billion to the final figure of $ 2.9 billion.[157]

## The Unger Letter

The impact of the Campaign, however, did not stop with the actual IPO. PetroChina's stock price sank below the stated offering price upon its debut and took months to recover.[158] A headline in The New York Times said it all: "China's No. 1 Oil Company Goes Public With Whimper."[159] The Chinese government absorbed their experience with this flagship offering and announced it would be delaying or shelving altogether the planned offering of several other industrial companies.[160] Meanwhile the emboldened participants in the PetroChina Campaign turned their attention to potential regulatory and institutional reform.

Responding to complaints from fund managers at major investment banks, the AFL-CIO began an effort to establish investment screens at the pension funds on whose boards they sat.[161] The fund managers claimed they had been "blindsided" by the Campaign and, fearing the loss of management fees, said they would be happy to implement the approach of the Campaign if given clear guidance by pension fund trustees. The most significant and successful effort came at CalPERS, the giant public employee retirement fund for California state employees. After months of research and lobbying, the labor trustees on the CalPERS board led by Sean Harrigan, a vice president of the United Food and Commercial Workers union and now president of CalPERS, and joined by sympathetic public officials such as Phil Angelides, California's state treasurer, and Willie Brown, San Francisco mayor and a gubernatorial appointee to the board, proposed and won the adoption of a new policy governing the fund's equity investments in the so-called "emerging market" countries, including China.

The new CalPERS policy required the $147 billion fund's staff to begin active management of its "emerging market" equity investments and to hire new fund managers with an active, as opposed to passive or indexed, investment approach. The trustees also approved a list of "investibility screens" aimed at shaping the Fund's investments in emerging markets. According to CalPERS, "the screens outline financial and economic factors, and three additional factors that include transparency, political stability and prohibitions on abusive labor practices. Managers will [now] be selected based on their ability to invest in emerging markets and adherence to the Global Sullivan Principles and the International Labor Organization's Declaration on Fundamental Principles and Rights at Work."[162] The substance of the new CalPERS policy reflected the same issues raised by the PetroChina Campaign and, in fact, many of the individuals involved in the Campaign took part in the effort to shape and implement the new CalPERS policy.

The impact of the new policy was soon felt when CalPERS announced that it would suspend future equity investments in several countries, including Indonesia, Thailand, Malaysia, and the Philippines. At the same time the fund announced it would open the door to new investment in Poland and Hungary due to improvements in those countries.[163] The announcement sent share prices in several Asian markets tumbling and set off an intense round of negotiations as those countries attempted to make changes in domestic policy in order to win back CalPERS investments.[164] Months of lobbying by the Philippine government convinced CalPERS to reverse its position against equity investments there. The fund agreed to back a new investment fund in Thailand sponsored by a private investment group and the International Finance Corporation (IFC), an arm of the World Bank, but, so far, none of the committed capital has been invested. The fund will "only make investments in companies that agree to comply with Government of Thailand and IFC environmental and social policies, including high standards of corporate governance and transparency."[165] A dialogue between CalPERS and senior Thai government officials is underway, and the implementation of domestic reforms there may open the door to future investment.[166] A similar policy is being considered by the New York City retirement system and the State of Connecticut public employees fund.[167]

A broader political campaign was underway as well. The AFL-CIO and others in the loosely organized "PetroChina Coalition" argued that disclosure documents filed by PetroChina and Goldman Sachs with the SEC all but ignored the risks highlighted by the Campaign. Responding to these concerns, a Congressionally-created United States Commission on International Religious Freedom issued a report in May of 2000 that called for greater disclosure by PetroChina, especially with respect to the use of proceeds from the IPO to pay off parent company CNPC debt. "Millions of those dollars from CNPC's sale of PetroChina shares may well end up benefiting" the joint venture in Sudan.[168] The Commission called on the SEC to "be especially careful to investigate the adequacy and reliability of representations made in any filings related to the recent sale by CNPC and PetroChina of PetroChina shares."[169]

This discussion led, in turn, to pressure for legislative or other regulatory reform with respect to disclosure by foreign corporations that attempt to issue securities in the U.S. capital markets. In March of 2001, Republican Congressman Frank Wolf, of Virginia, addressed a letter to Laura Unger, who was then serving as Acting Chairman of the Securities and Exchange Commission following the departure of longtime SEC Chairman Arthur Levitt.[170] Congressman Wolf noted the role that PetroChina's parent company CNPC played "in providing the Government of Sudan with unprecedented resources to carry out its war and atrocities against

Southern Sudan" and contended, "more people are suffering and have died because of the PetroChina listing."[171] He argued that the purchase of shares in the offering might have violated a 1997 Executive Order that imposed "comprehensive economic sanctions on Sudan."[172] He urged Chairman Unger "to vigorously investigate this matter and take appropriate action" and argued that the apparent violation of the Executive Order "offers grounds for de-listing PetroChina from the NYSE [the New York Stock Exchange]."[173] He sent nearly identical letters to Secretary of the Treasury Paul O'Neil and Chairman of the New York Stock Exchange Richard Grasso. He followed up the letter with a direct meeting with Unger and a second letter on April 2, 2001.

Chairman Unger replied to the Wolf letters and meeting on May 8, 2001 with a detailed five-page letter and the submission of a memorandum by David B.H. Martin, then Director of the Division of Corporate Finance of the SEC.[174] The Division has major responsibility for reviewing and assessing the disclosure provided by issuers of securities on a U.S. securities exchange, including the New York Stock Exchange where PetroChina had listed its securities.[175] The Unger Letter detailed the actions that the SEC had taken in response to the Wolf inquiries and outlined several initiatives it planned to undertake in the near future. The Chairman and staff of the SEC met or spoke with representatives of several of the organizations included in the PetroChina Campaign or knowledgeable about the offering, including the Center for Security Policy, the U.S. Commission on International Religious Freedom, the U.S. State Department, and the Treasury Department's Office of Foreign Assets Control (OFAC).[176] In the discussions with other federal agencies, the SEC "raised the possibility of interagency cooperation on Sudan."[177]

The Chairman met with Directors of each of the SEC's major divisions and she stated that "they are sensitized to this issue and will be looking for creative ways to enhance investors' access to material information about foreign investment in Sudan and its impact on the human rights situation there."[178] As suggested in the next section, this commitment is the crucial step taken by the Unger Letter, reinforced by the several initiatives promised by the

Chairman. These include: a proposed rulemaking to require electronic filing by foreign companies who register their securities with the SEC; a new requirement that the SEC will end selective review of filings by certain foreign issuers and instead "review all registration statements filed by foreign companies which reflect material business dealings with governments or countries subject to U.S. economic sanctions"; a requirement of "enhanced disclosure" in securities filings by foreign issuers doing business in sanctioned countries; a commitment to bring to the attention of OFAC any disclosure in registration statements filed by foreign companies which "reflect material dealings" with countries subject to sanctions; and support for the "formation of an interagency working group on Sudan."[179]

## Some Initial Arguments

Whether or not the Unger Letter was a "bombshell," as the Financial Times suggested, its release nonetheless certainly hit a nerve. It seemed to confirm the worst fears of leading financial figures like Federal Reserve Chairman Alan Greenspan, who quickly denounced efforts to attach political criteria to disclosure when given a chance in testimony to the Senate Banking Committee a few weeks after the release of the Letter.[180] His opportunity to begin a counter-attack on the PetroChina Campaign came when asked a very friendly question by then Chairman of the Committee, Senator Phil Gramm, Republican of Texas, in reference to proposed legislation that would limit China's ability to raise capital in the U.S. capital markets. Gramm noted:

> Mr. Chairman [referring to Greenspan], as you're aware, we have spent years battling the effort by [the] American government to use trade as a tool of foreign policy....And except for those pariah states, where we have virtually a state of war...we have gotten away from using economic trade as a tool of foreign policy. We now have a new proposal...that seeks for the first time to use access to our banking system as an instrument of American foreign

policy.... [These] tools that are being used represent, in my opinion, a very real threat to our prosperity....[181]

The Chairman of the Federal Reserve embraced the concerns of Senator Gramm wholeheartedly:

> Mr. Chairman, I certainly agree with the comments you have made, and I clearly understand the motives underlying Senator [Fred] Thompson's bringing this amendment forward.... It's the openness and the lack of political pressures within the [American financial] system which has made it such an effective component of our economy and, indeed, has drawn foreigners generally to the American markets for financing as being the most efficient place where they can in many cases raise funds.... To the extent that we block foreigners from investing, from raising funds in the United States, we probably undercut the viability of our own system.... I am not even sure how such a law would be effectively implemented.... If we were to block China or anybody else for that matter from borrowing in the United States, they could very readily borrow in London and be financed [there] by American investors.... And therefore I must say, Mr. Chairman, I join in your concerns about that amendment and I trust it would not move forward.... [182]

Chairman Greenspan's comments pose a serious challenge for proponents of human rights and other related "social" or "political" disclosure through the capital markets. Is there really a debilitating paradox at work here, as Greenspan suggests? Do efforts to advance the international human rights agenda through the capital markets have the effect of destroying the very functioning of those capital markets? Traditional approaches to securities regulation provide a useful but, in the end, only partial response to this question. A closer look at recent changes in the structure of the global capital markets, and in the political responses to the globalization process that underlies those structural changes, provides a useful supplement to our understanding. This Part reviews each of these three in turn and suggests both their value and their limitations.

## A. The Traditional Securities Law Approach

The core principle behind capital market regulation in the United States, and many other leading economies, particularly the United Kingdom, is quite straightforward.[183] No security can be offered or sold in the United States, unless the transaction is registered with the Securities and Exchange Commission or an exemption to that registration requirement is available. If a transaction is to be registered, then the seller of the security must provide adequate disclosure of all material information about the issuer and the security to potential purchasers. Even in transactions where the seller has an available exemption, disclosure that is almost the equivalent of that provided in registered offerings will occur because of demand from potential buyers. It is thought disclosure, like sunshine, is "the best of disinfectants."[184] The basic disclosure obligations were put in place in the 1930s in response to a major capital shock that brought the U.S. economy to a standstill. Rampant conflicts of interest and obscure and overly complex financial schemes were found to pervade the securities industry.[185] While the New Deal Era architects of the new regime had much more ambitious plans for restructuring of the U.S. financial and corporate system, the disclosure requirements were their longest lasting and perhaps most significant reform.[186]

A key word in this basic disclosure framework is the concept of materiality, which has been the subject of agency interpretation and judicial pronouncement ever since the passage of the original securities acts. And at one level the entire debate about whether or not human rights concerns belong inside the capital markets can be explored within the framework of the concept of materiality. Understandably, given the mandate of the SEC, that is the way in which the Unger Letter frames the question. Unger notes that as a result of the campaign against the PetroChina IPO, the SEC had become "sensitized" to issues involving human rights and the capital markets. She stated that the Commission and its staff would be "looking for creative ways to enhance investors' access to material information" about issuers who access the U.S. capital markets and have investments in countries like the Sudan - where PetroChina's parent company had significant operations - and the impact of such investments on human rights.[187]

A focus on materiality originally arose in the securities law regime because of important structural changes that were taking place in the forms of corporate organization and in the financial markets.[188] As economic activity became more complex and grew in scale and scope in the early part of the twentieth century, entrepreneurs were increasingly forced to widen their search for capital beyond family structures. The corporate form of economic organization became dominant along with its central structural characteristic - the separation of ownership and control - which was described so vividly in the landmark study by Berle and Means, written in the wake of the 1929 Crash.[189] Berle and Means were in a sense frightened by the emergence of a separation between ownership and control of the modern corporation, between a dispersed shareholder base and a centralized managerial group, because of the implications that a concentration of economic power in small groups of insiders had for a democracy. This structure was both a solution to an emerging problem - the increasing complexity of modern industry - and a cause of a new set of problems, namely problems of governance within the new framework and between this new corporate world and the surrounding polity.[190]

Modern securities regulation helped to solve the new problems by providing shareholders a consistent and reliable information package in the form of regular disclosure by publicly traded corporations and disclosure about securities offerings made by corporations. The concept of materiality - understood to mean all the information that a reasonable investor requires to make an informed investment decision[191] - lies at the heart of this disclosure regime. It is widely believed that the requirement that companies provide material information on a regular basis to shareholders and potential investors helps to close the gap between owners and managers, or, in the language of "law and economics," helps lower the costs associated with the principal-agent problem created by the separation of ownership and control.[192]

It should not seem like too big a step for the SEC to take when it acknowledges that disclosure about potential human rights violations by a corporation, or associated with a corporation's operations, could be considered material to a potential investor. The SEC already requires companies to disclose details about their environmental liabilities, potential problems related to intellectual property, and relationships with employees. The SEC long ago agreed to increase disclosure of so-called "soft" information, such as projections about the future course of a company's business model, even making available a safe harbor for forward-looking statements.[193] In fact, the triumph of the "efficient market hypothesis"[194] would appear to reinforce the requirement that progressive effort be made to expand the reach of disclosure requirements. Because the hypothesis mandates that past, or hard, information is of little use to the evaluation of a company's future prospects, the door was opened to the requirement that soft information about the impact of future events be disclosed to the markets.[195] More recently, the SEC signaled its interest in increasing the level of disclosure by companies of what are called "intangibles," such as human capital and intellectual property.[196] The mandate of the Unger Letter is entirely consistent with this approach.

Nonetheless, in addition to the competitive and other concerns raised by Alan Greenspan, some commentators worry that Chairman Unger opened up a kind of Pandora's box. A recent Note in the Harvard Law Review commented:

> One observer has suggested that the Unger Letter will "lead to lobbying for further measures by the SEC to demand additional disclosure on environmental or broader human rights grounds.' Indeed. Not to mention equal employment opportunity, workplace and consumer safety, and any other political or social concern implicated by corporate behavior. If the SEC has concluded that information unrelated to a firm's financial performance may nonetheless be material, then it has opened a door to all types of mandated disclosure.[197]

This comment reflects a disconcerting misreading of current securities law requirements which, as noted above, mandate a wealth of complex disclosure requirements that already can or do include much of what the Note's author worries about.[198]   In addition, the comment seems to have been made in ignorance of the origins of the Unger Letter in the PetroChina Campaign where, as this chapter demonstrates, it was not whether to disclose certain non-traditional risk factors (since PetroChina made extensive disclosures of non-traditional information) but how to disclose them in a manner that investors found meaningful.   As the Martin Memorandum transmitted to Congressman Wolf by Chairman Unger notes, "the Supreme Court has held that information is material if "there is substantial likelihood that a reasonable shareholder would consider it important in making an investment decision.'  TSC Indus. Inc. v. Northway, Inc., 426 U.S. 438, 449 (1976)."[199]   That disclosure about human rights violations or violations of U.S. economic sanctions are unusual or non-traditional is not to be doubted.   There is little basis, however, to suggest that that alone renders such disclosure non-material, even if one takes the traditional approach to materiality adopted by the SEC, which "generally focuses on matters that have affected, or will affect, a company's profitability and financial outlook."[200]   Indeed, that is the grounding provided by the SEC in the Martin Memorandum.  Equally important in securities law, however, is the meaningful nature of disclosure, something that is just as much, if not more, at issue in securities law since the PetroChina Campaign. One court stated, "the registration process established under the [Securities] Act [of 1933] is designed to require disclosure to investors in a meaningful manner of the material facts concerning securities which are offered to members of the public."[201]

The fact that the Harvard Law Review Note is grounded in a "law and economics" analysis may explain its limitations.[202]  The standard set of law and economics objections to the established securities law regime include concern about federal as opposed to state regulation of the financial markets, and stronger objections to the once widely accepted norm that the market itself is not likely to mandate such disclosure if left to its own devices.  These federalist and private ordering objections to the securities law regime do raise important concerns and often highlight flaws in regulatory practice.[203] Nonetheless, these issues are not triggered in particular by the efforts to add human rights disclosure to the regime. The decision about whether or not human rights disclosure is a good thing or not seems a priori to the discussion of what institutional means should be adopted to make sure the goals agreed upon are reached. Furthermore, the emergence of the PetroChina Syndrome reflects a change in the nature of the global economy. The institutions that have traditionally regulated economic activity must adapt to reflect those changes. Traditional law and economics analysis provides only a partial explanation for the PetroChina Syndrome, and thus will be inadequate to the task of mapping an institutional future for the global economy.

There is a further potential objection from law and economics, however, that might be more appropriately raised by the evolution in the disclosure regime indicated by the Unger Letter. Opponents of this kind of disclosure could conceivably argue that the requirements of the Letter amount to a regulatory taking[204] if it were found that the new disclosure regime was strict enough that it might either prevent companies from raising capital in the U.S. securities markets - as suggested is indeed possible by the Lukoil example[205] - or because it might force companies to restructure their operations in significant ways in order to provide the markets with positive sounding disclosure. The latter possibility assumes, of course, that companies will be reluctant to affirm that they do indeed violate international human rights or progressive corporate governance standards. For example, one of the arguments raised by the oil industry is that it is forced to operate in parts of the world where there are all sorts of bad actors. They have to go where the oil is and deal with whomever controls it, thus some level of association with human rights violations seems almost inevitable. There are problems with this view of international business activity and with the way that oil companies use this argument. There is, for example, an extensive and rapidly growing literature on socially responsible business activity that undermines the cogency of this position from within the business community itself.[206] Nonetheless, one could imagine the development of a counter-attack to the Unger Letter logic from business along these lines.[207]

There is a natural response to the potential takings complaint based in the analysis suggested above regarding the expansion of the disclosure regime mandated by the Unger Letter.[208] I argued there that the commitment by Chairman Unger to look for "creative ways to enhance investors' access to material information" about human rights violations was consistent with the general principles articulated for many years by the SEC with respect to disclosure.[209] There is, therefore, in the SEC's approach to disclosure, the kind of "structural habit" that Holmes suggested placed a limit on the application of the takings argument.[210] As Robert Brauneis has written:

> Holmes thought that the positive law of a jurisdiction could be described, not just as an accidental aggregation of specific, unrelated rules, but as a body of law that exhibited an internal structure, organized around a variety of principles or paradigm cases. Those "structural habits" provided a basis for assessing how much change in positive law a particular piece of legislation caused.... The "property" protected by the Constitution is not a theorist's ideal, but the actual, established practice of a particular legal tradition.... [The regulation in question] must be evaluated in terms of how different it is from established practice.... [Where] it "is not different in fundamental principle" - it does not amount to so drastic a change as to require compensation.[211]

Brauneis argues that Holmes' view was that only "radical, discontinuous alterations" in one's property rights where "change was measured as deviation from fundamental principles, or structural habits, embedded in the organized body of standing positive law" were deserving of constitutional protection.[212]

There is another deeper dimension to this argument that must be considered. The flip side of a regulatory taking, particularly in a world of global capital flows, is "regulatory arbitrage."[213] This occurs where corporations take advantage of the flexibility and liquidity of global capital markets to run around efforts by states to regulate corporate activity in the public interest.[214]   When this occurs it can be assumed to offend a particularly deep "structural habit."  Normally this is thought of as a "race to the bottom" as opposed to a "race to the top."[215] Typically, those who normatively favor government regulation argue that issuers will try to lower their costs by issuing securities, or chartering their corporation, in a jurisdiction with the least onerous, and perhaps least socially protective, regulatory schema. Thus an overarching regulatory framework is necessary to prevent issuer arbitrage that slowly but surely eats away at socially desirable standards.   Meanwhile, those who are more skeptical about the efficacy of government intervention argue that, in a competitive market, prices will accurately reflect investors' preferences for a particular regulatory regime, and thus an efficient market for the securities of a company can help police the regime choice.   Thus, Amir Licht argues that financial arbitrage can ameliorate the impact of regulatory arbitrage because in an efficient market the price of the company's stock will reflect the value that investors place on the company's choice or, in the case of a dual listing, its mix, of regulatory regimes.[216]   In some sense that is precisely what happened when PetroChina attempted its IPO.  The PetroChina Campaign was part of the process by which information about the company was integrated into the market price - a price, as indicated, that the underwriters adjusted downward as poor investor reaction during the road show accumulated.   Far from undermining the argument here about an expansion of the concept of materiality, this reinforces it.  Thus, the market has signaled the importance of the issues raised in the PetroChina IPO and the Unger Letter reflects that signal.

But I am suggesting a different kind of problem.  Issuers who wish to raise capital may not be able to assure investors of a high enough return on their investment to overcome the concerns raised in their home market, where the normal protections available to investors do not exist.  In such a case, the issuer may attempt to partially "expropriate" the reputation value possessed by a highly regulated and efficient market, such as that of the United States, in order to raise capital at a lower price than would otherwise be possible. Another way of stating the problem is to suggest that insiders may be able to obscure informational asymmetries that give them an advantage over outside potential purchasers of the company's securities by hiding behind the positive veil that listing in a well-established and highly-regulated market may offer. Some scholars appear to address this problem by identifying a subset of issues associated with the general set of issues called "international regulatory competition."[217] The subset looks at the possibility of "piggybacking" where issuers, as Licht points out, "may want to list their stocks on foreign markets with a view to improve their corporate governance, thereby creating shareholder value."[218] Licht argues that while most commentators conclude that this is evidence of a "race to the top" with the consequence of increases in shareholder value, his own research on Israeli companies that list extraterritorially in the United States provides evidence of a "race to the bottom," as managers take advantage of a weaker corporate governance regime in the United States.[219]

An issuer of securities in a wholly state-owned enterprise, however, could engage in an exceptional form of "managerial opportunism" in order to appropriate the value associated with the extraterritorial listing. This risk of opportunism seems likely to increase when one considers an SOE in an undemocratic society. The clash of competing interests of the multiple constituencies found in the SOE's of post World War II social democratic Europe, for example, would help mitigate the risk of managerial opportunism by greatly increasing the transparency and accountability of the offering process. But that is precisely what is absent in countries like China where the regime has delayed democratization while attempting to undertake market reforms. The legitimating impact of interest group pluralism, central to the structure of the post World War II democratic states, is entirely absent in the Stalinist form of state ownership.[220] Thus, what seems like a "regulatory taking" - the imposition of a particular disclosure regime regarding human rights - may be more properly understood as the only available corrective for this new form of regulatory arbitrage and, therefore, consistent with our established Holmesian "structural habits."

PetroChina knew that it had no chance to raise billions of dollars on its domestic Shanghai stock exchange. The Chinese government places far greater limits on capital liquidity than the United States or Europe, and institutional investors consider the level of corruption there to be intolerably high.[221] Thus, not surprisingly, the quality of the corporations that offer their shares only domestically in China is considered far worse than those that are able to make international offerings. Hence, Chinese issuers suffer a reputation effect or, rather, they add, perhaps inappropriately, to the value of their reputations if they can figure out a way to list successfully overseas, ideally in New York or London but at least in Hong Kong. For years, Chinese mainland companies have understood this problem and when seeking to raise their profile, and to raise significant amounts of new capital, have listed shares on the Honk Kong exchange.

PetroChina was not only formed to step around its parent company's operations in Sudan, but to attempt to sidestep the very serious issues that undermine the ability of China's own domestic stock exchanges to attract significant capital investment. China's new form of regulatory arbitrage was the equivalent of a kind of "social dumping"[222] when it attempted to foist the securities of its reorganized SOE's on unwitting foreign investors, who would otherwise never invest directly through a domestic Chinese exchange in the same company. As discussed above, little reassurance was offered to U.S. investors that somehow the listing requirements of the New York Stock Exchange or the rules and regulations that govern corporate behavior generally in the United States could actually be enforced against a company whose management would remain firmly in the hands of the Chinese Communist Party.[223]

B. A Structural Approach

At the core of the transition to a world of global capital markets is a shift away from commercial banks as the most important financial intermediaries to a range of new financial institutions, including pension funds, mutual funds, university endowments, and a new world of wealthy and sophisticated individual investors who provide funding for the private equity world of hedge funds, buyout groups, and venture capital. A 1996 study published by the American Enterprise Institute documented this significant development.[224] As the study noted:

> For more than two centuries banks in the United States were the main repository of households savings and the primary source of credit for businesses. They occupied the central role in the intermediation of credit. In the 1980s and 1990s all that ... changed. Innovations in financial markets ... allowed many borrowers to bypass banks entirely, and newly developed nonbank financial intermediaries ... invaded the traditional turf of banks by taking their customers and undercutting their profitability. During those two decades banks [saw] their share of traditional financial intermediation steadily eroded as non-bank financial intermediaries ... provided better substitutes for traditional banking services and as innovations in the financial markets ... enabled business borrowers to directly access credit markets for their funds.[225]

This is further evidenced by changes in the macro-economy. As a percentage of personal disposable income, U.S. savings have dropped steadily over the last twenty years, from a post World War II high of 10.9% in 1982 to a post-WW II low of 2.3% in 2001.[226] Meanwhile during the same time period there has been an explosion of borrowing through the capital markets. Credit market borrowing by the domestic non-financial sector of the economy grew explosively in the last twenty-five years from $ 194 billion per year in 1975 to $ 2 trillion in 2001.[227] Growth of total credit market debt outstanding for the domestic non-financial sector mirrored this expansion, rising from approximately $ 2.3 billion in 1975 to nearly $ 20 trillion in 2001.[228] This borrowing, of course, points to the new intermediaries, the financial players who are engaged in purchasing these debt instruments on behalf of the new creditors, namely pension funds and investment companies. As Edwards notes, "their share of intermediary assets grew from 20 percent in 1980 to almost 40 percent in 1994, and that growth shows no sign of abating."[229]   Pension funds alone owned more than 32% of the outstanding value of U.S. equities held by households in 2000.[230]

If pension funds and mutual funds, among others, are the key new financial players, this fact has not been lost upon those who manage such funds nor those who are the beneficiaries of such funds.   Most importantly, one of the central institutions of what could be called the older, and perhaps now exhausted, "Industrial Relations" era, the trade union movement, also plays a key role in this new "Capital Markets" era.[231]   Thus, as noted above, the AFL-CIO's affiliates directly control pension funds with financial assets currently valued at some $ 400 billion.   Indirectly, as trustees of plans jointly sponsored with employers or the public sector, the labor movement oversees funds with assets valued at approximately $ 5 trillion.   Under the new leadership of the AFL-CIO, which took office in 1995, the labor movement has established, in its Washington, D.C. headquarters, a Department of Corporate Affairs and an Office of Investment, and has sponsored the establishment of a non-profit entity called the Center for Working Capital.   These new organizations attempt to mobilize the financial resources found in the pension fund assets of union workforces in support of the labor movement's broad goals, including international labor standards and human rights, progressive forms of corporate governance and democratic political change in emerging markets, and other forms of socially responsible investment, while maintaining the long term returns to the funds.   In addition the AFL-CIO is working on an international effort to promote a similar approach by labor movements in other countries.   The major international labor umbrella group, the International Confederation of Free Trade Unions based in Brussels, is the sponsor of a Global Task Force that coordinates cross-border campaigns in the capital markets.

While the PetroChina Campaign became the signature event of this new movement, it is not the only example.   Just prior to its intervention in that effort - in late 1999 and early 2000 - the AFL-CIO responded to a call for assistance by the German trade union movement in the battle which erupted after a hostile takeover bid was announced by Vodafone, the upstart British mobile phone company, for Mannesmann, the giant century-old German industrial concern. In this Campaign, a further dimension of the labor movement's leverage in the financial markets became clear. While union pension funds owned only a small percentage of the shares of Mannesmann and, thus, could not likely have a significant effect on the outcome of the tender offer, the fund managers hired by pension funds to manage their investments controlled on behalf of their various clients some thirteen percent of the shares of Mannesmann.

In what has become the standard approach of the AFL-CIO in such campaigns, they issued a report to managers of pension funds that argued against the takeover bid, linking traditional union concerns with the fiduciary duty of fund managers and trustees to protect the asset value of their beneficiaries.[232]   The report was released publicly and brought to the attention of Wall Street analysts, many of whom, of course, work for the same financial institutions as the fund managers of the major pension funds.   The threat of opposition to the bid was taken seriously enough by the Vodafone team that Vodafone CEO Chris Gent made a strenuous effort to engage AFL-CIO President John Sweeney in discussions about the bid.   When Sweeney refused to engage in such discussions without the participation of German union leaders, Gent made several written public statements reassuring the German work force that the takeover bid would not disturb existing labor-management relations.   In the final days of the acquisition, Gent finally entered into face-to-face negotiations with the German union leadership - something he had thought he could avoid and that is indeed relatively rare in the mergers and acquisitions environment.

A more recent and ongoing example is the international campaign by the labor movement to support efforts to restore democracy in Burma, which has been ruled by a brutal military dictatorship for several decades.   Labor has joined with a wide range of non-governmental organizations to oppose companies that continue to invest in Burma.   Initially these efforts focused on Unocal, the California-based oil company, which built a natural gas pipeline across Burma in a joint venture with the military.

Widespread human rights abuses are known to have accompanied this project, including forced labor to build the project, forced relocations of villagers; and killings, beatings, and rapes of villagers who resisted the project. The AFL-CIO introduced a shareholder resolution calling on Unocal to respond to these charges and to set aside a portion of its profits from the pipeline in a trust fund for the future economic development of a democratic Burma.[233]    More recently, as noted above, the AFL-CIO joined with British unions to pressure Premier Oil, a British company, which continues to operate in Burma. In particular, the AFL-CIO asked the American oil company, Amerada Hess, to either use its twenty-five percent stake in Premier to pressure Premier to withdraw or else to sell its entire stake in the company.[234]

While many of these capital market campaigns focus on intervening in the capital markets to stop a transaction when organized labor believes its core principles are implicated, the trade union movement is also developing a framework for changing the way that Wall Street and corporations think about investment decisions.   It wants to broaden the core concepts that motivate basic investment decisions - in a sense, to endogenize human rights, democratic politics, and progressive corporate governance into the concept of materiality, on the investor side, and into the concept of valuation on the company side. An important example of this approach was the decision by CalPERS to put in place an "investment screen" to control the way its fund managers invest its members' assets in the equity markets of the so-called "emerging market countries." Now those investment decisions must include weighting for the core labor standards established by the International Labor Organization, which include the right to freedom of association, the right to engage in collective bargaining, prohibitions against the use of forced labor and abusive child labor, and against discrimination in employment. Thus, the PetroChina Campaign reflects in part a structural shift to a new environment where capital markets have important social and political effects. But that has not meant that the older institutional players, such as organized labor, have been left behind.

## C. A Political Approach

Because organized labor has lost the most as a result of the end of the Industrial Relations era, it is particularly motivated to develop its role as an institutional investor in the new Capital Markets era. But it is not just the labor movement that has begun to notice the potential for advancing a political agenda through the capital markets. In that earlier era, collective bargaining and union activity was understood to be a complement to traditional parallel political institutions. "Industrial democracy" on the shop floor stimulated workers' interest in and understanding of broader democratic processes.[235] In addition, the exercise of freedom of speech and association in the workplace, once fought for and won, was not likely to be given up lightly in society at large.[236] Thus, labor unions have been seen as a key force in civil society that serves as a counterweight to the concentration of power in financial, corporate, or government bodies. Some used this perspective to argue that unions are a natural component of U.S. politics and the American model of industrial capitalism. It was this kind of approach to labor-management relations that made industrial relations ideology a central part of U.S. foreign policy in the Cold War. There is more than coincidence in the fact that "Wild Bill" Donovan, the founder of the Office of Strategic Services (OSS), the forerunner of the Central Intelligence Agency (CIA), practiced labor law and that William Colby, head of the Phoenix counterinsurgency program in Vietnam and later a Director of the CIA, began his career after wartime service with the OSS as a labor lawyer first for Donovan's own Wall Street law firm and then for the National Labor Relations Board in Washington, D.C.[237] The OSS itself had a very active labor branch during World War II, "created to work with Socialist trade union groups in the European underground."[238] The CIA played a central role in attempting to use the American Industrial Relations system and ideology as part of a wider effort to combat the success of Stalinism during the Cold War. Colby, for example, was directly involved in such efforts in post-World War II Italy.[239] Other leading figures of the post-war era who came out of the Industrial Relations era included: Clark Kerr, President of the University of California during its Free Speech Movement; economists John Dunlop and John Kenneth Galbraith at Harvard; and George Schultz, first at the University of Chicago, and then Stanford, and later the holder of four Cabinet level positions, including Secretary of Labor, State, and Treasury. These are only intriguing bits of anecdotal evidence, of course, but there is little doubt that for most of the Cold War, the United States professed to support collective bargaining and unionization as a vital bulwark against "totalitarianism."[240]

In the post-Cold War era of globalized capital markets, this particular dimension of U.S. foreign policy and domestic legitimation has been undermined. Certainly this is one of the factors that motivate labor's interest in advancing a capital markets strategy. The Cold War era foreign policy establishment, however, has not simply disappeared into investment banks, business schools, or early retirement. While adherents of a neo-liberal free trade ideology have been the dominant force in American foreign policy over the last two decades or so, a group of "neo-conservatives" emerged from a pro-labor wing of the Cold War to fight what was often, until September 11, a rear guard battle to promote a foreign policy that it viewed as vital to the narrower national interests of the United States.[241] The idea of joining multilateral missions to stop "ethnic cleansing" in obscure European countries, like the newly recognized states of the former Yugoslavia, or genocide in Rwanda was not high on their list of priorities. In the first few months of the Bush Administration it looked as if this perspective on foreign policy was, in fact, gaining the upper hand. The appointment of a foreign policy team linked to the Ford Administration and the Cold War era (not to the era of globalization), the withdrawal of the United States from the Kyoto environmental treaty, and the confrontation with China over a downed spy plane, all hinted at the return of unilateralism defined by a vaguely defined "national interest" in contradistinction to the pure globalization, market *über alles* view of many in the Clinton era.

Some in this national interest layer in American politics saw the PetroChina Campaign as a way to put itself back on the political map at a turning point in American politics. Though of secondary importance relative to the weight on the AFL-CIO and large institutional investors, an important force in the campaign against the IPO was led by the Center for Security Policy, a Washington think tank with links to the neo-conservative William Casey Institute, headed by former investment banker Roger Robinson. This Center forms the core of a somewhat broader political group that has supported some of the Congressional activism that led to the issuance of the Unger Letter, including ties to Congressman Wolf and Senator Brownback, Republican of Kansas, and then Senator Fred Thompson, Republican of Tennessee, who have all been active on religious freedom, China, and human rights issues.

Of course, the literature issued by this wing of the PetroChina Campaign rarely mentioned the layoffs of nearly a million workers that would follow a successful restructuring of PetroChina, nor the absence in China of free and independent trade unions to provide workers a voice in the shock therapy now being implemented by that regime to its domestic economy. Instead their concern - one that was indeed shared by the labor movement - focused on the denial of religious freedom and the use of forced labor by the Chinese oil industry in Sudan.

Ironically, while the national interest perspective appears to have made some headway in the Bush Administration, that national interest is, of course, in the process of being radically redefined. And, ironically, one of the first beneficiaries of the new post-9/11 war against terrorism was Sudan. One of the promises dangled in front of the Sudanese regime in return for some kind of support for the anti-terror effort was the possibility of lifting the sanctions in place against that regime for its human rights violations. Some in the neo-conservative national interest camp are calling foul. "The Bush administration risks appearing craven where they too pretend that Sudan warrants a clean bill of political health based on Khartoum's assistance to fight terrorism," according to the Casey Institute's Roger Robinson.[242]

There is, of course, some reflection of national interest politics in today's labor movement. Its heaviest concentration remains in parts of the international affairs wings of the AFL-CIO. But, in general, the Cold War anti-communist character of the labor movement has disappeared. The effort of the Sweeney administration to establish a "new internationalism" as the basis of an independent foreign policy for the global labor movement has been successful within much of labor. This is the approach that animates labor's campaigns on international trade and finance as seen in labor's presence at the Seattle WTO demonstrations in 1999, and at the annual meetings of the International Monetary Fund and the World Bank. While this movement waned somewhat in reaction to the terrorist attacks on September 11, it is likely to be a permanent feature of international politics. The recent massive demonstrations against the war with Iraq indicate the persistent significance of an emerging independent world public opinion.[243]

In addition to these neo-liberal, national interest and new internationalist perspectives, there is also a mirror image to the national interest approach found in developing, or so-called "emerging market" countries. While having obtained some additional leverage over the world system because of their newfound "comparative advantage" (i.e., their ability to offer global corporations cheap labor),[244] many of these countries still find themselves locked out of key markets in the advanced countries and far behind in key areas of economic growth, like high technology. In response, there has emerged in many of these countries what might be called a neo-mercantilism as they negotiate their way around the new institutions of the global economy.[245] Examples of this dynamic include the debates underway over the value of capital controls[246] or the right to produce cheaply drugs to fight AIDS in the developing world.[247] The politics of neo-mercantilism is likely to be a source of resistance to efforts like the PetroChina Campaign, though domestic labor movements in some of these countries have welcomed the new internationalist approach of the AFL-CIO, which represents a significant shift from the Cold War era links to official U.S. foreign policy.

One can delineate, therefore, four different political camps in the post-Cold War period: neo-liberalism, neo-mercantilism, the national interest grouping, and new internationalism. The neo-liberal model has animated the core of U.S. international economic policy in the Capital Markets era and is the source of the strongest opposition to the use of the capital markets as an arena to advance human rights.[248] The neo-mercantilists of the Third World are also likely to oppose such efforts though for their own narrower interests, particularly as a bargaining chip to use inside the new global institutions like the WTO. Many, though not all, in the national interest or neo-conservative camp inside the United States welcomes the capital markets initiatives, but have a more limited agenda defined by their real focus on advancing a particularly hawkish approach to U.S. foreign policy. Finally, there is what I believe is the central motivating force behind the anti-globalization movement and the kind of capital markets initiative evidenced in the PetroChina Campaign - the new internationalism actively promoted by the AFL-CIO and its sister organizations in the global labor movement, and among its friends in environmental and human rights organizations.

## The New Era: From Keynes to Friedman

As I have suggested here, one could consider the recent turn in the SEC's behavior towards concern about human rights within the context of theoretical debates about materiality and the nature of our disclosure regime. Further, discussions of the new role of capital markets, institutional investors, and of the different political camps that have emerged in response to globalization add to our understanding of the PetroChina Syndrome. But there is another theoretical framework that is perhaps even more helpful in understanding its potential long-term significance. While the debate about corporate governance and the securities law regime is responsive to the issues raised by the separation of ownership and control, the same development in economic history - the rise of the large vertically-integrated multinational corporation - created another problem, one that is analyzed by Massimo De Angelis in his recently published book entitled *Keynesianism, Social Conflict and Political Economy*.[249]

De Angelis describes a problem with which both John Maynard Keynes and the Polish economist, Michal Kalecki, Keynes'

178

contemporary, grappled. The emergence of the large industrial manufacturing concern required the creation of a large industrial working class, both to work in the new factories, such as Henry Ford's massive River Rouge complex which employed 120,000 workers in a single site, and to consume the products of this new industrial economy, such as the Model A cars that started rolling off the Rouge assembly line in the late 1920s. De Angelis suggests Keynes and Kalecki understood that with this massive concentrated employment of industrial workers came a new confidence among those workers that employers needed them. They could no longer be pushed so easily into unemployment to serve as a "reserve army of labor" which had undermined, for many decades, efforts to form stable and effective trade unions. This new awareness emboldened workers to push for wage increases and improved working conditions, and was reflected in the strike waves that hit the American economy in the mid-1930s and throughout World War II, even in the face of difficult economic conditions. Thus, De Angelis notes, "the organizational and confrontational maturity of what was, following the Soviet revolution, Fordism and the Great Depression, a new kind of working class."[250]

Keynes and Kalecki, as economists, argued that this new era of social conflict gave rise to a phenomenon known as "wage stickiness" or "wage rigidity": the prospect of unemployment, even in the depths of the Great Depression, no longer frightened employees with jobs into lowering wage demands, thus interfering with the alleged self-correcting role of markets. De Angelis stated that "according to Keynes' biographer Skidelsky... 'the incomplete British recovery from the depression of 1920-1922 started Keynes on the road to the Keynesian Revolution.' This incomplete recovery had revealed the persistence of unemployment and at the same time the rigidity of real wages."[251] This forced economists to grapple with a new world. The heritage of "Say's Law" - the world of the nineteenth century where "market forces" (i.e. the reserve army of labor) would drive down the price of labor until it was once again profitable for capitalists to re-hire unemployed workers and hence end the Depression - had apparently been surpassed.[252] As De Angelis argues, "the recognition of unemployment as a problem by economic theory (namely Keynesianism) originated out of the failure of downward movements of the business cycle to provide the traditional disciplinary device for both the employed and unemployed labor force."[253] Unemployment ceased to play its counter-cyclical role in lowering wages to allow employers to once again begin expanding investment.

A new institutional structure had to be built to deal with this problem. Without new institutions, employers would lose control over the system of production and their motive for investing in new production.[254] This was not an idle threat. It had indeed happened in one extreme instance. In 1917, the working class of Russia overthrew a weak capitalist regime that only several months before had assumed power reluctantly after the ouster of the Russian monarchy by a broad revolutionary movement. While that workers' regime was later itself crushed in a brutal civil war as a new bureaucratic authoritarian government rose to power under Stalin, the risk of conceding to workers' power was clear to capitalist theoreticians like Keynes:

> Keynes' revolution in economics can be understood as a reaction to working-class struggles in Europe and general insurgency in other parts of the world. It is the product of the change in the balance of forces between classes during the struggles of the 1920s and 1930s and during the Second World War.[255]

Keynes, in fact, personally witnessed a dramatic version of these events when Britain's government was nearly toppled by the General Strike of 1926. On the eve of the Strike, Keynes admitted, "the trade unions are strong enough to interfere with the free play of the forces of supply and demand, and public opinion ... supports the trade unions in their main contention that coal-miners ought not to be the victims of cruel economic forces which they never put in motion."[256] The events of 1926 had a particularly deep impact on Keynes' re-thinking of the role of class power in economic theory:

> Repressive policies had been called [for by some] on the basis of the fact that the strikers had broken the law. "To those who clamoured that the General Strike was illegal and

stepped outside the limits of constitutional action, Keynes gave a short reply: 'That may be so, but so what?'" The balance of forces has changed and [Keynes understood that] "legality must be adjusted to fit the new situation."[257]

Without a new institutional arrangement, the only alternative would be the kind of repression that was indeed taking place in the emerging Stalinist and fascist countries. As Keynes admitted, "it is only in a highly authoritarian society, where sudden, substantial, all-round changes could be decreed that a flexible wage-policy could function with success. One can imagine it in operation in Italy, Germany or Russia, but not in France, the United States or Great Britain."[258]

Thus, a central institutional outcome of the "Keynesian Revolution" was the emergence of the industrial relations system that dominated economic life in the advanced economies of the post-war world well into the late 1970s.[259] At the heart of this new structure was what many stylized as a "social contract" between employers and workers under government supervision (or even at times control) where wage increases were granted over time in exchange for productivity increases. In some countries these deals were, and remain, explicit (as in European and Japanese corporatism) or exalted (as in the Stalinist regimes), while they remained only implicit in others (as in the collective bargaining systems in the United States and the United Kingdom). This industrial relations system promised a relatively equitable distribution of income, stability in economic growth, and only moderate divergence in growth patterns between countries. De Angelis terms this solution to the "wage rigidity" problem identified by Keynes and Kalecki as "the social microfoundations of Keynesianism."[260]

However, the system could not last forever. As early as the 1960s, it became clear that firms were living on borrowed time, as De Angelis describes:

From the mid-1960s many basic economic indicators showed a turning point. Investments that were flourishing in the

1950s and 1960s turned sour and worsened after the 1974 oil crisis. Business and manufacturing investment collapsed.... Industrial profit rates began their downturn in the mid-1960s.... Inflation began to approach double digits by the late 1960s. The welfare state appeared to crumble under weight of increasing deficits and exponential increase of the public debt. All these trends could be translated into DM [Deutschemarks], lire, or pounds because the turning point was more or less evident in all major capitalist countries....[261]

At the center of this crisis were the institutions, such as collective bargaining, that regulated labor-management relations. What had once been a boon to capitalist success, the use of the industrial relations framework to regulate wages and productivity, became an albatross. The industrial relations system tended to lock in older technology due to management's attempts to constrain worker power on the shop floor or management reluctance to confront that power. This was linked to a second problem: the collective bargaining system was imposed from above to try and break the back of the idea that workers had independent power in a "full employment" economy.[262] Thus, the social microfoundations were political too, and the imposition of a political system, while offering some newly found stability or equity to workers, also chafed at the level of the rank and file worker. Productivity was thus under attack.

If the "golden age" had seen an impressive increase in productivity growth, the subsequent period suffered what numerous observers have called the "productivity slowdown." What is more important, productivity in most OECD countries grew less than money wages, thus leading to inflationary pressures as business tried to restore profit margins.[263]

Senator Edward Kennedy, a leading pro-labor Democrat, noted at the time:

The effect that worker discontent has on productivity. The National Commission on Productivity states that in at least one major industry, absenteeism increased by 50%, worker turnover by 70%, worker grievances by 38% ... and disciplinary lay-offs by 44% in a period of 5 years. How much does that cost the economy in terms of low productivity?[264]

The answer appeared to be significant. One contemporaneous follower of the events noted:

Absenteeism has important effects on production.... The cost of all this to management is enormous. For example in 1971, in the Oldsmobile Division of GM alone, the cost of absenteeism (considering only fringe benefits) was about $ 50 million. Turnover costs were another $ 29 million.... GM's labour costs rose from 29.5% of sales in 1962 to 33% in 1972.... The firm's investment per worker rose from $ 5,000 in 1950 to $ 24,000 in 1969. James Roche, Chairman of GM, commenting on these figures, said: "tools and technology mean nothing if the worker is absent from his job" and went on to stress the domino effect of absenteeism on co-workers, on quality and efficiency, and on other GM plants with related production. "We must receive a fair day's work for which we pay a fair day's pay...."[265]

As productivity and profitability slowed in the late 1960s, employers began to use the same institutional structure to ratchet up the pressure on workers. Bargaining became tougher and the resolution of grievances through negotiations and arbitration slower. Some employers began to break away from the institutional structure to engage in aggressive union busting or runaway shops. In the newly formed General Motors Assembly Division (GMAD), for example, management became particularly aggressive. United Auto Workers Union President Leonard Woodcock called it "the roughest and toughest in GM."[266] At the Lordstown, Ohio GMAD plant, there were 100 unresolved grievances when the Division took over. That soon skyrocketed to 1400. Workers began to react. Sabotage of cars became frequent, absenteeism exploded, and informally workers began to leave a certain percentage of cars unfinished as they sped along the assembly line. The workers' protests became so apparent that they even caught the eye of the national media when Time Magazine noted that at Lordstown, "autos regularly roll off the line with slit upholstery, scratched paint, dented bodies, bent gear-shift levers, cut ignition wires, and loose or missing bolts. In some cars the trunk key is broken off right in the lock, thereby jamming it."[267] The number of cars needing repairs before they left the plant ran so high the plant was often forced to close for lack of space. A mini strike wave occurred in the United States, including a strike at Lordstown[268] and numerous other auto plants and a wave of wildcat, or unofficial, strikes in several industries. An even more intense strike wave hit much of Western and Eastern Europe. France nearly descended into civil war in 1968, as factory occupations spread across the country. Meanwhile, to the south, Italy experienced its "Hot Autumn" led by rank and file workers in 1969. These battles were echoed in the Eastern Bloc where only Soviet tanks could suppress the Prague Spring of 1968, and in Poland where major strike waves took place in 1970 and 1976 in the run-up to the emergence of the Solidarity Movement in late 1980.

Partially in response to this unrest in the 1970s, De Angelis argues, the advanced economies shifted gears and gutted the decades old Industrial Relations system. For De Angelis, the archetypal figure of the twenty-five year period following World War II was Keynes, but for the new era, Milton Friedman emerged as the archetype.[269] Friedman promoted the idea of liberalized exchange rates and, of course, the expansion of free market institutions. These ideas began to take hold, first in the Nixon Administration and later more aggressively under Presidents Carter and Reagan. The U.S. decision to suspend convertibility of the dollar into gold in 1971 signaled a break with the older institutional framework. Now, increasingly, employers could expand their operations internationally as market institutions were spread to more and more countries, and deregulation of currency trading increased their operational flexibility.[270] These steps were crucial building blocks of the phenomenon now called "globalization." They heralded the arrival of a new disciplining force that could replace the Industrial Relations system, and perhaps solve the problem of declining productivity and profitability. No longer did employers have to engage in collective deals or social contracts with workers in order to trade wage gains for productivity increases, nor did they have to engage in pitched battles at the factory gates and on the shop floor to raise productivity. Now employers could rely on the entrance into the labor market, a new global labor market, of hundreds of millions of previously unavailable workers. After all, if Mexico instituted genuine contract and property rights and a liberalized exchange regime, and also offered cheap labor, it would become far more attractive to auto industry executives to break up their troublesome, aging, and expensive workforces in places like Flint, Michigan and move operations to the new non-union maquiladora zone in northern Mexico. This would replicate the runaway shop policy that the textile industry had put to such good use in moving to the southern United States to avoid Northern unions in the middle of the twentieth century.[271]

Note here the important role that the capital markets can play. Now that more than a trillion dollars are traded back and forth every day in the currency markets alone, those markets provide a kind of daily vote by key financial institutions on the attractiveness for investors of every country in the world. Social welfare spending, union influence over business decision making, and other dimensions of the Keynesian era are now seen by many participants in these markets as introducing inefficiency and rigidity into economic development. Sovereign debt instruments and domestic currencies are ripe for speculative attack as a form of political pressure. As De Angelis notes: "In a context of open capital markets, the simple announcement of a government's Keynesian intentions may well be sufficient to bring the government to its knees via a massive capital outflow."[272]

In the run-up to the Brazilian elections, for example, global speculators began a sell-off of Brazilian debt instruments and the Brazilian currency.[273] This forced the government to raise interest rates on financial assets denominated in the domestic currency to try and stop the sell-off.[274] That, in turn, only made the domestic economic situation worse as the cost of financing the government budget increased dramatically. The prospect of the election of leftist former labor leader, Luis Inacio da Silva, known popularly as

"Lula," "had Wall Street freaked. Ever since last spring, when the first polls showed Lula with the lead, credit agencies and New York investment banks ... issued dire warnings and downgraded Brazil's [credit] ratings, causing Brazil's currency to plummet and helping to precipitate" an IMF bailout.[275] The government was forced to negotiate a stringent agreement with the International Monetary Fund that placed a severe restriction on government spending. In a highly unusual development, candidates in the ongoing presidential campaign were forced to sign on to a commitment to abide by the IMF restrictions if they were elected. In the new era, the post-Keynesian era, the global capital markets provide capitalism with the essential disciplinary device necessary to assure profitability.[276]

In this environment, industrial relations, collective bargaining, even unions themselves, are not just out-gunned; they at first glance appear to be truly irrelevant. As De Angelis noted, "financial integration and liberalization allows capital mobility to serve as a disciplinary device to limit the scope of any concessions by individual governments that could harm national competitiveness and to present "adjustment' in terms of cuts in welfare spending and entitlements as a necessity posited from the outside."[277]

Confronting the Legitimation Deficit

As powerful as this argument is in explaining the new era, however, it leaves out a second concern triggered by globalization, a concern that is at the heart of our legal system, a concern about legal process, secured in part by the institutions of labor law. Only an understanding of this dimension of the Industrial Relations era allows us to see the potential for a progressive, labor-led response to the issues posed by the new Capital Markets era. While De Angelis emphasizes in his assessment of the Keynesian era the economic effects of a particular institutional arrangement, he fails to recognize an equally important aspect of the industrial relations system, namely, its ability to put in place a workplace rule of law that helped to legitimate the outcome of wage-productivity bargaining. What some have called "American approach to industrial relations"[278] was based on the promotion of a common law of the shop floor that developed out of organizing campaigns, grievance processing, and contract negotiations. This system was created by a series of statutes, beginning with the National Labor Relations Act of 1935 (often referred to as the "Wagner Act" after its chief legislative author, Senator Wagner),[279] and later institutionalized by several important Supreme Court decisions, notably the famous Steelworkers Trilogy cases of the early 1960s.[280] As Justice Douglas said in one of those crucial opinions:

> The collective bargaining agreement states the rights and duties of the parties. It is more than a contract; it is a generalized code to govern a myriad of cases which the draftsmen cannot wholly anticipate.... The collective agreement covers the whole employment relationship.... It calls into being a new common law - the common law of a particular industry or of a particular plant.... A collective bargaining agreement is an effort to erect a system of industrial self-government.[281]

This new approach was as much a result of popular protest through widespread strikes in the 1930s, including three general strikes in San Francisco, Minneapolis, and Toledo, as it was a product of legislative and judicial effort. The centerpiece of the new industrial relations system was the National Labor Relations Board, established by the 1935 Act. Its role in monitoring and adjudicating labor-management conflict was an attempt to take the emerging class warfare then breaking out on the streets of major American cities back to the negotiating table, by setting up a process for union recognition while limiting the ability of workers to continue more radical efforts to control the production process. As a 1961 study cited by labor law scholar Katherine Van Wezel Stone concluded: "The gains from this system [of industrial relations] are especially noteworthy because of their effect on the recognition and dignity of the individual worker.... Wildcat strikes and other disorderly means of protest have been curtailed and an effective work discipline generally established."[282] The Wagner Act, therefore, can be seen as a "double-edged sword" - a legal instrument that cut both ways, in favor initially, it seemed, of workers, but over time providing the framework for severely curtailing worker power. As labor law historian Karl Klare noted, "the liberal model of industrial democracy simultaneously invites and limits employee participation in workplace governance."[283] The fact that it provided procedures such as mandatory bargaining and grievance procedures for workers to attempt to secure basic improvements in their lives helped cement acceptance of the compromise.[284]

A broader claim was also made for the industrial relations system. Figures like John Dunlop, George Schultz, and Clark Kerr argued more or less explicitly that it provided a base for the vision of liberal pluralism they felt was essential to govern industrial society. In the view of these "strong IR" figures, modern industrial capitalism was a world where competing centers of power - labor, government, and business - each had a legitimate role in broader political and social life. Thus, a more formalized tripartite relationship was the stabilizing core of a system that allowed the rapid change and development, inherent in capitalism's waves of "creative destruction," to take place without triggering radical or destructive reactions. Clark Kerr, for example, wrote of

> the contribution of the unions to a sense of consensus in industrial society, to the sense that the rules and rewards are just and acceptable, and to how they thus lead to social tranquility.... The overall impact of unionization has been to contribute to a sense of fair play, a sense of acceptance of the arrangements of industrial society.[285]

This is not just a matter of appearances. The basic building blocks of an active and democratic labor movement are the right to organize, the right to bargain collectively, and the right to strike. These rights run parallel to basic political rights found in general social life - the right to assembly, the right to freedom of speech, and the right to petition the government for the redress of grievances. Thus, the "common law of the shop floor" runs parallel to democratic governance in society at large.[286] Just as the common law that emerges inside the workplace guarantees that there is some check against arbitrary power in economic life, federal and constitutional structures provide a countervailing force against abuse of power in the polity as a whole, whether as checks on the assumption of power by a single individual or unrestricted abuse of majoritarianism. In fact, there is an essential link between these two parallel processes that explains the fact that with the exception of authoritarian or totalitarian societies, labor movements inevitably become involved in political activity. There is a reciprocal relationship between the expression of civil liberties inside a workplace and in society at large. A vibrant and effective trade union is impossible to sustain as an island of freedom in a sea of authoritarianism. The right to organize, for example, depends vitally on the freedom of speech. Thus, to preserve their successes at the workplace, labor unions must also continually defend civil liberties in the outside political realm. Conversely, those in society at large who value civil liberties recognize their importance inside the workplace as well. Thus, in recent years, human rights organizations like Amnesty International and Human Rights Watch have paid increasing attention to labor rights issues. The existence of a vibrant trade union movement, then, is often a litmus test for a country's progress towards democracy and freedom. This is the substance of the "pluralism" of the Industrial Relations era. The value we place on a process of "deliberative and pluralistic decision-making"[287] is central to the legitimation of the outcomes of that decision-making.

For De Angelis, this perspective on the role of trade unions is a difficult one to comprehend. He views the new trade union movement of the 1930s not as an adversarial effort to represent the interests of workers, but as bodies "institutionalized by the state ... to control the grass-roots...."[288] Of course, if this were an accurate description, it would not have been possible for the unions to play the role that Kerr describes. Only an organization that has some legitimacy with its own membership could have engaged in the compromises he describes and survive.[289] Nor would an institution whose only role was to impose outcomes negotiated in smoke filled back rooms on a compliant rank and file be able to animate the wider activity of that same rank and file in general political and social life, as the "strong IR" view suggests was the case. The labor movement must inevitably wrestle with its need to confront employers and, on occasion, the state, in order to win material improvements for its membership while simultaneously remaining concerned with survival in a persistently hostile environment. This is not a dynamic that De Angelis seems to understand. In one sense, Kerr and De Angelis are flip sides of the same coin, with Kerr hoping for the integration of the trade unions into a wider capitalist apparatus, and De Angelis thinking the deed has been done. De Angelis mistakes the more conservative pronouncements of some trade union officials for the actual labor movement itself.[290] Kerr, at least, would acknowledge the existence of an adversarial relationship, while De Angelis at the end of the day cannot see this as a realistic phenomenon. That is why he cannot see any role for the adversarial process in creating legitimacy in the Keynesian era.

If the transition from a collective bargaining dominated system to one where global capital markets play a central role preserves the disciplinary function still so crucial to modern capitalism, it has left behind the central legitimating impact of the sophisticated system of process generated by industrial relations. The missing element in today's environment is precisely what figures like Clark Kerr thought was so crucial about the earlier framework - the institutions that developed "a sense of consensus." Kerr went even so far as to suggest that unions' ability to help generate this consensus "may well be their one great justification. It is easier to get the appearance of economic justice than to be certain about its reality - and the unions give the appearance."[291] While many may argue with Kerr's suggestion about the actual impact of unionization, there can be little argument that this contribution to "consensus" is absent in the era of globalization. Unions still exist, of course, but they have suffered significant losses in the face of rapid technological change fed by the emergence of new global labor markets. No institutional framework remotely comparable to that of the Keynesian era exists to mediate class conflict over the process of economic development. Instead, unforgiving global capital markets force reluctant players into line, but with little or no opportunity for impacted social groups to debate or engage decision makers. Instead of constructive dialogue and conscious planning of economic activity that addresses the entire social cost of rapid economic change, those most intimately impacted by such change are often left with only violence or apathy as a way out. This takes a very mild form in the United States, for the time being,[292] but it is altogether different in many parts of the world.

Thus, there is no sense emerging that this is a system committed to what Kerr called a "sense of fair play." Quite the opposite, in fact, as a broad sector of the population in both advanced and developing countries have begun to express their view that the new era is an intensely unfair one. This was manifested most openly at the demonstrations against the World Trade Organization in Seattle in 1999. The protests there ranged across the political and social spectrum, including both middle class environmentalists and working class trade unionists. Thus, this legitimation deficit suggests the emergence of a vacuum in social and political life. Whether it will be filled by regulation, or altered private behavior, or open social conflict, or perhaps all three is not yet clear. But the anti-globalization/pro-globalization divide is not simply about the division of spoils, not simply about the fights between winners and losers, it is also about power - power to influence, power to participate, power to debate. This concern with power is the emerging content of process in the anti-globalization era. The possibility that this content will be shaped by destructive conflict or even reactionary or fundamentalist movements is what leads me to suggest the possibility of an emerging PetroChina Syndrome, where social groups with significant concerns about the impact of the new era are locked out of decision-making processes and are forced to turn to more radical solutions. A legal order that promises to protect the general interest but fails to provide accessible, transparent, and accountable mechanisms to generate legitimate outcomes can only be said to be suffering a legal pathology.

## Conclusion

The PetroChina Campaign represented an important and innovative first step in the constructive forging of a genuinely legitimate new world order, and thus is evidence of that pathology but also points to its resolution. By its tactics, agenda, and choice of methods, it sent a strong signal about the inadequacies of the current neo-liberal regime. It represented the emerging outline of a new model of global economic development. On a tactical level, it chose to bring politics into the capital markets where they are manifestly unwelcome. Thus, it forced the recognition of the political impact and relevance of those markets. The capital markets can no longer be seen, as Alan Greenspan would prefer, as simply passive intermediaries betweens savers and investors. They are inherently political because they impact social outcomes. But they violate the fundamental precepts of a legitimate political order. They provide no institutional mechanism to hold them accountable for their impact. What the PetroChina Campaign illustrated was that the normal mechanisms that are supposed to guarantee the so-called "integrity" of the markets broke down when they attempted to digest the mix of an authoritarian economy with a democratic one. The PetroChina IPO represented an attempt to impose a particular social and economic order that corresponds to the needs of those few with the resources and ability to take advantage of those markets. The fact that the Chinese regime was forced to bring an abrupt halt to its global capital markets strategy indicates the effectiveness of the tactical choice to intervene in those markets made by the Campaign.

The agenda of the Campaign grew largely out of the range of issues raised by the "new internationalism" fostered by the Sweeney Administration at the AFL-CIO, but it was also reflective of the efforts of many NGO's in the human rights and environmental activist communities. In what are likely to be only fortuitous circumstances linked to China's particular political history, the agenda was fortified by the presence of conservative religious groups concerned about religious freedom. But even among conservatives there is a growing concern about the impact that neo-liberal globalization is having on traditional ways of life.[293] The agenda expanded into arguments about the appropriate forms of corporate governance in the new era. In the post-Enron environment, such a concern looks remarkably prescient. Thus, it can be fairly said that in a single effort, the Campaign raised awareness of some of the most significant dimensions of the globalization process. In many ways, the Campaign is an echo of the efforts by organizers like Walter Reuther and A.J. Muste in the early 1930s to call attention to the social costs of the new-market driven industrial order. A similar effort was made by figures like the future Justice Brandeis and labor activists Florence Kelley and Rose Schneiderman in the Progressive movement of the early twentieth century against sweatshops and harsh conditions in the workplace.

Finally, in its choice of methods - addressing its concerns first to the stewards of the retirement assets managed by large institutional investors, and then to regulators - the Campaign found a new way to press for progressive reform. Institutional investors are significant new players in the global economy. They are becoming aware of the weight of that responsibility, and cannot afford to hide behind narrow definitions of "fiduciary duty" while their assets are manipulated by Wall Street fund managers and investment banks at significant cost to the values and goals of the fund beneficiaries, American workers. Using the power and influence of these institutions to force the Securities and Exchange Commission to acknowledge the importance of the Campaign's agenda to investors, as the Commission did with the issuance of the Unger Letter, represents a small but notable step in response to the legitimation deficit created by the globalization process.

The outcome of this process cannot be predicted. What can be recognized and accepted, however, is that we are confronting an entirely new set of problems. In the past, for example in the era of Holmes or Douglas, constructive and progressive responses to such problems have emerged by first recognizing that a problem exists, and, second, by asking, through research and argument, what the real dimensions of that problem are. Only then can we move to constructive institution building that helps resolve the problems. The emergence of the PetroChina Syndrome can be seen as a social variant of the miner's canary - warning us that there is, indeed, the possibility of an explosion.

Postscript

Late in the night on December 23, 2003, a natural gas well owned by PetroChina and operated by CNPC burst, and sent a cloud of toxic gas over the countryside in Chongqing in southwestern China.[294] In what Chinese media called a "zone of death," at least 243 people died while hundreds more suffered skin burns and poisoning.[295] Within a few days, the *New York Times* reported that the Chinese government admitted that CNPC "cut corners" including not having the right safety equipment on site, improperly dismantling equipment needed to prevent such a blowout and waiting hours to ignite the gas in order to prevent its deadly spread to the surrounding area.[296] The *Times* noted, "China also forbids workers to organize independent unions that might make safety a higher priority."[297]

# Conclusion

The optimism that accompanied the fall of the Berlin Wall in 1989 has long since dissipated. But the argument that the globalization process would render possible the spread of a legitimate democratic capitalist system has lingered. The essays collected here, however, suggest a darker and more complex picture. The trade union has been seen since the end of the Second World War as a key constituent part of democratic capitalism. Yet, it is in decline across the globe. Instead, globalization has triggered both a race to the bottom for millions of workers in advanced and developing countries alike, with layoffs and restructuring as much a part of the Chinese economy as they are at the heart of industrial change in the advanced European and North American economies. Sweeping into the vacuum left by the decline of democratic capitalism as a viable form together with its traditional industrial relations ideology are new forms of authoritarianism whether influenced by the experience of Che Guevara and the Sandinistas in Central and Latin America or by the expanding role of China's ACFTU inside the international labor movement.

What then can be said today about the role of the traditional democratic labor movement in the new global economy? While the final outcome will be settled on the ground in and around the workplaces of the new economy, some preliminary comments are possible.

It needs to be more widely understood that, in fact, despite appearances, the genuine democratic trade union has no natural stable place inside capitalism. Trade unions are, by their nature, a force that is hostile to the control exerted by management inside the workplace and thus unions have always engendered opposition from the employers. Rather, I would argue, the defensive position that organized labor now finds itself in is its natural place in modern capitalism. The myth that trade unions ever had a secure role in the capitalist economy is largely kept alive by what might be called an "accommodationist" ideology, which argues that unions can be smoothly integrated as one power center among many within a pluralist and democratic capitalism. Classic industrial relations theory was one form taken by this ideology. The post war

Keynesian era reinforced the accommodationist illusion for several decades for a certain layer of the industrial working class in the advanced economies. However, in fact, collective bargaining was, at best, a social compromise between two inexorably opposed forces, not a permanent "capitalist" institution. Of course, for most of the world's workers over the last fifty years, even this social compromise was unattainable.

The left itself is largely responsible for the intellectual mistake represented by this approach to trade unionism. On the social democratic side of the ledger, accommodationism replaced more radical approaches and became the substance of its politics. As discussed at the outset of this collection, liberal labor historians such as David Brody and Nelson Lichtenstein as well as labor economists Gary Fields and Robert Flanagan typify this view and many in the trade unionism's official hierarchy would be in accord with these intellectuals. They cannot comprehend the notion of an autonomous, as opposed to accommodationist, labor movement that could lead the way to a genuinely just and democratic society. Perhaps the best example in the recent period comes from those who, fancifully, see in the Chinese ACFTU the basis of something akin to American company unions that can then evolve into genuine trade unions.[1]

On the far left, on the other hand, trade unionism is mistaken for the accommodation form itself and thus dismissed as irrelevant to "revolutionary" struggle. The work of Massimo De Angelis examined in Chapter Five falls into this perspective. This group does not comprehend that the capitalist process of value creation serves as a kind of natural sabotage against any notion of an accommodating form of trade unionism thus constantly pushing even the most conservative labor leaders into opposition movements such as the "Battle of Seattle" against the WTO discussed in Chapter Three. What I call here a genuine and democratic labor movement is, in essence, a *non sequitur*, inevitably contradictory to the ordinary functioning of capitalism.

To put the matter more starkly, a viable labor movement inevitably creates a form of dual power inside capitalism, and just as such situations are unstable and short lived in the world of grand politics, such a condition cannot be easily tolerated inside the workplace. The International Confederation of Free Trade Unions was right when it concluded a 1993 report on corporate campaigns against unionization by stating: "Viewed globally the offensive is aimed at putting a definitive end to trade unionism."[2] Thus, we begin to see the outlines of the fundamental problem today: capitalism has a totalitarian edge to it that has now found new allies in the explicitly authoritarian regimes of China and elsewhere. This is, perhaps, an uneasy alliance since the myth of a potential global democratic capitalism lingers, but the economic force of the alliance cannot be dismissed.

The grand compromise that capital was willing to make with a portion of the labor movement after 1945 has now been permanently broken. The recent credit crisis is only the latest sign of the volatility and instability of the current period. The attack on organized labor has been from two directions: an intensification of capital accumulation since the late 1970's through the use of semiconductor based technology combined with a life sucking appropriation of value through sweat shop conditions in the so-called developing world. The Stalinist regimes of the earlier era are now restructuring in order to perfect the new global alliance with western forms of capital. It is to animate that alliance that new forms of authoritarian "trade unionism" have emerged.

A re-conceptualization of the trade union is required to break the intellectual stalemate of the current period and, perhaps, in turn, lead to practical progress on the ground for the labor movement itself. If mistaken views of the accommodationist approach have hobbled thinking about labor on the left, then that re-conceptualization should begin with the exploration of a potential *autonomous* role for the trade union. Promoting the union as an arm of its rank and file members that advocates for their interests independently of the consequences for capitalism must become central to the purpose of the labor movement. In the United States this most clearly means the move by unions to political independence, cutting the slavish ties between organized labor and the Democratic Party. In China, it means the

197

organization of workers into unions that are both independent of the Chinese state and Communist Party but also independent of any ideology that sees a coherent future for the Chinese worker in the globalization process.

One practical proposal made in this volume has the potential to tie labor movements of the developed and developing world together in a renewed response to globalization: the promotion of a wages, hours and working conditions approach within the debate about international labor rights.[3] The heart of such an effort would be advocacy for significant improvements in pay and conditions endured by millions of workers in the United States and China. Concretely, such an effort would move the labor rights debate outside of the confining halls of the ILO annual conferences, where it has been limited to process standards such as the *right* to engage in bargaining as opposed to substantive improvement in workers' lives, directly to the labor movement itself and more importantly to the millions of workers in both parts of the globe who are now forced to survive the new global economy outside the protections offered by that labor movement.

The advocates of accommodation inside and around the U.S. labor movement will likely view such a campaign as "impractical." They fail to recognize the value – to workers in China and elsewhere - of western unions especially those in the United States taking the lead in such an effort. It is precisely because it will send a signal that the era of accommodation to globalization is over that such an effort could resonate powerfully among Chinese workers. Of course, the effort will be dismissed as another version of accommodation by the far left. But they fail to see the impact of breaking through the increasingly totalitarian hold of the emerging authoritarianism in the new global economy. A view which understands the trade union as an inherently dissenting voice also can understand the significant potential impact of what some dismiss all too easily as "bread and butter" demands by ordinary workers. The history of the labor movement teaches us an altogether different lesson – one that now must be re-learned for that movement to move forward.

## Introduction

[1] *See* R. J. FLANAGAN AND W. B. GOULD IV, EDS., INTERNATIONAL LABOR STANDARDS: GLOBALIZATION, TRADE AND PUBLIC POLICY (Stanford Univ. Press 2003) which sets up a straw man version of the "race to the bottom" thesis and then, as expected, proceeds to knock it down.

[2] *See* G. S. FIELDS, ED., PATHWAYS OUT OF POVERTY (Springer 2003).

[3] *See* R. FLANAGAN, GLOBALIZATION AND LABOR CONDITIONS (Oxford Univ. Press 2006) and FLANAGAN AND GOULD *supra* note 1.

[4] *See* Wong and Bernard, *Labor's Mistaken Anti-China Campaign,* NEW LABOR FORUM, Fall/Winter 2000 at 19. For the perspectives of Brody and Lichtenstein see Debate on Wal-mart and labor rights in China at Alameda Public Affairs Forum, Oct. 13, 2007.

## Chapter One

[1] The Frente Sandinista de Liberación Nacional ("FSLN"), or Sandinista Front for National Liberation, was founded in the 1961 in the wake of the Cuban Revolution. Relying on classic third world national liberation movement tactics, it led a mass movement to overthrow the corrupt Somoza dictatorship in 1979. It lost power in 1990 elections only to regain power in the 2006 presidential elections.

The nature of the FSLN today is hotly disputed, with several splinter groups having broken from the Ortega-controlled party itself. *See,* for example, Cardenal, *Sandinistas: no voten por el falso sandinismo,* EL NUEVO DIARIO, Oct. 26, 2006. *See also* Smith, *Renovation and Orthodoxy: Debate and Transition Within the Sandinista National Liberation Front,* 24 LATIN AMERICAN PERSPECTIVES 102 (Mar. 1997). A detailed discussion of this process is beyond the scope of this chapter.

[2] Interview with Alejandro Solórzano, Secretary General for International Relations, Confederación General de Trabajadores - Independiente, member of the Central Committee of the Partido Socialista de Nicaragua, former head of the Construction Workers' Union, in Managua, Nicaragua (Jan. 1989). "*Contras*" was short hand for "*contrarevolucionarios,*" the armed force recruited, trained and armed by the United States to overthrow the Nicaraguan government. *See* L. HORTON, PEASANTS IN ARMS: WAR AND PEACE IN THE MOUNTAINS OF NICARAGUA, 1979-1994 (Ohio Univ. Press 2000) and W. I. ROBINSON, A FAUSTIAN BARGAIN: U.S. INTERVENTION IN THE NICARAGUAN ELECTIONS AND AMERICAN FOREIGN POLICY IN THE POST-COLD WAR ERA (Westview Press 1992).

[3] *Nicaragua: Trade Union Heads Held,* LABOR NEWS (Amnesty International, New York) Winter 1984; Amnesty International, NICARAGUA: HUMAN RIGHTS RECORD (1986).

[4] Americas Watch, HUMAN RIGHTS RECORD IN NICARAGUA (1984).

[5] International Labour Office. Two Hundred and Thirty-third Report of the Committee of Freedom of Association. (Feb. 25-Mar. 3, 1984); International Labour Office. Report of the Committee on Freedom of Association: 226th Governing Body of the International Labour Office. May, 1984); International Labour Office. Report of the Committee of Experts on the Application of Conventions and Recommendations. (1984); International Labour Office. Two Hundred and Thirty-sixth Report of the Committee on Freedom of Association. (Nov. 12-16, 1984); International Labour Office. Two Hundred and Thirty-eighth Report of the Committee on Freedom of Association. (Feb. 25-Mar. 1, 1985).

[6] International Labour Office. Two Hundred and Thirty-third Report of the Committee of Freedom of Association, *supra* note 5.

[7] *Id.*

[8] Burbach, *The Radical Challenge to the US: Bolivia, Ecuador and Venezuela*, Apr. 19, 2007, (http://globalalternatives.org/video/lectures).

[9] *Id.*

[10] *See* Chapter Four *infra*.

[11] The appearance recently of two biographical films of Guevara indicate his continuing popularity. *See Che* (2007, Starring Benicio del Toro; Director: Steven Soderbergh) and *The Motorcycle Diaries* (2004, Starring Gael Garcia Bernal; Director: Walter Salles). Together the two films cover three of the four most important periods of Che's life. This paper fills in part of the essential missing piece: Che's role and outlook on the early Cuban revolution.

[12] E. Guevara. Venceremos! The Speeches and Writings of Che Guevara. (John Gerassi, Panther 1969) (1968).

[13] Unless noted otherwise, this chapter describes the policies of the FSLN during its first period in power in Nicaragua from 1979 until 1990.

[14] V.T. López, Nicaragua: Una Nueva Democracia en el Tercer Mundo 52, 299 (Vanguardia 1986).

[15] *See* I. Deutscher, Soviet Trade Unions: Their Place in Soviet Labour Policy (Royal Institute of International Affairs 1950).

[16] H. Ortega S., Sobre la Insurrección 73 (Editorial de Ciencias Sociales 1986).

[17] During my fieldwork in Nicaragua in the late 1980s I often heard the AFL-CIO referred to as the "AFL-CIA."

[18] Interview with Sandinista Defense Committee Leader (Jan. 1989); *See also* T. Borge, Carlos, The Dawn is No Longer Beyond Our Reach: The Prison Journals of Tomás Borge remembering Carlos Fonseca, Founder of the FSLN (New Star Books 1984).

[19] There were several smaller independent unions that may have grown larger in a more open Nicaragua. These were affiliated with various political parties, including a social Christian group, a union close to the AFL-CIO, and several associated with sectarian left parties. All of these groups found themselves harassed and worse by the FSLN.

[20] R. Fagen, C. D. Deere and J. L. Coraggio, Transition and

DEVELOPMENT: PROBLEMS OF THIRD WORLD SOCIALISM 15 (Monthly Review/Center for the Study of the Americas 1986) (Emphasis in original).

[21] *Id.* (Emphasis in original).

[22] I met and traveled with Tirado López on one such trip.

[23] (Verso 1987).

[24] http://globalalternatives.org/taxonomy/term/21.

[25] *Supra* note 23 at xii.

[26] *Id.* at 6.

[27] *Id.* at 1.

[28] *Id.* at 42.

[29] *Id.* at 6.

[30] *Id.* at 1, 2.

[31] *Id.* at 45-6

[32] *Id.* at 38.

[33] *Id.* at 24.

[34] *Id.* at 38.

[35] *Id.* at 42-3.

[36] *Id.* at 7.

[37] *Id.* at 7.

[38] *Id.* at 7-8.

[39] *Id.* at 49.

[40] *Id.* at 48.

[41] *Id.* at 49.

[42] *Id.* at 53. Burbach has now distanced himself somewhat from the FSLN structure, instead pointing to the potential "new socialism" of figures like Venezuela's Hugo Chavez, who presumably has a more attractive means of exercising power. *See* Burbach, *A Bolivarian Socialist at the UN Hugo Chavez's Mission*, COUNTERPUNCH, Sept. 24/25, 2005 ("a 'democratic postmodern revolution' is unfolding in Venezuela as hundreds of thousands of local organizations and movements are taking root among the multitude, enabling them to take control of their lives and their destinies").

[43] *Id.* at 56.

[44] *Id.* at 59-60 (emphasis added).

[45] *Id.* at 61.

[46] *Id.*

[47] *Id.* at 58 (emphasis added).

[48] Núñez Soto, *Las Fuerzas Clasistas de la Revolucion Popular Sandinista.* CUADERNOS DE SOCIOLOGICA, Sept., 1986, at 4 (Managua: Universidad Centroamericana).

[49] F. CASTRO, HISTORY WILL ABSOLVE ME 33 (Lyle Stuart 1961) *cited in* Núñez, *The Third Social Force in National Liberation Movements*, LATIN AMERICAN PERSPECTIVES, Spring, 1981 at 7.

[50] Núñez Soto, *The Third Social Force in National Liberation Movements*, LATIN AMERICAN PERSPECTIVES, Spring, 1981 at 7. For a contemporary

portrait of the massive potential size of such a Third Force, *see* M. DAVIS, PLANET OF SLUMS (Verso 2006).

[51] *Id.* (emphasis added).

[52] Núñez Soto, *Ideology and Revolution Politics in Transitional Societies* in R. FAGEN, C. D. DEERE AND J. L. CORAGGIO op. cit. n. 20 at 238.

[53] *Id.* at 232.

[54] *Id.* at 234-7.

[55] *Id.* at 234-7.

[56] *Id.* at 236, 237.

[57] *Id.* at 235.

[58] C.M. VILAS, THE SANDINISTA REVOLUTION: NATIONAL LIBERATION AND SOCIAL TRANSFORMATION IN CENTRAL AMERICA 108 (Monthly Review Press 1986) (Emphasis in original).

[59] *Id.* at 283. Ruiz, trained in Moscow and a key figure during the rise to power of the FSLN, remains an active leader of the left today in Nicaragua, but in a breakaway group from the original FSLN.

[60] *Id.* at 118

[61] *Id.*

[62] *Id.* at 179 (emphasis in original).

[63] *Id.* at 204.

[64] *Id.* at 191 (emphasis in original).

[65] *Id.*

[66] Castillo, *La participación de los trabajadores en la gestión de las empresas.* (CONAPRO "Heroes y Martires" 1983) in *Id.* at 190.

[67] *Id.* at 184.

[68] *Id.* at 185.

[69] *Id.*

[70] *Id.* at 189

[71] *Id.* at 182.

[72] *Id.* at 164.

## Chapter Two

[1] This chapter is based on a talk presented at a conference sponsored by the MacArthur Foundation and Social Science Research Council on democracy and the transition from communism in Eastern Europe at the Central European University, Prague, Czechoslovakia, in 1993.

[2] *See* COOPERS AND LYBRAND'S EASTERN EUROPEAN BUSINESS AND INVESTMENT GUIDES, CZECHOSLOVAKIA (Sept. 24, 1992).

[3] *Skoda Plzen To Dismiss More Than 1200 People in October,* CTK NATIONAL NEWS WIRE, Sept. 22, 1992.

[4] *See Hungary Fights Unrest with New Social Contract,* NEW YORK TIMES, Nov. 29, 1992, p.8; COOPERS AND LYBRAND, *supra* note 2.

[5] Melloan, *Yeltsin Must Turn to the People Once More,* WALL ST. J., November 23, 1992, p. A15.

[6] United States International Trade Commission, *Review of Trade and Investment Liberalization Measures by Mexico and Prospects for Future United States-Mexican Relations: Phase I and II* (USITC, 1990).

[7] *See* F. FAJNZYLBER, UNAVOIDABLE INDUSTRIAL RESTRUCTURING IN LATIN AMERICA (Duke Univ. Press 1990)

[8] Jonathan Zysman, "Technology and Power in a Multi-Power Global Economy," Seminar, Graduate School of International Relations and Pacific Studies, 1990.

[9] Michael Piore, "Critical Notes on Dunlop's *Industrial Relations System*," Colloquium paper, Les Systèmes de relations professionelles," Paris, March, 1989.

[10] "A Benign Scenario," FIN. TIMES, Jun. 3, 1989.

[11] Sanderson and Hayes, *Mexico – Opening Ahead of Eastern Europe*, HARV. BUS. REV., Sept.-Oct., 1990.

[12] M. Anderson (Jun. 28, 1990). Statement before the Subcommittee on Trade, Committee on Ways and Means, U.S. House of Representatives.

[13] Pear, *Rich got Richer in 80's; Others Held Even*, N.Y. TIMES, Jan. 11, 1991.

[14] Reich, *Secession of the Successful*, N.Y. TIMES MAGAZINE, Jan. 20, 1991.

[15] International Labor Rights Education and Research Fund, *Worker Rights in a Changing International Economy*, (1988).

[16] Coalition for Justice in the Maquiladoras, (n.d.) *Maquiladora Standards of Conduct.*

[17] *California AFL-CIO News*, 1988; Interviews by author of various regional and national AFL-CIO officials, 1990-1991.

[18] Jorge Castañeda, conversation with author, 1991.

## Chapter Three

[1] This chapter originally appeared at 29 PEPPERDINE L. REV. 115 (2001). It has been revised slightly for inclusion in this volume and appears with the permission of the Pepperdine Law Review which claims the copyright to the original article.

[2] Grass & Bourdieu, *A Literature From Below*, THE NATION, Jul. 2, 2000, at 26. "Since the Communist hierarchies fell apart, capitalism has come to believe that it can do anything, that it has escaped all control. Its polar opposite has defaulted. The rare remaining responsible capitalists who call for prudence do so because they realize that they have lost their sense of direction, that the neoliberal system is now repeating the errors of Communism by creating its own dogma, its own certificate of infallibility." *Id.* at 26.

[3] Lloyd, *The Trial of Jose Bove*, FIN. TIMES, Jul. 1, 2000, at 9.

[4] The concept "globalization" remains controversial and difficult to pinpoint. I consider globalization to represent the expansion of cross-border flows of capital in both its fictitious and physical forms (i.e., investment and trade) that has been so marked in the last twenty years.

In addition to the increase in flows, the ability to locate first class production facilities in low cost areas around the globe, a process facilitated by financial and technological developments, gives a new significance to capital mobility and threatens long-standing social and economic arrangements together with the political and institutional frameworks that accompanied those arrangements. For a generally favorable view of the impact of globalization, *see* T. FRIEDMAN, THE LEXUS AND THE OLIVE TREE (Farrar, Straus and Giroux 2000). For critical views from the left, *see* P. GOWAN, THE GLOBAL GAMBLE: WASHINGTON'S FAUSTIAN BID FOR WORLD DOMINANCE (Verso 1999) and W. GREIDER, ONE WORLD READY OR NOT: THE MANIC LOGIC OF GLOBAL CAPITALISM (Simon and Schuster 1998). For a critical assessment from the right, *see* J. GRAY, FALSE DAWN: THE DELUSIONS OF GLOBAL CAPITALISM (New Press 1998).

[5] Wilkinson, *The changing face of protest: Idealists or subversives?*, FIN. TIMES, Jul. 31, 1999, at 12.

[6] Paulson, *Clinton Says He Will Support Trade Sanctions for Worker Abuse*, SEATTLE POST-INTELLIGENCER, Dec. 1, 1999, at A1.

[7] *Id.*

[8] Pruzin, *United States Submits Proposal for WTO Working Group on Labor*, DAILY LABOR REP., Nov. 2, 1999, 211 DLR A-4. Only a few weeks before, United States Trade Representative Charlene Barshefsky explained that the "U.S. proposal did not cover the enforcement of labor rights with trade sanctions." Jessup, *Update on WTO Labor Working Group*, NEW ECONOMY INFORMATION SERVICE. They are "not on the table," she stated in a November 1, 1999 press conference. The United States-proposed WTO working group is "very limited" and "quite focused" on analyzing such issues as job growth and trade, or the relationship between market opening and living standards, she said. In a statement issued by the United States Government in advance of the Seattle meeting, it stated that "the objective of the Working Group in the first two years will be to produce a report on its discussions for consideration by WTO Members at the Fourth Ministerial Conference." *Id.*

[9] See for example the divergent view presented in a recent issue of NEW LABOR FORUM by, on the one hand, the heads of two of the country's most important labor education centers attacking the AFL-CIO for its anti-PNTR campaign, and, on the other, a defense of the campaign by two leading in-house AFL-CIO intellectuals. Wong & Bernard, *Labor's Mistaken Anti-China Campaign*, NEW LABOR FORUM, (Fall/Winter 2000), at 19; Levinson & Lee, *Why Labor Made the Right Decision* NEW LABOR FORUM (Fall/Winter 2000).

[10] International Labor Organization (www.ilo.org). The ILO was designed by a Labor Commission established by the Peace Conference that convened in 1919, first in Paris and then at Versailles. The Commission was chaired by Samuel Gompers, head of the American Federation of Labor. It was seen as a necessary step for humanitarian, political and economic reasons. The first of these may be obvious given the poor

working conditions that persisted in the new industrial era. The second motivation, though, emerged as part of an explicit effort to avoid social unrest, even revolution, through the establishment of a tripartite organization that addressed labor conditions. Finally, the economic rationale made explicit a concern still echoed today to avoid the so-called "race to the bottom" whereby certain countries are able to use relatively cheaper labor and minimal health and safety standards to their comparative advantage. The Preamble to the Constitution of the ILO, adopted by the Peace Conference, states that "the failure of any nation to adopt humane conditions of labor is an obstacle in the way of other nations which desire to improve the conditions in their own countries." The ILO is now a Specialized Agency of the United Nations. *Id.*

[11] *Id.* "The ILO's standards take the form of international labor Conventions and Recommendations. The ILO's Conventions are international treaties, subject to ratification by ILO Member States. Its Recommendations are non-binding instruments, typically dealing with the same subjects as Conventions, which set out guidelines that can orient national policy and action. Both forms are intended to have a concrete impact on working conditions and practices in every country of the world." *Id.*

[12] H. FRUNDT, TRADE CONDITIONS AND LABOR RIGHTS: U.S. INITIATIVES, DOMINICAN AND CENTRAL AMERICAN RESPONSES 41 (Univ. Press of Florida 1998). One analyst speaks of a "consensus" around certain core labor rights among business, labor and government.

[13] *Id.* There are now more than 180 ILO Conventions and more than 185 Recommendations. Formally, the core or "fundamental" ILO Conventions include the following: FREEDOM OF ASSOCIATION AND PROTECTION OF THE RIGHT TO ORGANIZE CONVENTION, 1948 (No. 87); RIGHT TO ORGANIZE AND COLLECTIVE BARGAINING CONVENTION, 1949 (No. 98); FORCED LABOR CONVENTION, 1930 (No. 29); ABOLITION OF FORCED LABOR CONVENTION, 1957 (No. 105); DISCRIMINATION (EMPLOYMENT AND OCCUPATION) CONVENTION, 1958 (No. 111); EQUAL REMUNERATION CONVENTION, 1951 (No. 100); MINIMUM AGE CONVENTION, 1973 (No. 138); WORST FORMS OF CHILD LABOR CONVENTION, 1999 (No. 182). *Id.* There are 174 ILO Member States. None of the above Conventions have received unanimous ratification, though a large majority of states have ratified all of the above but for those related to Child Labor. *Id. See generally,* V. LEARY, *The Paradox of Workers' Rights as Human Rights in* L. A. COMPA AND S. F. DIAMOND, HUMAN RIGHTS, LABOR RIGHTS AND INTERNATIONAL TRADE (University of Pennsylvania Press 1996) [*hereinafter* COMPA & DIAMOND] (discussing the relative weaknesses and strengths of these core standards).

[14] S.F. Diamond, *Labor Rights in the Global Economy: A Case Study of the North American Free Trade Agreement in* COMPA & DIAMOND (1996) [*hereinafter* Diamond, *Nafta Case Study*].

[15] *See* LEARY, *supra* note 13.

[16] *Id.*

[17] *Id.*

[18] NORTH AMERICAN FREE TRADE AGREEMENT, Dec. 17, 1992, U.S.-Can.-Mex., H.R. Doc. No. 103-159 (1994).

[19] NORTH AMERICAN AGREEMENT ON LABOR COOPERATION, ("NAALC") (Sept. 14, 1993) *32 I.L.M. 1499 (1993).* The NAALC entered into force on January 1, 1994. *See* 19 U.S.C. ß 3311(b) (2000) (enabling each member country to monitor enforcement by other member countries of their respective labor laws).

[20] *See* U.S. Department of Labor, PUBLIC REPORT OF REVIEW OF NAO SUBMISSION NO. 940001 (HONEYWELL) and NAO SUBMISSION NO. 940002 (GENERAL ELECTRIC) and MEXICO NAO REPORT ON PUBLIC SUBMISSION 9501 (SPRINT). For an analysis of the inherent structural tensions in the NAFTA side agreement on labor, *see* Diamond, *Nafta Case Study, supra* note 13.

[21] Goodman, *Recent Developments: The North American Agreement on Labor Cooperation: Linking Labor Standards and Rights to Trade Agreements,* 12 AM. U.J. INT'L L. & POL'Y 815, 870 (1997).

[22] Bacon, *Labor agreement's final blow: Strikers beaten at NAFTA hearing,* S.F. BAY GUARDIAN, July 26, 2000.

[23] CARIBBEAN BASIN ECONOMIC RECOVERY ACT OF 1983, 22 I.L.M. 1381, 1383 *(1983).*

[24] *Id.*

[25] 19 U.S.C. ß 2702 (2000); *see also* FRUNDT, *supra* note 12, (discussing a valuable study of the impact of labor rights provisions in the CBI).

[26] TRADE ACT OF 1974, 19 U.S.C. ß 2461 (1999).

[27]TRADE AND TARIFF ACT OF 1984, UNITED STATES, 24 INT'L LEGAL MATERIALS 823 (1984).

[28] TRADE ACT OF 1974, 19 U.S.C. ß 2467 (1999).

[29] OMNIBUS TRADE AND COMPETITIVENESS ACT OF 1988, 19 U.S.C. ßß 2901-10013 (1988).

[30] URUGUAY ROUND TRADE AGREEMENTS, WORKING PARTY ON WORKER RIGHTS, 19 U.S.C. ß 3551 (2000).

[31] *See generally,* J.R. MACARTHUR JR., THE SELLING OF "FREE TRADE": NAFTA, WASHINGTON, AND THE SUBVERSION OF AMERICAN DEMOCRACY (Hill and Wang 2000).

[32] *See* Compa & Hinchliffe Darricarrere, *Private Labor Rights Enforcement Through Corporate Codes of Conduct, in* COMPA & DIAMOND, *supra* note 13.

[33] *See Industrial Countries Agree to New Guidelines on Multinational Business,* FIN. TIMES, Jun. 27, 2000; *see also* OECD GUIDELINES ON MULTINATIONAL ENTERPRISE.

[34] 28 U.S.C. ß 1350 (2000). "[A] court applying the [Alien Tort Statute] must determine 'whether there is an applicable norm of international law, whether it is recognized by the United States, what its status is, and whether it has been violated.'" Burma v. Unocal, Inc., 176 F.R.D. 329, 345 (C.D. Cal. 1997) (quoting *In re* Estate of Ferdinand E. Marcos Human Rights Litigation, 978 F.2D 493, 502 (9th Cir. 1992)); *see also* John Doe I v. Unocal Corp., 963 F. SUPP. 880 (C.D. Cal. 1997)

[35] *See*, The Global Compact, *at* http://www.unglobalcompact.org (last visited Jul. 12, 2009).

[36] *See* http://www.aflcio.org/mediacenter/prsptm/pr02232000.cfm (last visited Jul. 12, 2009).

[37] *Union Leaders From 145 Different Countries Seek Enforceable Labor Standards in Trade Pacts*, 70 DAILY LABOR REP. (BNA), Apr. 11, 2000, at A-1.

[38] *Id.; see also* Press Release, "AFL-CIO, Union Leaders from 145 Developing and Industrial Countries Launch New Campaign Calling for Enforceable Workers Rights in Trade Agreements and International Economic Institutions" (Apr. 7, 2000) (on file with author).

[39] J.J. Sweeney, President of TUAC, Comments to G-8 Heads of State available *at* http://www.aflcio.org/mediacenter/prsptm/sp07192001.cfm (last visited Jul. 12, 2009).

[40] *Id.*

[41] *See id.*

[42] *E.g., Nike Terminates Contract With Brown University After University Seeks Compliance With Code*, 64 DAILY LABOR REP. (BNA), Apr. 3, 2000, at A-2; *see also. e.g., Nike, University of Michigan End Apparel Licensing Relationship*, 84 DAILY LABOR REP. (BNA), May 1, 2000, at A-6.

[43] As Leary has pointed out, "norms" "are binding in international law either through international agreement or as customary international law." FRUNDT, *supra* note 12 at 31. Thus, even in the absence of ratification by some individual state, it is conceivable that a widely accepted norm, such as freedom of association, is enforceable as customary international law. It remains hotly debated, though, whether even such "core" standards have achieved that status. *See* Alston, *Labor Rights Provisions in U.S. Trade Law: 'Aggressive Unilateralism'?, in* COMPA & DIAMOND, *supra* note 13.

[44] Self-executing treaties, once ratified, do not require the further step of legislation implementing the requirements of the treaty into domestic law. Warren v. United States, 340 U.S. 523, 526 (1951). Thus, in one of the rare instances where the ILO is even mentioned in American jurisprudence, an ILO Convention on maritime health and safety was found to be "operative by virtue of the general maritime law and ... no Act of Congress is necessary to give [these provisions of the Convention] force." *Id.* This was an example of the self-execution of portions of an ILO Convention into American law. Unfortunately, the United States has ratified only two of the eight Conventions that make up the "core" standards: No. 105 on Abolition of Forced Labor and the recently enacted No. 182 on Worst Forms of Child Labor. The latter was signed into law by President Clinton during the WTO meetings in Seattle.

[45] *See* CONST. OF THE INT. LABOR ORG., June 28, 1919, Art. 24, (allowing a national or international labor or employees organization to make "representations" that a Member State has failed to apply an ILO Convention it had previously ratified); *see also id.* at Art. 26 (allowing

formal complaints against a Member State and providing a separate mechanism to supervise the Conventions on the freedom of association).

[46] *See id.*

[47] *See id.* at Art. 33 (providing that the ILO may take "such action as it may deem wise and expedient to secure compliance" with the recommendations of a Commission of Inquiry or the findings of the International Court of Justice). The International Court of Justice can hear the appeal by a Member State from a Commission of Inquiry finding, but it cannot take any independent enforcement action. It serves as a last-gap defense step for a Member State found in violation.

[48] Press Release, "International Labor Conference Adopts Resolution Targeting Forced Labor in Myanmar" (Burma) (June 4, 2000) (on file with author). Sanctions had already been imposed by the European Union and the United States. COUNCIL REGULATION (EC) NO. 552/97 of 24 March 1997 temporarily withdrawing access to generalized tariff preferences from the Union of Myanmar. PROHIBITING NEW INVESTMENT IN BURMA, EXEC. ORDER NO. 13047, 62 FR 28301, 1997.

[49] CONST. OF THE INTER. LABOR ORG., *supra* note 45.

[50] *Id.*

[51] Some have argued that the step taken by the ILO to ask its constituents to raise the Burma issue with *other* international agencies is an unusual step with some additional teeth. *Labor calls for Burmese (Myanmar) sanctions: ILO alleges forced labor, divided on timeline for action,* REUTERS, June 12, 2000. However, the point here is that these remain normative recommendations not legal duties. And, of course, there is nothing in the ILO Constitution nor the governing documents of other international institutions that obligates any further action, despite the clear finding of a violation of the ILO Convention on forced labor.

[52] International Labor Conference, Special sitting concerning the application by Myanmar of the FORCED LABOUR CONVENTION, 1930 (No. 29), in application of the resolution adopted by the International Labour Conference at its 88th (2000) Session, 89th Sess., pt. 3.

[53] S.F. Diamond, Class and Power in Revolutionary Nicaragua: The Rise and Decline of the Sandinista Movement, (1990) (unpublished doctoral dissertation, University of London, United Kingdom) (on file with author).

[54] The ILO decision on Burma made immediate headlines in Asia and became the basis of a shareholders' intervention against a multinational mining company with operations in Burma. Editorial, *Laboring over Burma Relations,* BANGKOK POST, Jun. 26, 2000.

[55] This author was able to make significant use of ILO monitoring efforts during his doctoral research on labor rights under the Sandinista regime in Nicaragua during the 1980s. *See* Diamond, *supra* note 53, at 283-331 (describing the period that relies on ILO monitoring).

[56] MacShane, *Human Rights and Labor Rights: A European Perspective,* COMPA & DIAMOND, *supra* note 13, at 54.

[57] It is worth recalling one classic example, the repression of the Democracy Movement in China in June 1989. The repression came about only after it became clear that the initial efforts by students were impacting a broad range of workers, culminating in a march in Beijing of more than one million people. Efforts during that period to form autonomous and democratic unions were brutally suppressed. Leaders of that effort were jailed or forced into hiding and exile. Dozens of those jailed union activists remain in prison today. *See generally,* Chan & Unger, *China After Tiananmen: It's a Whole New Class Struggle,* THE NATION, Jan. 22, 1990, at 79; *see also* various issues of the CHINA LAB. BULL., Hong Kong.

[58] *See* COMPA & DIAMOND, *supra* note 13.

[59] *Id.*

[60] "We are no longer writing the rules of interaction among separate national economies. We are writing the constitution of a single global economy." Press Release, "WTO Director-General to the United Nations Conference on Trade and Development ("UNCTAD") Trade and Development Board", TAD/INF/2687 (Oct. 8, 1996).

[61] The title of Dean Acheson's autobiography is PRESENT AT THE CREATION: MY YEARS IN THE STATE DEPARTMENT (1987), a reference to the famed diplomat's central role in the post-World War II era establishment of the Bretton Woods institutions, including the International Monetary Fund, the World Bank and the proposed International Trade Organization. The latter was rejected by an isolationist American Congress and thus the somewhat weaker GATT emerged. The WTO is seen by some as a continuation of the original post-war vision.

[62] MacARTHUR, *supra* note 31, at 155.

[63] "The political problem is that our [Democratic Party] base hates [NAFTA]," stated Tom Nides, chief of staff to Clinton's first United States Trade Representative Mickey Kantor, and that was a base of people "who believe they helped you get elected. You have a President who kind of ran against Washington ... and then you're trying to pass a major piece of legislation that your base - ... labor unions, Midwestern Democrats, industrial Democrats, the majority of African-American members [of Congress], women - were opposed to. That's a pretty significant challenge." *Id.* at 176.

[64] *Id.* at 231-32.

[65] Billings, *Reich says Clinton may name new labor secretary as early as December 13,* 240 DAILY LABOR REP., Dec. 13, 1996, at D4.

[66] MacARTHUR, *supra* note 31.

[67] A very much-weakened version of the same approach continues today in the form of the Advisory Committee on Labor Diplomacy, housed in the Bureau of Democracy, Human Rights and Labor in the Department of State. The Committee was initially chaired by Tom Donahue, the former head of the AFL-CIO and a long time member of the cold war wing of the American social democratic movement.

[68] B. SIMS, WORKERS OF THE WORLD UNDERMINED: AMERICAN LABOR'S ROLE IN FOREIGN POLICY (South End Press 1992).

[69] *Id.* at 97.

[70] In a 1998 speech at the Moscow University of International Relations, President Clinton delivered a particularly blatant encomium on this theme to his Russian audience. *See* The White House, Office of the Press Secretary, Remarks to the Next Generation of Russian Leaders (Sept. 1, 1998) ("no nation, rich or poor, democratic or authoritarian, can escape the fundamental economic imperatives of the global market").

[71] This possibility has been recognized for some time by the international labor movement, since, of course, it is a development that affects labor organizations in all countries. A report issued by the Executive Board of the International Confederation of Free Trade Unions in 1993 stated that "the current threat to [trade union] rights stands out as an unprecedented attack upon" organized labor, "unprecedented in its extent, in the variety of forms in which it appears, and in the persuasive nature of its ideological underpinnings and legitimation (sic)." "Viewed globally," the ICFTU continues, "the offensive is aimed at putting a definitive end to trade unionism." International Confederation of Free Trade Unions, "TRADE UNION RIGHTS UNDER THREAT," REPORT OF THE EXECUTIVE BOARD, BRUSSELS, ICFTU (Dec. 1-3, 1993).

[72] Lee, *Presentation by Thea Lee, Economic Policy Institute,* 12 AM. U.J. INT'L L. & POL'Y 857 (1997).

[73] Trumka, Speech at Labor and the Global Economy Conference (Nov. 21, 1996) *at* http://www.aflcio.org/mediacenter/prsptm/sp11211996.cfm (last visited Jul. 12, 2009). This approach was reflected in the emphasis on solidarity in AFL-CIO campaigns such as the Campaign for Global Fairness. Thus, in announcing this Campaign in February 2000, President Sweeney promised the Federation "will escalate [its] efforts to stand with [its] sisters and brothers around the globe ... to support a broader development agenda that can create equitable, sustainable, and democratic economic growth." Sweeney, Remarks at Press Conference on Campaign for Global Fairness (Feb. 16, 2000). A genuine effort to re-orient the AFL-CIO's international policy appears to be underway under the leadership of the Federation's first post-Cold War president, John Sweeney. Speaking at a Trades Union Congress meeting in London in 1996, Sweeney called for the international labor movement "to engage in a seamless garment of activism." He has carried out a reorganization of the Federation's international bodies, combining them into the newly formed American Center for International Labor Solidarity. The Federation's International Affairs Committee recommended that the Center "be funded without government supervision, foreign or domestic." Currently, the Center receives most of its financial backing from the United States Agency for International Development and the National Endowment for Democracy. Parks, *International focus shifts to organizing and solidarity,* (Dec. 23, 1996).

[74] Many developing countries were still stung by the decline in power, once the WTO had been established, of such UN institutions as UNCTAD and the Center on Transnational Corporations. UNCTAD operates on a one country, one vote structure, while the WTO operates on "consensus," which has, until Seattle, effectively rested control of the organization in the major economic powers. Bello, *Time to Lead, Time to Challenge the WTO, in* K. DANAHER & R. BURBACH, GLOBALIZE THIS! THE BATTLE AGAINST THE WORLD TRADE ORGANIZATION AND CORPORATE RULE (Common Courage Press 2000).

[75] A WTO Working Party is the second lowest organizational form in the WTO hierarchy. Only Working Groups are lower than Parties. Above them stand Committees, Councils, Plurilaterals, and then the Ministerial level General Council (which also serves as the Trade Policy Review Body and the final level of appeal for dispute settlement). Only the Ministerial Conference stands over the General Council.

[76] *U.S. May Refuse to Sign GATT Accord Over Labor Rights Issues, Official Says*, 1994 DAILY LABOR REP. 65, Apr. 6, 1994, at D10.

[77] Opposition was so intense, that at one point the director general of the ILO was formally "disinvited" from the WTO meetings. His mere presence was thought to lend credibility to the concept of a link between labor issues and trade. Parry, *ILO Director Michael Hansenne "Disinvited" From World Trade Organization Meeting*, 234 DAILY LABOR REP. A-1, Dec. 5, 1996, at D7.

[78] The Australian position has been the subject of heated debate. The Opposition Labor Party has been facing increasing pressure from its trade union base to impose "social tariffs" as a means of combating imports made with cheap, non-union labor. *See* Norington, *Free Trade Stand Puts Beazley at War with Unions*, SYDNEY MORNING HERALD, Jun. 28, 2000, at 1; Robinson *Unions attack Beazely on tariffs*, THE AGE, June 28, 2000; and Long and Martin, *Union leaders Unveil New Agenda*, FIN. REV., June 26, 2000.

[79] SINGAPORE MINISTERIAL DECLARATION, Dec. 13, 1996, P4, *reprinted in* 36 INT'L LEGAL MATERIALS 218, 221 (Jan. 1997) (reproduced from World Trade Organization Doc. WT/MIN(96)/DEC/).

[80] The tensions that the language causes are reflected in the record of discussions held by WTO Member States in the form of its Trade Policy Review Body. There, the EU and the United States regularly query certain Member States about their compliance with core labor standards. Just as regularly, the target State will bat such questions away with the standard comment that the ILO, not the WTO, is the appropriate forum for such a discussion. Occasionally another Member State, usually from the developing world, will come to the rescue. *See, e.g.*, Press Release, "World Trade Organization, Trade Policy Reviews: First Press Release – Bangladesh" (May 1, 2000) (where India comes to the rescue of Bangladesh after a verbal assault from the European Union).

[81] Vaca v. Sipes, 386 U.S. 171, 177 (1967). "Under this doctrine, the [union's] statutory authority to represent all members ... includes a

statutory obligation to serve the interests of all members without hostility or discrimination toward any, to exercise its discretion with complete good faith and honesty, and to avoid arbitrary conduct." *Id.* (*quoting* Humphrey v. Moore, 375 U.S. 335, 342 (1963)).

[82] *See* Wong & Bernard, *supra* note 9; Levinson & Lee, *supra* note 9. Unfortunately, the source of the wording used by the WTO is the ILO itself. Its 1998 DECLARATION ON FUNDAMENTAL PRINCIPLES AND RIGHTS AT WORK uses identical language on the comparative advantage question. DECLARATION ON FUNDAMENTAL PRINCIPLES AND RIGHTS AT WORK, International Labor Conference, 86th Sess. (June, 1998).

[83] International Confederation of Free Trade Unions, A NEW STRATEGY FOR TRADE AND DEVELOPMENT, Nov. 1999, at 3.

[84] The Auto Workers, the Teamsters, and the Steelworkers each withheld a decision on the endorsement, despite pressure from the AFL-CIO leadership. The Steelworkers subsequently endorsed Gore, but that was before Seattle and before the China announcement. They later expressed some doubts about their decision. The Auto Workers first stated that they were considering an endorsement of Ralph Nader, but later backed Gore. The Teamsters leader Jimmy Hoffa, Jr., appeared publicly with Ralph Nader and, while stopping short of an endorsement, issued a call that Nader be included in the publicly televised debates with the major presidential candidates, Gore and George W. Bush. After the major party conventions, the Teamsters announced their support for Gore.

[85] One clear hint about the IFG perspective comes in a preliminary report on the WTO prepared by a Task Force that it sponsors. The preliminary report was issued in advance of the Seattle events and the final report, promised for June 2000, has yet to be released. Participants on the task force include Walden Bello (Focus on the Global South), John Cavanagh (Institute for Policy Studies), Martin Khor (Third World Network), and Lori Wallach (Public Citizen). No representatives from the trade union movement are part of the Task Force. The preliminary report calls for "respect" for international labor rights but when it comes to enforceable standards it includes only a prohibition on forced labor. There is no mention of incorporating labor rights in the WTO. BEYOND THE WTO: ALTERNATIVES TO ECONOMIC GLOBALIZATION, Prelim. Rep. by Task Force of the International Forum on Globalization (Nov. 26, 1999).

[86] 1999 Country Rep. on Human Rights Practices, Malaysia, Bureau of Democracy, HUMAN RIGHTS AND LABOR (Feb. 25, 2000).

[87] Ratifications of the FUNDAMENTAL HUMAN RIGHTS CONVENTIONS by country in Asia & Pacific, ILOLEX, July 9, 2000.

[88] 112/113 THIRD WORLD RESURGENCE, Dec. 99-Jan. 2000.

[89] *Supra* note 30. *See also* Thaitawat, *UNCTAD Conference - Hopes world trade tensions will ease at Bangkok meeting,* BANGKOK POST, Dec. 11, 1999.

[90] Once available at http://www.citizen.org (last visited Dec. 8, 2001), the letter has now been removed from the Public Citizen website.

[91] The cover of the Spring 2000 issue of FOREIGN POLICY asked "Why is This Woman Smiling?" next to a photo of Wallach. The answer: "Because she just beat up the WTO in Seattle, that's why." The editorial board of FOREIGN POLICY includes such mainstream pro-free trade figures as C. Fred Bergsten, Donald F. McHenry, and Joseph S. Nye and is published by the Carnegie Endowment for International Peace in Washington, D.C.

[92] Interview with author, Nov. 15, 2000.

[93] "Tariffs collected on imports have been a major source of the revenues used to support China's social welfare system. WTO membership will reduce these revenues. ... 'China used to be able to say with some validity that while their system did not protect individual liberties, it did provide for social and economic rights better than a free market economy such as the United States. Now, increasingly, the Chinese system combines the worst features of capitalism and socialism.'" Anderson, Cavanagh, & Athreya, *Don't Strengthen the WTO by Admitting China*, 4 THE PROGRESSIVE RESPONSE, No. 19, May 4, 2000. This is the kind of argument that was so familiar in the Cold War era used by sympathizers with Stalinism to justify the alleged benefits of that system. For another, even more egregiously pro-Chinese regime example, *see* Bello & Mittal, *Dangerous Liaisons: Progressives, The Right, and the Anti-China Trade Campaign*, 6 FOOD FIRST, No. 1, Institute for Food and Development Policy (2000).

[94] To his credit, John Cavanagh and his co-workers at least understood the impact on the WTO of allowing China to accede:

> We do not support the permanent normalization of trade relations with China at this time for the same reasons that we do not support any efforts to strengthen the current trade and investment institutions without explicitly addressing social and environmental concerns. The massive protests in Seattle against the WTO, as well as recent protests against the World Bank and International Monetary Fund in Washington, D.C., have only underscored the widespread public rejection of the trade and investment liberalization agenda.

[95] I do not mean to endorse a "go it alone" strategy, of course, but only wish to point out that it may be all that is available to labor. This is where the earlier discussion of the Cold War legacy of United States labor plays some role. The AFL-CIO has not completely broken with that past and this provides some fertile ground for the assertion of the neo-Third World camp that United States labor is once again engaging in "aggressive unilateralism," to quote one international legal scholar who has looked at this issue. *See* Alston, *supra* note 43. Of course, the facts make clear that this link with United States foreign policy is all but dead. What remains is for the AFL-CIO to articulate its own foreign policy, independent of funding and other ties to the United States government.

[96] There is some effort underway inside the AFL-CIO to articulate such alternatives. *See* T. PALLEY, THE CASE FOR CORE LABOR STANDARDS IN THE INTERNATIONAL ECONOMY: THEORY, EVIDENCE, AND A BLUEPRINT FOR IMPLEMENTATION, Rep. Submitted to the International Financial Advisory Commission of the Department of the Treasury by the AFL-CIO (Not dated.) To date, however, their approach tends to rely on a form of "global Keynesianism." *See* Faux, *Slouching towards Seattle*, 11(2) AMERICAN PROSPECT, December 6, 1999. It is hard to imagine how one expects Keynesianism to be reestablished on an international scale after its dismantling on a national level.

[97] *See* MacARTHUR, *supra* note 31.

[98] International Confederation of Free Trade Unions, A NEW STRATEGY FOR TRADE AND DEVELOPMENT, Nov. 1999 at 3.

[99] For a milder approach to expanding the "core" to include a wider agenda, see Compa, *Promise and Peril: Core Labor Rights in Global Trade and Investment, in* G. ANDREOPOULOS, ED., INTERNATIONAL HUMAN RIGHTS: A HALF CENTURY AFTER THE UNIVERSAL DECLARATION (2002).

[100] Protests that the WTO is not technically equipped to deal with these issues do not make a great deal of sense. Even today the dispute resolution process calls upon the talents of law professors with varying skills and backgrounds. Including some with backgrounds in labor law and economic development would not be particularly difficult. The ILO has a wealth of data and professional resources that could be tapped for such an effort. For an indication of the potential in this approach, *see* R. ROTHSTEIN, DEVELOPING REASONABLE STANDARDS FOR JUDGING WHETHER MINIMUM WAGE LEVELS IN DEVELOPING NATIONS ARE ACCEPTABLE, Final Rep., Sept. 3, 1996, Economic Policy Institute, Washington, D.C. In the developed countries campaigns for a "living wage" are increasingly supplanting those for just a minimum wage. These take into account regional differences in the cost of living.

## Chapter Four

[1] This chapter originally appeared in the *U.C. Davis Journal of International Law and Policy*, Volume 10, No 1, Fall, 2003. It has been revised slightly for inclusion in this volume.

[2] CRIMINAL VERDICT: YAO FUXIN AND XIAO YUNLIANG (Intermediate People's Court of Liaoyang Municipality, Liaoning Province, May 9, 2003) translated in *The Liaoyang Workers' Struggle: Portrait of a Movement*, CHINA LAB. BULL., July 2003, at 71, *available at* http://www.china-labour.org.hk (on file with author) [*hereinafter Liaoyang Workers' Struggle*].

[3] Descriptions of these events are found in Press Release, "Human Rights in China, Liaoyang Labor Activists' Daughters Detained" (Mar. 3, 2003) and *Liaoyang Workers' Struggle*, *supra* note 2, CHINA LAB. BULL. at 26.

[4] *Liaoyang Workers' Struggle*, *supra* note 2, at 71.

[5] "Human Rights in China", *supra* note 3.

⁶ 1998 CHINA STATISTICAL YEARBOOK (China Stat. Info. & Consultancy Service Centre) at 105.

⁷ *See* P. HIRST & G. THOMPSON, GLOBALIZATION IN QUESTION: THE INTERNATIONAL ECONOMY AND THE POSSIBILITIES OF GOVERNANCE (Polity 1996).

⁸ Montwieler, *'High Productivity Poverty' Threatens Workers Labor, Professor Warns Machinists Meeting*, DAILY LABOR REP., Sep. 13, 2000, at C-1.

⁹ *Id. See also*, H. SHAIKEN, MEXICO IN THE GLOBAL ECONOMY: HIGH TECHNOLOGY AND WORK ORGANIZATION IN EXPORT INDUSTRIES (Center for U.S.-Mexican Studies, U.C. San Diego 1990).

¹⁰ R. DUNCAN, THE DOLLAR CRISIS: CAUSES, CONSEQUENCES, CURES 144 (Wiley 2003).

¹¹ J.M. KEYNES, THE GENERAL THEORY OF EMPLOYMENT, INTEREST AND MONEY at 26 (Macmillan and Co. 1932; 1964). There is enormous controversy within the field of economic history on the actual definition of Say's Law and on Keynes' interpretation of it. In fact, the Law itself is better understood as the "law of markets" - which holds that where there is no "interference" with the markets they will find an equilibrium whereby all output can be sold. Only what W.H. Hutt called "defects in pricing" can interfere with the exchange of all output for other goods and services. W.H. HUTT, A REHABILITATION OF SAY'S LAW at 8 (1974). But there is very little controversy about what Keynes meant on a substantive level, that the power of the labor movement constrained the ability of the private sector and the government to use wage cutting as a means of jumpstarting economic growth in a depression. "To suppose that a flexible wage policy is a right and proper adjunct of a system which on the whole is one of laissez-faire, is the opposite of the truth. It is only in a highly authoritarian society, where sudden, substantial, all-round changes could be decreed that a flexible wage-policy could function with success. One can imagine it in operation in Italy, Germany or Russia, but not in France, the United States or Great Britain." KEYNES at 269. Recall, of course, that this was when fascism or Stalinism ruled the first set of states, while democracy continued to function in the latter set. Hutt expressed the more traditional laissez-faire view that the power of unions was a key "defect in pricing" rather than the inevitable byproduct of modern capitalism. HUTT at 134-144. On Say generally, *see* E.L. FORGET, THE SOCIAL ECONOMICS OF JEAN-BAPTISTE SAY: MARKETS AND VIRTUE (Routledge 1999).

¹² Xie, *Asia Pacific: The Chinese Decade*, MORGAN STANLEY GLOBAL ECON. FORUM, Feb. 10, 2003.

¹³ Paulson, Jr., *More Than the Bloom of One I.P.O.*, N.Y. TIMES, Apr. 15, 2000, at 17.

¹⁴ Wong & Bernard, *Labor's Mistaken Anti-China Campaign*, NEW LABOR FORUM, (Fall/Winter 2000). ("Labor needs to encourage critical engagement with China. ... Labor leaders should take a bold step and seek

to open up dialogue and cultivate relationships with workers and trade unions [sic] in China.").

[15] Pei, *Don't hold your breath for openness in China*, FIN. TIMES, May 7, 2003 at 15 (discussing "sclerotic authoritarian regime syndrome" that afflicts Chinese leaders); *ACFTU-ICFTU: A Modern Love Story in the Making?*, 52 CHINA LAB. BULL., Jan.-Feb. 2000, available at http://www.china-labour.org.hk (last visited Aug. 4, 2003; on file with author) (noting that "aspirations of the international trade union movement and the international work of the ACFTU stand contrary to each other"); E. FINGLETON, IN THE JAWS OF THE DRAGON: AMERICA'S FATE IN THE COMING ERA OF CHINESE HEGEMONY (Thomas Dunne Books 2008).

[16] E.g., INTERNATIONAL COVENANT ON ECONOMIC, SOCIAL AND CULTURAL RIGHTS, pt. III, art. 8(1)(a), opened for signature Dec. 16, 1966, G.A. res. 2200A (XXI), 21 U.N.GAOR Supp. No. 16, at 49, U.N. Doc. A/6316 (1966) (entered into force Jan. 3, 1976) recognizes the right of individuals "to form trade unions and join the trade union of his choice ... [and] the right to strike" [*hereinafter* ICESCR]. *See* Lehl, *China's Trade Union System Under the International Covenant on Economic, Social and Cultural Rights: Is China in Compliance with Article 8?*, 21 U. HAW. L. REV. 203, 226 (1999). The ICESCR is, in some ways, stronger than the ILO DECLARATION as it not only incorporates the crucial principle of freedom of choice of labor organizations but also recognizes the right to strike.

[17] Gould, *Labor Law for a Global Economy: The Uneasy Case for International Labor Standards*, 80 NEB. L. REV. 715 (2001) ("there is no evidence of a 'race to the bottom' internationally in the labor arena" but "there are substantial arguments for international regulation" because "the outlier countries coupled with China make it possible that the 'race to the bottom' phenomenon could yet become a pressing one").

[18] Williams, *Corporate Social Responsibility in an Era of Economic Globalization*, 35 U.C. DAVIS L. REV. 705, 731 (2002), *citing* Press Release, "ILO, Global Employment Levels in Textile, Clothing and Footwear Industries Holding Stable as Industries Relocate" (Oct. 16, 2000), *available at* http://www.ilo.org/public/english/bureau/inf/pr/2000/38.htm.

[19] *See Chapter Three.*

[20] Roach, *Global: China - Externally or Internally Driven?*, MORGAN STANLEY GLOBAL ECON. FORUM, April 2, 2003.

[21] J. STUDWELL, THE CHINA DREAM: THE QUEST FOR THE LAST GREAT UNTAPPED MARKET ON EARTH 34 (Grove Press 2002).

[22] *Id.* at 38.

[23] *Id.* at 34.

[24] B. NAUGHTON, GROWING OUT OF THE PLAN: CHINESE ECONOMIC REFORM 1978-1993 (Cambridge University Press 1995); John McMillan & Christopher Woodruff, The Central Role of Entrepreneurs in Economic Reform (2002) (unpublished paper, on file with author); John McMillan, China's Nonconformist Reforms (1994) (unpublished paper, on file with author).

[25] *See generally* A.R. KHAN & C. RISKIN, INEQUALITY AND POVERTY IN CHINA IN THE AGE OF GLOBALIZATION (Oxford University Press 2001).

[26] STUDWELL, *supra* note 20, at 229; *The 2003 Fortune 500*, FORTUNE, Apr. 14, 2003, *available at* http://www.fortune.com (last visited Dec. 4, 2003).

[27] *Id.* at 231-32.

[28] KHAN & RISKIN, *supra* note 25, at 105.

[29] *Id.* at 151.

[30] *Asia's Top 50*, FORTUNE, Jul. 21, 2003, *available at* http://www.fortune.com (last visited Dec. 4, 2003).

[31] Naughton, Opening the Red Box: Explaining Economic Policy Regimes in China, Walter Shorenstein Forum, Asia/Pacific Research Center, Stanford University, Feb. 6, 2003.

[32] *See* N. HARRIS, THE MANDATE OF HEAVEN: MARX AND MAO IN MODERN CHINA (Quartet Books Limited 1978).

[33] *See* Chapter Five.

[34] STUDWELL, *supra* note 21, at 215.

[35] *50,000 Daqing Oilfield Workers Organise Independent Trade Union*, CHINA LAB. BULL., Mar. 6, 2002; *Mass Paramilitary Deployment Quells Daqing Demonstrations*, CHINA LAB. BULL., Mar. 26, 2002.

[36] KHAN & RISKIN, *supra* note 25, at 107.

[37] STUDWELL, *supra* note 21, at 51 (noting that a "particularly perverse ... effect of the aftermath of the Tienanmen killings was that the government was able to see through its austerity programme ... without a murmur of dissent. The population was too terrified to object. ... Urban wages were held down and the urban unemployment rate reached its highest level since the start of the decade.").

[38] STUDWELL, *supra* note 21, at 211-212.

[39] *Id.* at 214.

[40] DUNCAN, *supra* note 10, at 159.

[41] STUDWELL, *supra* note 21, at 206.

[42] S.F. Diamond, *The PetroChina Syndrome*, 29 JOURNAL OF CORPORATION LAW 39, 127 (2003).

[43] *Id.* at 65.

[44] *Id.* at 213.

[45] *Id.* at 226.

[46] KHAN & RISKIN, *supra* note 25, at 152-53.

[47] Leggett, *The Outlook: Under Pressure, China Blesses Private Sector*, WALL ST. J., Mar. 13, 2000, at A1 ("20 million new job seekers enter the labor market every year); Andy Xie, *China: The Virtuous Cycle Continues*, MORGAN STANLEY GLOBAL ECON. FORUM, Mar. 6, 2001 ("China's biggest challenge is to create 20 million jobs a year to absorb the entire labor surplus over two decades").

[48] King, *Trade With China is Heating Up As a Business and Political Issue*, WALL ST. J., Jul. 30, 2003, at A1; Barboza, *Textile Industry Seeks Trade Limits on Chinese*, N.Y. TIMES, Jul. 25, 2003, at C1; Leggett & Wonacott,

*Surge in Exports From China Gives a Jolt to Global Industry*, WALL ST. J., Oct. 10, 2002, at A1.

⁴⁹ DUNCAN, supra note 10, at 201.

⁵⁰ *Id.*

⁵¹ Zhao, *The Fed is in a dangerous game with China*, FIN. TIMES (London, England), Jul. 30, 2003, at 11; DeRosa, *Everybody Is Prodding China to Revalue the Yuan*, BLOOMBERG NEWS, Jul. 11, 2003.

⁵² *See supra* text accompanying notes 1-3.

⁵³ *Liaoyang Workers' Struggle, supra* note 2, at 11.

⁵⁴ *Id.*

⁵⁵ *See* CRIMINAL VERDICT, supra note 2, at 71.

⁵⁶ Press Release, CHINA LAB. BULL., Mar. 6, 2002 (on file with author).

⁵⁷ Int'l Confederation of Free Trade Unions Executive Bd., ICFTU CHINA POLICY (November 27-29, 2002) (on file with author) ("noting that the ACFTU is not an independent trade union organization and, therefore, cannot be regarded as an authentic voice of Chinese workers").

⁵⁸ Int'l Confederation of Free Trade Unions, ANNUAL SURVEY OF VIOLATIONS OF TRADE UNION RIGHTS (2003) [*hereinafter* ICFTU SURVEY]. The ICFTU has now been renamed the International Trade Union Confederation.

⁵⁹ *Id.*

⁶⁰ *See* discussion *infra* at notes 85-93.

⁶¹ Amnesty Int'l, REPORT 1999 (1999). Amnesty Int'l, PEOPLE'S REPUBLIC OF CHINA: LABOUR UNREST AND THE RIGHT TO FREEDOM OF ASSOCIATION AND EXPRESSION: "WORKERS WANT TO EAT - RORKERS WANT A JOB," AI INDEX: ASA 17/015/2002 (Apr. 2002).

⁶² Amnesty Int'l, REPORT 1999 (1999).

⁶³ *Feature: Unemployment*, 50 CHINA LAB. BULL. (Sept.-Oct. 1999).

⁶⁴ *See Workers' Forum: The Struggle Continues*, 51 CHINA LAB. BULL. (Nov.-Dec. 1999).

⁶⁵ *Radio Broadcast Transcript, Daqing Oilfield Workers' Struggle*, CHINA LAB. BULL., Mar. 6, 2002.

⁶⁶ Press Release, Amnesty Int'l, "'Subversion' Charges Must Not Be Used to Imprison Rights Activists" (Jan. 14, 2003).

⁶⁷ Lee, *From the Specter of Mao to the Spirit of the Law: Labor Insurgency in China*, 31 THEORY & SOC'Y 189 (2002) [*hereinafter Labor Specter of Mao*].

⁶⁸ The Four Cardinal Principles include: 1) To keep to the socialist road; 2) To uphold the people's democratic dictatorship; 3) To uphold the leadership by the Communist Party; and 4) To uphold Marxism-Leninism and Mao Zedong Thought. *See* CONSTITUTION OF THE COMMUNIST PARTY OF CHINA (CPC) amended and adopted at the 16th CPC National Congress on Nov. 14, 2002 (on file with author).

⁶⁹ Int'l Union of Foodworkers, REP. OF THE INT'L UNION OF FOODWORKERS ON MISSION TO CHINA 18 (1997) [*hereinafter* IUF MISSION TO CHINA].

⁷⁰ *Id.* at 4.

⁷¹ *Id.*

72 Cited in *Analysis of the New Trade Union Law*, CHINA LAB. BULL., Feb. 28, 2002.

73 *Id.*

74 *Id.*

75 The official figures can be found in WANG, *Labor Issues and Foreign Direct Investment in the PRC,* in ADVANCES IN CHINESE INDUSTRIAL STUDIES - THE MANAGERIAL PROCESS AND IMPACT OF FOREIGN INVESTMENT IN GREATER CHINA 177 (C. Jayachandran and L. Guijin, eds., Emerald Group Publishing Limited 1999). The CHINA LABOUR BULLETIN estimates are described in their study *Feature: Unemployment, supra* note 63.

76 *See* FEI-LING WANG, *Id.* at 40.

77 *See id.* at 178.

78 On the hukou system and the contemporary Chinese labor market, *see* Wang, *Floaters, moonlighters, and the underemployed:  A national labor market with Chinese characteristics,* 7 J. CONTEMPORARY CHINA 459 (1998); *see also* Section 301 Petition, AFL-CIO, Mar. 16, 2004.

79 The following summary of independent worker activity is based on *Worker Passivity in China: A Maoist Myth,* CHINA LAB. BULL., Nov. 2003.

80 Lee, *Pathways of Labor Insurgency,* in E. PERRY AND M. SELDEN, CHINESE SOCIETY: CHANGE, CONFLICT AND RESISTANCE at 48 (Routledge 2000) [hereinafter *Labor Insurgency*].

81 *Id.* at 56, Lee notes the "Beijing students' disdainful stance towards workers' participation in the Tiananmen protests." Eventually, though, several students became active leaders of the WAF movement.

82 *Worker Passivity, supra* note 79.

83 *Labor Insurgency, supra* note 80, at 49.

84 *Id.*

85 *Worker Passivity, supra* note 79.

86 *Id.*

87 When the huge Daqing oil reserves were exploited during the reign of Chairman Mao, the workers of Daqing were widely hailed as heroes. The oil workers were the basis of a classic Stalinist labor emulation campaign as Mao told China to "learn from Daqing" and rewarded so-called "Iron Man" Wang Jinxi for his prodigious productivity. This approach to labor discipline originated in the Soviet Union under the term Stakhanovism. Gittings, *Strikes Convulse China's Oil-Rich Heartlands,* THE GUARDIAN, Mar. 21, 2002 at 20.

88 *Labor Insurgency, supra* note 80, at 51.

89 *Id.*

90 *Id.*

91 Press Release, Amnesty Int'l, "China: One Thousand Executed in Strike Hard Campaign Against Crime" (July 2, 1996) (condemning campaign as "state killing on a massive scale" and "widespread arbitrary violation of the most basic right to life"). A revival of this approach is underway now in China. *China Punishes 12,000 Criminals Involved in Organized Crimes,* PEOPLE'S DAILY (Beijing), Mar. 11, 2002.

92 Wei, Conscientiously Implement the Spirit of the Fifth Plenary Session of the 15th Central Committee and Speed Up the Organising and Establishing of Trade Unions in New Enterprises, Address at Work Meeting on Organising and Establishing Trade Unions in New Enterprises (Nov. 12, 2000), in Leung, *ACFTU and Union Organizing*, CHINA LAB. BULL., Apr. 2002.

93 *Worker Passivity, supra* note 79.

94 DUNCAN, *supra* note 10, at 233.

95 DUNCAN, *supra* note 10, at 238.

96 *See Bridging the Divide, supra* note 19.

97 ILO, DECLARATION ON FUNDAMENTAL PRINCIPLES AND RIGHTS AT WORK, 86th Session, Geneva (June, 1998). The fundamental rights are made up by eight fundamental ILO Conventions, including: 1) FREEDOM OF ASSOCIATION AND PROTECTION OF THE RIGHT TO ORGANIZE CONVENTION, 1948 (No. 87); 2) RIGHT TO ORGANIZE AND COLLECTIVE BARGAINING CONVENTION, 1949 (No. 98); 3) FORCED LABOUR CONVENTION, 1930 (No. 29); 4) ABOLITION OF FORCED LABOUR CONVENTION, 1957 (No. 105); 5) DISCRIMINATION (EMPLOYMENT AND OCCUPATION) CONVENTION, 1958 (No. 111); 6) EQUAL REMUNERATION CONVENTION, 1951 (No. 100); 7) MINIMUM AGE CONVENTION, 1973 (No. 138); 8) WORST FORMS OF CHILD LABOUR CONVENTION, 1999 (No. 182). Int'l Labour Organisation, FUNDAMENTAL ILO CONVENTIONS.

98 Press Release, CalPERS, "CalPERS Board Takes Action on Investment and Other Measures", Nov. 15, 2000.

99 SINGAPORE MINISTERIAL DECLARATION, Dec. 13, 1996, P4, 36 I.L.M. 218, 221.

100 TREATY OF VERSAILLES, Jun. 28, 1919, pt. XIII I headnote, 225 CONSOL. T.S. 188.

101 Gould, *supra* note 17, at 720. Oddly, Professor Gould seems to accept the notion that Congress had it right about the impact of a race to the bottom on interstate commerce in 1935 when it passed the NLRA but that the international labor movement has now got it wrong in suggesting that the weight of hundreds of millions of workers barely paid a subsistence wage are no longer an obstacle to the progressive development of international commerce.

102 *Confusion at the ILO - China's Government Elected to Governing Body as ... Worker Delegate,* CHINA LAB. BULL., Jun. 19, 2002.

103 *Id.*

104 ICFTU SURVEY *supra* note 56; *ICFTU Denounces Prison Sentences on Worker Rights Activists,* CHINA LAB. BULL., May 12, 2003; Press Release, "Int'l Confederation of Free Trade Unions, ILO Keeps Pressure on Several Anti-Union Governments," (Apr. 4, 2003); Press Release, "Int'l Confederation of Free Trade Unions," ICFTU China Policy: ICFTU Executive Board, (Nov. 27-29, 2002) [*hereinafter* ICFTU China Policy].

105 ICFTU China Policy, *id.*

106 *Id.* (emphasis added).

107 *Id.*

[108] Wong & Bernard, *supra* note 13; Jenkins, *US unions resume talks after 20 years*, SOUTH CHINA MORNING POST, Sept. 27, 2002; Gregory Mantsios, *Tea for Two: Chinese and U.S. Labor: A Report from China*, FALL/WINTER 2002, NEW LAB. F. 61 [*hereinafter* Mantsios Report].

[109] Mantsios Report, id. at 15.

[110] *Id.* at 7.

[111] *Id.* at 1.

[112] *Id.* at 9.

[113] *Id.* at 17.

[114] *See* discussion *supra* note 59.

[115] *See* arts. 9-12, TRADE UNION LAW OF THE PEOPLE'S REPUBLIC OF CHINA (2001), Adopted at the 5th Session of the 7th National People's Congress on Apr. 3, 1992, amended in accordance with the DECISION ON AMENDING THE TRADE UNION LAW OF THE PRC made at the 24th Meeting of the Standing Committee of the 9th National People's Congress on Oct. 27, 2001.

[116] *See id.* art. 9.

[117] *Id.*

[118] *Id.*

[119] *See id.* art. 11.

[120] *See id.* art. 42-44.

[121] *Analysis of the New Trade Union Law, supra* note 72.

[122] ICFTU SURVEY *supra* note 58.

[123] *Labor Insurgency, supra* note 80, at 49.

[124] Sec. 77, Ch. X, LABOR LAW OF THE PEOPLE'S REPUBLIC OF CHINA, Adopted at the 8th Meeting of the Standing Committee of the 8th National People's Congress on Jul. 5, 1994, promulgated by ORDER NO. 28 OF THE PRESIDENT OF THE PEOPLE'S REPUBLIC OF CHINA on Jul. 5, 1994, and effective as of Jan. 1, 1995. (Emphasis added.)

[125] ICESCR, *supra* note 16, art. 8.

[126] ICESCR, *supra* note 16, art. 2.

[127] DECLARATIONS AND RESERVATIONS, INTERNATIONAL COVENANT ON ECONOMIC, SOCIAL AND CULTURAL RIGHTS, Feb. 5, 2002, U.N. Treaty Collection (on file with author).

[128] Jenkins, *supra* note 108.

[129] Shailor, *Letter to the Editor*, SOUTH CHINA MORNING POST (on file with author).

[130] IUF MISSION TO CHINA, *supra* note 69, at 29.

[131] *Id.* at 39.

[132] *Id.* at 30.

[133] *Id.* at 40.

[134] Id. at 42.

## Chapter Five

[1] This chapter originally appeared in 29 JOURNAL OF CORPORATION LAW 39 (2003).

2 Alden, *SEC Chief Inherits Disclosure Bombshell*, FIN. TIMES, May 11, 2001, at 1. Note that the SEC continues to use the word "Chairman" despite widespread usage of gender-neutral titles in other parts of the government.

3 Letter from Laura Unger, Acting Chairman, Securities and Exchange Commission, to Frank P. Wolf, Congressman, U.S. House of Representatives (May 8, 2001) (on file with author) [*hereinafter* Unger Letter].

4 The Federal Reserve's Second Monetary Policy Report for 2000: Hearing Before the Senate Comm. on Banking, Housing and Urban Affairs, 106th Cong. 13 (2000) (statement of Alan Greenspan, Chairman, Board of Governors, Federal Reserve System) [*hereinafter* Greenspan].

5 Beard, *Russia's Lukoil Disappoints US Investors with London Listing*, FIN. TIMES, Jul. 2, 2001, at 23.

6 Leahy & Van Duyn, *Spy Plane Incident Hits Bond Sale in US*, FIN. TIMES, May 16, 2001, at 31 ("Recent changes to SEC procedures regarding the amount of documentation required from foreign borrowers might also have delayed the process of issuing a bond into the US market....").

7 Greenspan, *supra* note 3 ("To the extent that we block foreigners from investing, from raising funds in the United States, we probably undercut the viability of our own system.").

8 *Union Peak Body Calls for Amerada Hess Vote on Triton, Oil & Gas Today*, Aug. 8, 2001.

9 In late 2002, AHC and Premier Oil gave in to shareholder and public pressure and sold off their Burmese assets to a Malaysian company friendlier to the dictatorial regime. Macalister, *Premier Oil Gets Out of Burma*, THE GUARDIAN, Sept. 17, 2002; Press Release, The Burma Campaign UK, "Campaigners Celebrate as Premier Oil Pulls Out of Burma" (Sept. 16, 2002).

10 Press Release, "AFL-CIO, Worker Shareholders Challenge Unocal's Plans for New Investment in Burma and Ask for Commitment to Global Labor Standards" (May 20, 2002).

11 On the WTO protests in Seattle, *see* Stephen F. Diamond, *Bridging the Divide: An Alternative Approach to International Labor Rights after the Battle of Seattle*, 29 PEPP. L. REV. 115 (2002) [*hereinafter* Diamond, *Bridging the Divide*].

12 I write of the Anglo-American model in distinction from the European and Asian models. The Anglo-American model, as will be clear from discussion below, relies heavily on arms-length capital markets, as opposed to friendly creditors, as a source of capital for, and as a device for the discipline of, corporations. The core principles (and principals!) of this model have become central to the globalization process of the last twenty years. *See* MICHEL ALBERT, CAPITALISM AGAINST CAPITALISM (Basic Books 1993) (arguing that a "new phase of capitalism" emerged with the rise to power of Margaret Thatcher in 1979 and Ronald Reagan in 1980); RONALD DORE, STOCK MARKET CAPITALISM: WELFARE CAPITALISM - PAPAN AND GERMANY

VERSUS THE ANGLO-SAXONS (Oxford University Press 2000) (discussing emergence of new model of capitalism where "firms run primarily, even exclusively, for the benefit of their shareholders").

[13] On legitimacy and capitalism generally, *see* J. HABERMAS, LEGITIMATION CRISIS 19 (Beacon Press 1973, 1975) ("Private ownership of the means of production ... in the long run threatens social integration [but] within the framework of a legitimate order of authority, the opposition of interests can be kept latent and integrated for a certain time. This is the achievement of legitimating world-views or ideologies."); 1 M. WEBER, ECONOMY AND SOCIETY 213 (Bedminster Press Incorporated 1968) ("Experience shows that in no instance does domination voluntarily limit itself to the appeal to material or affectual or ideal motives as a basis for its continuance. In addition every such system attempts to establish and to cultivate the belief in its legitimacy."), *cited in* HABERMAS, *supra*, at 97.

[14] For an exploration of the internal political dynamics of the Stalinist and neo-Stalinist regimes, *see* S.F. Diamond, Class and Power in Revolutionary Nicaragua: The Rise and Decline of the Sandinista Movement (1991) (unpublished Ph.D. dissertation, University of London) (on file with author).

[15] *See* E.P. THOMPSON, WHIGS & HUNTERS 265 (Penguin Books Ltd. 1977) ("The notion of the regulation and reconciliation of conflicts through the rule of law - and the elaboration of rules and procedures which, on occasion, made some approximate approach towards the ideal - seems to me a cultural achievement of universal significance.").

[16] In the West, the general acceptance of this view was signaled by the emergence of the "difference principle" arguments of J. Rawls in A THEORY OF JUSTICE at 75 (Harvard University Press 1971) ("The intuitive idea [of the difference principle] is that social order is not to establish and secure the most attractive prospects of those better off unless doing so is to the advantage of those less fortunate."). As Philip Selznick summarized this view:

> In a doctrine he calls the "difference principle," Rawls asserts that social and economic inequalities may be necessary and desirable, but their moral worth must be judged by what they contribute to the welfare of the least advantaged ... . The difference principle is founded in rationality and reciprocal advantage, not in sympathy and benevolence ... . Yet the difference principle, as Rawls understands it, is an expression of human solidarity. Within his theory of justice, the abstract ideal of fraternity takes on a new and more specific meaning. What began as a shrewd calculation - a hedge against unfavorable outcomes - generates a spirit of brotherhood and is a building block of community ... . Rawls imagines a social contract in which free, equal, and rational persons agree on the terms of their future cooperation by choosing principles of

justice. Behind a veil of ignorance about their individual circumstances, they choose the least bad or safest alternatives. No one can be sure of not ending up highly vulnerable to loss of liberty or at the bottom of the social ladder. Therefore he or she wants to insure against the worst alternative. The outcome is a set of principles - compelled by rationality - that protect the interests of the least advantaged and the basic liberties of all.

Selznick, *The Idea of a Communitarian Morality*, 75 CAL. L. REV. 445, 446 (1987) (citations omitted). This was expressed more cynically and with pointed humor in the eastern bloc. Russian workers in the Soviet era were heard to quip: "They pretend to pay us, we pretend to work." On games that workers in the Stalinist world played to survive, *see* M. HARASZTI, A WORKER IN A WORKER'S STATE (Universe Books 1978).

[17] John Lloyd, *Radical Islam Sees Itself Just as Communism Did - In a Battle With a Hostile World*, FIN. TIMES, Jan. 11-12, 2003, at I.

[18] In the case of the trade unions, this is much more the case in the West where the labor movement retained some level of independence from the system throughout the Cold War. In the east, the so-called trade unions were merely party appendages unable, for the most part, to generate any independent life after the collapse of the regimes.

[19] This chapter signals the existence of a deeper concern about the nature of law itself. The author belongs to a tradition marked by the work of E.P. Thompson who noted that law is not simply "another mask for the rule of a class," rather law is the outcome of complex social conflict: "What was often at issue [in Thompson's examination of 18th century battles between independent hunters and royal land-owners] was not property, supported by law, against no-property; it was alternative definitions of property-rights ... ." THOMPSON, *supra* note 15, at 259-61. In a word, men and women make law, but not just as they please. Thus, an important challenge for legal scholarship in the twenty-first century is to expose the unique social conflicts emerging in a new global environment, a new form of what Justice Holmes called "experience," and examine and debate the appropriate legal forms and institutions necessary to resolve those conflicts. This intellectual challenge is similar to the one that confronted legal thought in the late nineteenth century as the emerging era of industrial capitalism posed a new intellectual challenge. As Justice Holmes wrote of his approach to the problem: "The life of the law has not been logic: it has been experience." O. W. HOLMES, THE COMMON LAW 1 (Dover 1991) (emphasis added). *See also* his dissent in Lochner v. New York, 198 U.S. 45, 76 (1905) where with his memorable comment, "general propositions do not decide concrete cases," Holmes signaled the emergence of a battle against "Mr. Herbert Spencer's Social Statistics." A valuable reprise of Holmes' thinking, particularly his approach to "experience," is found in L. MENAND, THE METAPHYSICAL CLUB 337-47 (Farrar, Straus and Giroux 2001). Thompson, much like Holmes, believed in the importance

of reason, noting in the foreword to one of his most important works: "I commenced to reason in my thirty-third year, and, despite my best efforts, I have never been able to shake the habit off." E.P. THOMPSON, THE POVERTY OF THEORY AND OTHER ESSAYS I (1978). Both Holmes and Thompson, can "be distinguished ... from ... skeptics, who question ... the power of legal reasoning of any kind." Robert Brauneis, *The Foundation of Our "Regulatory Takings" Jurisprudence: The Myth and Meaning of Justice Holmes's Opinion in Pennsylvania Coal Co. v. Mahon*, 106 YALE L.J. 613, 644 (1996).

[20] Diamond, *supra* note 11.

[21] The Unger Letter is a hybrid instrument, most similar to the more standardized "Interpretive Releases" that the SEC issues regularly. It combines an interpretation of existing rules with a proposal for modification of those rules and also relays to Congress a staff memorandum that discusses the Commission's research and investigation of the issues involved.

[22] *See* FINAL PROSPECTUS, PETROCHINA COMPANY LIMITED (Mar. 27, 2000) (on file with author) [*hereinafter* PETROCHINA PROSPECTUS].

[23] Indeed, the frustrations of the laid off workers boiled over into open protest in the Spring of 2002, as part of what one close observer has called a "veritable labor insurgency" now underway in the PRC. C.K. Lee, *From the Specter of Mao to the Spirit of the Law: Labor Insurgency in China*, 31 THEORY & SOC'Y 189, Apr. 2002. Conflict was particularly acute in the Daqing oilfields now owned by PetroChina. *See* S.F. Diamond, *The Chinese Market: An Enigma Unraveled*, DISSENT 95 (Summer 2002). These strikes were widely expected, yet PetroChina told potential investors that its relationship with its employees was "good" and provided no information or background on the potential for worker unrest. PETROCHINA PROSPECTUS, *supra* note 22, at 143.

[24] Though beyond the scope of this chapter, it is important to note that while the lack of basic civil liberties and trade union rights are extreme in the PRC, a variation on these conditions is increasingly the norm in the newly industrializing areas of the so-called emerging market countries, thus feeding into the "legitimation deficit" discussed here.

[25] *See* PETROCHINA PROSPECTUS, *supra* note 22, at 31-33 (stating that PetroChina "will be controlled by CNPC, whose interests may differ from those of our other shareholders").

[26] Many details of the IPO remain confidential to this day. For example, there were reports that the entire restructuring of the oil industry was planned by the Chinese regime secretly with the World Bank. However, neither the Bank nor the PRC have made a report or other form of public accounting of this process.

[27] On the restructuring, *see* PETROCHINA PROSPECTUS, *supra* note 22, at 73.

[28] *Id.* CNPC and Sinopec do engage in foreign investments to supplement shortfalls in domestic oil production. In particular, CNPC is a joint

venture partner in an oil production effort underway in the Sudan. This triggered the opposition of several human rights and religious groups to the PetroChina IPO. Wonacott & Johnson, *PetroChina Hopes to Shake Off Its Past*, WALL ST. J., Jan. 14, 2000, at A13. As we will see below, the Sudan link is a major factor in the process that led to the Unger Letter.

29 Clifford & Roberts, *Can this Giant Fly: China's Oil Company Hopes for $5 Billion from Wall Street*, BUS. WK., Feb. 7, 2000, at 94B [*hereinafter* Clifford, *Can this Giant Fly*].

30 Xiangwei, *PetroChina in Pledge to Slash Costs*, S. CHINA MORNING POST, Jan. 31, 2000, at 1 (stating "about one million workers ... have been made redundant through the restructuring"); Forsythe, *Chinese Minister Says More Must Be Done to Help Fired Workers*, BLOOMBERG NEWS, Apr. 12, 2002 (explaining that in 2001 CNPC and Sinopec "fired 600,000 workers between them").

31 In fact, since the IPO, PetroChina has engaged in a series of layoffs, despite reported profitability and aggressive expansion plans, in response to investor expectations. *See Petrochina to Invest 2.2 bln Yuan in 1,500 Petrol Stations this Year*, AFX ASIA, Aug. 29, 2002 ("The company will continue to lay off employees to further improve operating efficiencies"); J.V. Cruz, *Jr., Hither and Thither - The Chinese Way*, BUS. WORLD (Philippines), Aug. 30, 2002, at 5, stating:

> Exxon Mobil, with revenues almost six times bigger than PetroChina's, has about 123,000 employees. PetroChina's employee headcount is about 1.4 million. Each employee of Exxon Mobil thus accounts for US$ 1.5 million of revenues, while each employee of PetroChina accounts for US$ 21,000. ... PetroChina seems overstaffed. If it is, it's only because China is trying to minimize the pain of a program that has already brought on considerable anguish.

32 Clifford, *Can this Giant Fly*, *supra* note 28, at 94B.

33 *Id. See also* PETROCHINA PROSPECTUS, *supra* note 22, at 55-59.

34 PETROCHINA PROSPECTUS, *supra* note 22, at 139.

35 Hongru, Executive Profiles, PetroChina.com.

36 Franco Bernabe, Executive Profiles, PetroChina.com.

37 Xu & Ho, PetroChina: International Corporate Governance with Chinese Characteristics, Center for Asian Business Cases, School of Business, The University of Hong Kong, HKU183, Feb. 15, 2002, at 8.

38 *Id.* at 17.

39 *See infra* text accompanying notes 105-107.

40 Basapa, *China Launches "World Class" Petro Giant*, CHEMICAL NEWS & INTELLIGENCE, Nov. 10, 1999.

41 Yihe, *China's Petroleum Industries Undergoing Major Management Overhaul*, Jan. 19, 2000.

42 *Id.* As will be discussed below, the PetroChina IPO is the lead project in a planned stream of public offerings by Chinese SOE's.

43 *Id.*

44 Ogden, *Shareholders Remain Pawns in Party Line*, S. CHINA MORNING POST, May 8, 2002, at 12 ("Picture the amazement if a table of Exxon Mobil executives featured United States Energy Secretary Spencer Abraham telling the press Exxon would not be buying ChevronTexaco because he deemed the price too high.").

45 *Id.*

46 *List of Alternate Members of the 16th CPC Central Committee*, XINHUA ECONOMIC NEWS SERVICE, Nov. 15, 2002.

47 Forsythe, *China Names Former PetroChina Head Top Cop, People's Daily Says*, BLOOMBERG NEWS, Dec. 9, 2002.

48 For an overview of the reform process, *see* Diamond, *supra* note 11.

49 There are roughly 380,000 SOE's in China. The largest of these are controlled by the central government as in the case of CNPC. Smaller and medium size SOE's are controlled by local and provincial governments. It is estimated that this sector employs directly more than 100 million people, and supports the livelihood of an additional 200 million people. Sun, *Reform of China's State-owned Enterprises: A Legal Perspective*, 31 ST. MARY'S L.J. 19 (1999); *see also* STUDWELL, *supra* note 21, Ch. 4 (arguing that "government's response to looming fiscal crisis ... is to claim that the state owns all kinds of valuable assets that it can sell to cover its expenditures"); Diamond, *supra* note 11.

50 International Union of Foodworkers, HONG KONG: IUF MISSION REPORT, Dec. 1977, at 3 [*hereinafter* IUF MISSION REPORT].

51 Sun, *supra* note 49 at 32. Also, "the SOE's are linked closely with ... government agencies. ... The managers of these SOE's are state cadres ... assigned to an SOE to work not as an enterpriser [sic] but as a bureaucrat." *Id.* at 46. This introduces a further complexity: as cadre, managers are not subject to unemployment risk if the SOE fails - only the rank and file workers are, as the Chinese saying goes, "pushed into the sea" of unemployment.

52 Eckholm, *Amid Garbage and Disdain, China Migrants Find a Living*, N.Y. TIMES, Feb. 11, 2000, at A1.

53 Xiangwei, *PetroChina Sets Out Stall of Sweeteners for Investors*, S. CHINA MORNING POST, Jan. 24, 2000, at 1.

54 *CNOOC Says Listing Withdrawal Due to Change in U.S. Policy/Weak Confidence*, AFX-ASIA, Nov. 11, 1999. Chan, *China Plays Suffer as Move Seen Putting Damper on Beijing's Plans to Fund State Reform, CNOOC Postpones Dual Listing*, S. CHINA MORNING POST, Oct. 16, 1999, at 1.

55 Lin, *Shortfall in Beijing Airport Equity Offering*, FIN. TIMES, Jan. 28, 2002, at 33.

56 *See* Kynge & McGregor, *Chinese Old Guard Gives Way to New in Orderly Handover*, FIN. TIMES, Nov. 15, 2002, at 11; McGregor, *Rising Star Named New Shanghai Mayor*, FIN. TIMES, Feb. 21, 2003, at 9; *see also*

McGregor, *"Shanghai Gang" Faces Life Without Benefactor Jiang: China's Leader Surrounded Himself with Acolytes from Shanghai. Will They Survive Without Him?*, FIN. TIMES, Nov. 8, 2002, at 9 ("Known collectively as the 'Shanghai Gang,' these comrades act as a tight network at the commanding heights of the central government."); *Five Clear Jiang Allies in New China Leadership*, AFX EUROPEAN FOCUS, Nov. 15, 2002.

[57] Lin, *Baoshan Iron and Steel Group Sets $1bn Target for Share Issue*, FIN. TIMES, Feb. 9, 2000, at 33.

[58] *See* Lam, *Leftists Make Late Bid to Slow Reforms*, S. CHINA MORNING POST, Feb. 10, 2000, at 9 (noting that "heavyweight leftists, or quasi-Maoists" oppose privatization as "succumbing to the temptation of 'bourgeois liberalisation'").

[59] Lafitte, TIBET'S NATURAL RESOURCE HERITAGE ON SALE TO WALL STREET BIDDERS: A REPORT FROM MILAREPA FUND (DRAFT), Jan. 2000, at 2, 23-24 (arguing that "Chinese state policies in recent years have deliberately shut down CNPC's competitors" noting that "all three oil SOE's are jostling to recapitalize by floating their shares" and noting "the lengths CNPC managers have gone to in order to win official permission to list their enterprises' shares"). *Interview with Ho Swee Lin, Author*, FIN. TIMES, Hong Kong/Beijing Bureaus (Mar. 10, 2000).

[60] *Id.*

[61] Basapa, *China Launches "World Class" Petro Giant*, CHEMICAL NEWS & INTELLIGENCE, Nov. 10, 1999.

[62] *Id.*

[63] Nixon, ed., *PetroChina's IPO - More to it Than Meets the Eye?*, HART'S ASIAN PETROLEUM NEWS, Jan. 31, 2000.

[64] The figures presented here are drawn from *China and Long-range Asia Energy Security: An Analysis of the Political, Economic and Technological Factors Shaping Asian Energy Markets* (BAKER INSTITUTE STUDY NO. 11, Center for International Political Economy and James A. Baker III Institute for Public Policy, Rice University, Apr. 1999) [*hereinafter* BAKER INSTITUTE STUDY].

[65] *Id.*; *see also* BP STATISTICAL REVIEW OF WORLD ENERGY, June 2003, at 4.

[66] BAKER INSTITUTE STUDY, *supra* note 64; *see also China Accelerates Shift in Energy Policy, Restructuring of State Petroleum Firms*, OIL & GAS J., Jan. 10, 2000.

[67] It is the latter project that is the source of domestic U.S. opposition to the PetroChina IPO raised by a number of religious and other groups. *See* Ottoway, *Chinese Fought on NYSE Listing; Groups Cite Oil Firm's Role in Sudan*, WASH. POST, Jan. 27, 2000, at E01 (noting that "conservative religious and human rights groups have launched a campaign to block" PetroChina offering); Landler, *China's No. 2 Oil Company Prepares to Go Public*, N.Y. TIMES, Oct. 12, 2000, at W1 (noting that investment by PetroChina parent in Sudan "led human rights and labor groups to organize a bitter campaign against PetroChina's offering").

[68] On the impact of joining the WTO, *see* G.C. CHANG, THE COMING COLLAPSE OF CHINA (Random House 2001).

[69] *Restructuring of China's Oil Industry Continues as Doubts About its Success Loom,* OIL & GAS J., Jan. 3, 2000, at 19.

[70] Nixon, *supra* note 63.

[71] PETROCHINA PROSPECTUS, *supra* note 22, at I-31 (stating that "CNPC, as the majority shareholder of the Company, may seek to influence the determination of the amount of dividends paid by the Company with a view to satisfying its cash flow requirements including those relating to its obligations to provide supplementary social services to its employees and a limited number of third parties").

[72] Nixon, *supra* note 63.

[73] *Id.*

[74] Lafitte, *supra* note 59, at 2.

[75] *Id.*

[76] *Id.*

[77] *2,000 Falun Gong Members Arrested During Spring Festival,* JAPAN ECON. NEWSWIRE, Feb. 10, 2000.

[78] *Id.*

[79] Sui, *China Using Asylums to Suppress; Banned Movement's Followers Reportedly Institutionalized,* WASH. POST, Feb. 12, 2000, at A17.

[80] Lam, *Jiang Compares Sect's Threat to Solidarity,* S. CHINA MORNING POST, Feb. 12, 2000.

[81] *Id.*

[82] *Id.*

[83] *Id.*

[84] IUF MISSION REPORT, *supra* note 50, at 17.

[85] AI REPORT 1999: CHINA, Amnesty International, 1999 [*hereinafter* AI REPORT 1999].

[86] *Id.*

[87] *Id.*

[88] *Id.*

[89] *Id.*

[90] AI REPORT 1999, *supra* note 85.

[91] Turack, *The New Chinese Criminal Justice System,* 7 CARDOZO J. INT'L. & COMP. L. 49, 58 (1999).

[92] *Id.* at 59.

[93] *Id.* at 58.

[94] The Laogai Research Foundation, A RARE INSIGHT INTO CHINA'S LAOGAI ECONOMY: DUN & BRADSTREET DIRECTORY LISTS FORCED LABOR CAMPS, at 13 (Jun. 30, 1999) [*hereinafter* Laogai Research Foundation].

[95] *Id.* at 9.

[96] Wei Jingsheng's activities on behalf of democratic rights extend back to the "Democracy Wall" movement of 1970s. Wang Dan was a leader of the student movement that took over Tiananmen Square in 1989, sparking widespread support among Chinese workers.

[97] PR Newswire, *The Laogai Research Foundation: Dun & Bradstreet Provides Rare Insight Into Financial Scope of Chinese Forced Labor Camps* (Jun. 30, 1999).

[98] AI Report 1999, *supra* note 85. Amnesty International, People's Republic of China: Labour Unrest and the Suppression of the Rights to Freedom of Association and Expression (Workers Want to Eat - Torkers Want Jobs), Mar. 4, 2002.

[99] AI Report 1999, *supra* note 85.

[100] *Unemployment in China*, China Lab. Bull No. 50 (Sept.-Oct. 1999).

[101] Pringle, *Industrial Unrest in China - A Labour Movement in the Making?*, China Lab. Bull. (Jan. 30, 2002).

[102] *Id.* (noting that "although the figures [for labour disputes] reflect widespread dissatisfaction and an increase in rights awareness among workers, they do not tell the whole story").

[103] Daqing Oilfield Workers' Struggle (China Lab. Bull. radio broadcast, Mar. 5, 2002).

[104] The death penalty was later withdrawn, but the two union activists are now serving four-year prison terms. Press Release, "'Subversion' Charges Must Not Be Used to Imprison Rights Activists", Amnesty International, Jan. 14, 2003. *See* Stephen F. Diamond, *The "Race to the Bottom" Returns: China's Challenge to the International Labor Movement*, 10 U.C. Davis J. Int'l L. & Pol'y 39 (2003).

[105] Lee, *supra* note 23.

[106] IUF Mission Report, *supra* note 50, at 17-18.

[107] The four cardinal principles include: 1) To keep to the socialist road; 2) To uphold the people's democratic dictatorship; 3) To uphold the leadership by the Communist Party; and 4) To uphold Marxism-Leninism and Mao Zedong Thought. *See* Const. of the Communist Party of China (CPC) (amended and adopted at the 16th CPC National Congress on Nov. 14, 2002) (on file with author).

[108] IUF Mission Report, *supra* note 50, at 18.

[109] *Id.*

[110] The official figures can be found in Wang, *Labor Issues and Foreign Direct Investment in the PRC* at 112, *supra* note 75, Ch. 4. The China Labour Bulletin estimates are described in their study *Feature: Unemployment*, *supra* note 100.

[111] *Id.* Wang.

[112] *Id.* at 178.

[113] *Id.*

[114] PetroChina Prospectus, *supra* note 22 at I-31.

[115] Kynge, *China Seeks to Ease Fears on CNPC Float, Oil Minister Says IPO Funds Will Not Go on Redundancies*, Fin. Times, Jan. 26, 2000, at 34; Nixon, *supra* note 63 ("[A] very large part of the monies raised will not go into new technologies and equipment, but rather into paying off debts and compensating a massively overstocked workforce, for it is a cardinal policy of the government that social stability must be maintained.").

[116] CHINESE LABOUR BULLETIN, *supra* note 103.

[117] BLACK'S LAW DICTIONARY 625 (6th ed. 1990).

[118] *Id.*

[119] Meinhard v. Salmon, 249 N.Y. 458, 464 (N.Y. 1928).

[120] For a discussion of the ability of investors in U.S. capital markets to be able to rely on "the integrity of the market price," *see* Basic Inc. v. Levinson, 485 U.S. 224, 247 (1988). A significant intellectual challenge to the efficient markets hypothesis that underlies the Court's opinion has been mounted in the last decade by the emergence of increasing evidence that even in developed economies the stock market is not an efficient allocator of capital but, instead, responds to irrational human behavior. *See* Shiller, *From Efficient Markets Theory to Behavioral Finance*, 17 J. ECON. PERSP. 83, 102 (2003) ("The recent worldwide stock market boom, and then crash after 2000, had its origins in human foibles and arbitrary feedback relations and must have generated a real and substantial misallocation of resources. The challenge for economists is to make this reality a better part of their models."); R.J. SHILLER, IRRATIONAL EXUBERANCE (Princeton University Press 2000) (analyzing the recent stock market boom); A. SHLEIFER, INEFFICIENT MARKETS: AN INTRODUCTION TO BEHAVIORAL FINANCE (Oxford University Press 2000) (using behavioral finance as a basis for critique of the efficient market hypothesis); and H. SHEFRIN, BEYOND GREED AND FEAR: UNDERSTANDING BEHAVIORAL FINANCE AND THE PSYCHOLOGY OF INVESTING 4 (Oxford University Press 2002) (arguing that "psychological phenomena pervade the entire landscape of finance").

[121] Wine, *Calpers Sticks to Ethical Stance*, FIN. TIMES, Feb. 20, 2003, at 17 (explaining that the "largest and most powerful public pension fund in the US ... signals ... staunch support for its socially responsible investing (SRI) policy").

[122] Goto, *China Oil Firms Prepare for the Big Time, Massive Streamlining Underway to Help Them Take on Foreign Giants*, THE NIKKEI WKLY., May 29, 2000, at 24 (stating that the PetroChina "issue has ... continued to flounder in both [Hong Kong and New York] markets, keeping ... funds actually raised below one-third the original target of 10 billion"); Nielsen, *PetroChina Begins Trading; Sinopec Postpones, Reduces IPO*, CHEM. WK., Apr. 19, 2000, at 25 (describing how PetroChina's weak reception by investors caused PRC to delay entry of other planned IPOs).

[123] BP is the new corporate name for British Petroleum.

[124] Lobe, *Activists Win on Petrochina, Target BP-Amoco*, INTER PRESS SERV., Apr. 5, 2000 ("The only major buyers [of PetroChina stock] to date, in addition to BP Amoco, are four Hong Kong-based companies" considered "under Beijing's influence.").

[125] Merolli, *PetroChina IPO Garners Tepid Response*, OIL DAILY, Apr. 3, 2000.

[126] *Id.*

[127] "EBITDA" is a widely used financial metric that gives a measure of the cash flow earned by a corporation. It stands for "earnings before interest, taxes, depreciation and amortization."

[128] Wonacott & Johnson, *PetroChina Prepares to Go Public: Changes Fail to Break its State Ties*, WALL ST. J. INTERACTIVE EDITION, Jan. 14, 2000, at A13.

[129] *"Use of Proceeds Verification,"* PETROCHINA PROSPECTUS, *supra* note 22, at 119-20.

[130] Lin, *Investors to Tread Warily in China Oilfields*, FIN. TIMES, Dec. 23, 1999 at 8.

[131] *Id.*

[132] *Id.* ("To top it all, CNPC has a lot of debts to repay: more than Rmb 115.3bn at the end of" 1998).

[133] Lee, *supra* note 23.

[134] *Restructuring of China's Oil Industry Continues as Doubts Regarding its Success Loom*, OIL & GAS J., Jan. 3, 2000, at 19.

[135] Lin, *Western Wiles to Woo the Market*, FIN. TIMES, Mar. 14, 2000, at 18.

[136] Wong, *Securities Regulations in China and Their Corporate Finance Implications on State Enterprise Reform*, 65 FORDHAM L. REV. 1221, 1242 (1996); Simon, *The Legal Structure of the Chinese "Socialist Market" Enterprise*, 21 J. CORP. L. 267 (1996); *see also* Lam & Jie, *China's State-Owned Share Dilemma*, Financeasia.com.

[137] Wong, *supra* note 136, at 1242.

[138] *See*, e.g., PETROCHINA PROSPECTUS, *supra* note 22, at 30-47.

[139] A recent example included efforts to delay bond offerings by Russian and Chinese corporations in the U.S. in 1997. *See* Clark, *Move to Curb Chinese Access to US Capital*, FIN. TIMES, Nov. 6, 1997, at 4; McKay, *Russian Bond Offerings Delayed Due to Turmoil*, WALL ST. J., Nov. 7, 1997, at A16. These moves were linked to elements within the conservative wing of the Republican Party, and appeared to have been motivated by national security concerns, and included proposals by Republican congressmen to establish an Office of National Security within the Securities and Exchange Commission to review planned offerings for national security implications. *See* William J. Casey Institute, *Russian Bonds Rocked by Second Hearing in a Week Focusing on Undesirable Foreign Penetration of U.S. Markets*, PERSPECTIVE, NO. 97-C 169 (Nov. 10, 1997). Such a national security-related effort may have more traction in a post-September 11th world.

[140] Claims that corporations violate an array of human rights appear to be on the rise. Notable examples include the ongoing litigation against the Unocal Corporation for its role in Burma and the recently settled claims of WWII Holocaust victims against Swiss banks. *See* Doe v. Unocal, 248 F.3d 915 (9th Cir. 2001). *See generally* Collingsworth, *ILRF Cases to Enforce Labor, Human Rights Under Alien Tort Claims Act*, WORKER RIGHTS NEWS, VOL. 5 NO. 1, Spring 2002, at 3; Stephens, The *Amorality of Profit: Transnational Corporations and Human Rights*, 20 BERKELEY J. INT'L. L. 45,

46 (2002) (stating that "morally defensible or not, business as usual or not, if corporations are complicit in human rights violations, the victims of the abuses have a legal right to compensation from those corporations"); Williams, *The Securities and Exchange Commission and Corporate Social Transparency*, 112 HARV. L. REV. 1197, 1201 (1999) (evaluating "whether the Securities and Exchange Commission (SEC) has the power to require social as well as financial disclosure by public reporting companies to promote social transparency"); Note, *Should the SEC Expand Nonfinancial Disclosure Requirements?*, 115 HARV. L. REV. 1433, 1435 (2002) [*hereinafter Should the SEC Expand*] (arguing "for a mandate bounded by considerations of investor welfare and underpinned by the same economic logic that supports mandatory financial disclosure").

[141] CNPC's partners included Talisman Energy, Inc., a Canadian concern that faced similar political pressure. In late 2002, in another sign of the significance of the new movement sparked by the PetroChina Campaign, Talisman announced the planned sale of its stake in the Sudan. Talisman CEO Jim Bucklee expressly acknowledged the impact of the protests over the human rights abuses when he announced his company's exit from the region: "Talisman shares have continued to be discounted based on perceived political risk in-country and in North America to a degree that was unacceptable for 12% of our production. Shareholders have told me they were tired of continually having to monitor and analyze events relating to Sudan." Press Release, Talisman Energy, Inc., "Talisman to Sell Sudan Assets for C$1.2 Billion" (Oct. 30, 2002). The sale was finally completed only in March of 2003 when Talisman announced at the signing ceremony of the sale to a state-owned Indian company that it was done "under US pressures." *Talisman Transfers Sudan Stake to Indian Company "Under US Pressure,"* AGENCE FRANCE PRESSE, Mar. 9, 2003.

[142] PETROCHINA PROSPECTUS, *supra* note 22, at 4 (emphasis added).

[143] *Id.* at 119-20.

[144] In late 1997, President Clinton invoked his emergency economic powers to impose sanctions on the Government of Sudan. EXEC. ORDER NO. 13,067, 62 Fed. Reg. 59,989 (Nov. 3, 1997).

[145] An Open Letter to President William Jefferson Clinton (Dec. 9, 1999).

[146] Press Release, Office of Public Affairs, Treasury Department, Treasury Applies Sudan Sanctions to Joint Oil Venture No. LS-393 (Feb. 16, 2000).

[147] Letter to James Burton, CEO of CalPERS (Jan. 24, 2000).

[148] *Can This Giant Fly, supra* note 29, at 94B (the PetroChina offering "will provide an important blueprint for overhauling state enterprises ... [that] could mark the emergence of China's new corporate giants on the world scene").

[149] *Id.*

[150] Ottaway, *Chinese Fought on NYSE Listing; Groups Cite Oil Firm's Role in Sudan*, WASH. POST, Jan. 27, 2000, at E01.

[151] I prepared the initial draft of the AFL-CIO report.

[152] Fidler & Labate, *Left and Right Unite in Protest over PetroChina Offering: Concern Over Chinese Group has Brought Seattle-Style Activism to Financial Markets*, FIN. TIMES, Mar. 21, 2000, at 6 (stating "an extraordinary ad hoc coalition ... has united left-leaning protest groups, trade unions and conservative national security types against the offering"); Cox, *AFL-CIO Flexes Muscle Against China IPO*, USA TODAY, Mar. 10-12, 2000, at B3.

[153] Telephone interview with William Patterson, Director, Office of Investment, AFL-CIO (Feb. 28, 2003); *see also* Labate & Lin, *China Oil IPO Fires Up Union Campaign*, FIN. TIMES, Mar. 10, 2000, at 6.

[154] Melcher & Soukup, *PetroChina Dustup: The Start of Something Big*, Potomac Global Equity Research Perspective, PRUDENTIAL SECURITIES (Mar. 22, 2000).

[155] Shell, *Goldman Moves Pitch for IPO to Avoid Clash, AFL-CIO Urges Investors to Avoid PetroChina Stock*, USA TODAY, Mar. 23, 2000, at 2B; Phillips, *PetroChina's IPO Roadshow Opens, While Opposition Forces Rally Nearby*, WALL ST. J., Mar. 23, 2000, at A14.

[156] Letter to President Clinton (Mar. 31, 2000).

[157] *See supra* text accompanying notes 122-124.

[158] Lin, *PetroChina Shares Plunge After Float*, FIN. TIMES, Apr. 8, 2000, at 8.

[159] Landler, *China's No. 1 Oil Company Goes Public With Whimper*, N.Y. TIMES, Apr. 8, 2000, at C2.

[160] Lin, *Poor Investor Response Forces China to Delay Two Listings*, FIN. TIMES, Apr. 1, 2000, at 17. In late 2000, an offering of stock by a second Chinese oil company, Sinopec, was made and ran into similar political opposition. Its shares trade down significantly from their offering price. Roger W. Robinson, International Security Dimension of Portfolio Management, Remarks at the Investor Responsibility Research Center, Inc. Conference (Oct. 26, 2001). One report suggested that China had planned an additional 120 stock offerings on the international capital markets. Those ambitious plans, if genuinely intended, were quietly withdrawn. Landler, *Stakes in China Suddenly Seem Less Appealing*, N.Y. TIMES, Mar. 31, 2000, at C1.

[161] The discussion that follows is based on contemporaneous interviews with William Patterson, Director of the Office of Investment at the AFL-CIO, a leading participant in the PetroChina Campaign.

[162] Press Release, CalPERS, "CalPERS Board Takes Action on Investment and Other Measures" (Nov. 15, 2000).

[163] Press Release, CalPERS, "CalPERS Adopts New Model for Investing in Emerging Markets" (Feb. 20, 2002).

[164] Einhorn, *Will CalPERS Kill Asia's Rally*, BUS. WK., Feb. 25, 2002 ("Thailand's market dropped 6.7% ... after the CalPERS news hit. The Philippines and Malaysia fell 3.9% and 1.7%, respectively ... ."); Braunschweig, *LPs Carry Their Weight Beyond Venture Capital*, BUYOUTS,

Sept. 9, 2002 (Philippines and Thailand "sent high-level delegations to Sacramento to ask CalPERS to reconsider its decision.").

[165] Press Release, CalPERS, "CalPERS Invests $ 75 million in Thailand Equity Fund" (Oct. 29, 2001).

[166] Barnes, *Can Thailand Win Back Calpers?*, FIN. TIMES, June 11, 2002, at 46.

[167] Collier, *State Employees' Pension Fund Flexes Its Muscle Around the World*, SAN FRANCISCO CHRON., Jul. 21, 2002, at A12. CalPERS recently reaffirmed their approach to the EMC screens. Telephone Interview with William Patterson, Director of Office of Investment, AFL-CIO (Feb. 28, 2003) (on file with author).

[168] REPORT OF THE UNITED STATES COMM. ON INTERNATIONAL RELIGIOUS FREEDOM, May 1, 2000, at 3.

[169] *Id.* at 5.

[170] Letter to Ms. Laura Unger, Acting Chairman of Securities and Exchange Commission, from Frank Wolf, Member of Congress (Mar. 8, 2001).

[171] *Id.*

[172] *Id.*

[173] *Id.*

[174] *See id.*; Memorandum from David B.H. Martin to Acting Chairman Laura Unger (May 8, 2001) [*hereinafter* Martin Memorandum].

[175] American investors in PetroChina would purchase "American depositary shares," or ADS's, "securities representing an ownership interest in a foreign company's common stock." MODERN DICTIONARY FOR THE LEGAL PROFESSION (3d ed. 2001). In the case of the PetroChina IPO, the Bank of New York would act as the depositary for the ADS's, each of which would represent 100 underlying shares in PetroChina. PETROCHINA PROSPECTUS, *supra* note 22, at 5, 19.

[176] OFAC is responsible for administering the sanctions on Sudan. *See supra* note 124.

[177] Unger Letter, *supra* note 3, at 1-2.

[178] *Id.* at 2 (emphasis added).

[179] *Id.* at 2-4.

[180] Greenspan, *supra* note 4.

[181] The Federal Reserve's Second Monetary Policy Report for 2000: Hearing Before the Senate Comm. on Banking, Housing and Urban Affairs, 106th Cong. 12 (2000) (statement of Sen. Phil Gramm, Chairman (R-TX)).

[182] Greenspan, *supra* note 4. Senator Gramm was so pleased with the response of Chairman Greenspan that he released a press release the same day headed "Gramm, Greenspan Share Concerns About Limits on China's Access to U.S. Capital." Press Release, Senate Banking Committee, Jul. 20, 2000.

[183] *See* SECURITIES ACT OF 1933 (codified as amended at 15 U.S.C.S. 77a (2003)); and SECURITIES EXCHANGE ACT OF 1934 (codified as amended at 15 U.S.C.S. 78a (2003)).

[184] L.D. BRANDEIS, OTHER PEOPLE'S MONEY AND HOW BANKERS USE IT 62 (National Home Library 1933). Although this requirement is simple enough, the content of that disclosure is outlined in a complex set of rules and regulations issued by the Securities and Exchange Commission.

[185] *See* J. SELIGMAN, THE TRANSFORMATION OF WALL STREET 29 (Houghton Mifflin 1982) (*citing* 1933 inaugural address of President Franklin Delano Roosevelt that Senate investigation of Wall Street led to the conclusion that the "practices of the unscrupulous money changers stand indicted in the court of public opinion, rejected by the hearts and minds of men").

[186] *Id.* Under the leadership of SEC Chairman William O. Douglas, significant changes in bankruptcy law (The Chapman Act of 1938) and the structure of the utility industry (The Public Utility Holding Company Act of 1940) were made. Douglas and other members of Roosevelt's "Brain Trust," actually hoped to make more far-reaching changes that ran into resistance from Wall Street and the more limited vision of FDR himself. *Id.* at 40-41. At one point, for example, Justice Douglas had been in favor of "public" directors serving on the boards of major corporations, a move he believed the SEC had the power to impose. *See* Karmel, *The Future of Corporate Governance Listing Requirements*, 54 S.M.U. L. REV. 325 (2001). However, as Karmel concludes, "the views of Justice Douglas remain controversial. The more common view is that the Securities Act is a full disclosure, rather than a merit, statute and the SEC does not have the power to regulate corporate governance." *Id.* at 337. In the wake of the Sarbanes-Oxley reforms put in place in the post-Enron era, that widely accepted conclusion is undergoing some, though not major, erosion.

[187] *See supra* text and accompanying notes 158-179.

[188] There exists important literature on industrial organization that receives too little attention in legal scholarship on corporations. *See* S.R. BOWMAN, THE MODERN CORPORATION AND AMERICAN POLITICAL THOUGHT: LAW, POWER, AND IDEOLOGY (Penn State University Press 1996); W.G. ROY, SOCIALIZING CAPITAL: THE RISE OF THE LARGE INDUSTRIAL CORPORATION IN AMERICA (Princeton University Press 1997); M.J. SKLAR, THE CORPORATE RECONSTRUCTION OF AMERICAN CAPITALISM, 1890-1916: THE MARKET, THE LAW AND POLITICS (Penn State University Press 1988); and M. ZEITLIN, THE LARGE CORPORATION AND CONTEMPORARY CLASSES (Rutgers University Press 1989). An important exception to my contention that this literature remains largely outside of legal scholarship is O.E. WILLIAMSON, THE ECONOMIC INSTITUTIONS OF CAPITALISM: FIRMS, MARKETS, RELATIONAL CONTRACTING (Free Press 1985), who relied heavily in his transaction cost theory of the corporation and its governance on the work of A. CHANDLER, THE VISIBLE HAND: THE MANAGERIAL REVOLUTION IN AMERICAN BUSINESS (Belknap Press of Harvard University 1977).

[189] A.A. BERLE & G.C. MEANS, THE MODERN CORPORATION AND PRIVATE PROPERTY (Transaction Publishers 1932, 1968) [*hereinafter* BERLE & MEANS].

190 The Berle Means thesis has been viewed as a foundation for both what might be called the "social protection" framework (probably most important to Berle and Means themselves) that animated securities law analysis in the New Deal, and much of the Keynesian era, but also for the "agency cost" perspectives of law and economics thinking that has dominated the securities law field for the past two decades. Whereas Berle and Means saw the problem as one of using law to shape the behavior of managers now in "control" of the new powerful monopolistic, post-private property industrial groups to enhance the larger "community" interest, the "law and economics" school attempted to use the concept of "agency" costs to mount a market driven counter-revolution against what they see as the potential for opportunistic managerial behavior in firms that are still living in a world of private property. *See* BERLE & MEANS, *supra* note 188, at 351, 356; Berle, *High Finance: Master or Servant*, 23 YALE L.J. 43 (1933), *cited in* Seligman, *supra* note 184; Jensen & Meckling, *The Theory of the Firm: Managerial Behavior, Agency Costs and Ownership Structure*, 3 J. FIN. ECON. 305 (1986). A recent appraisal of both approaches is considered in Bratton, *Berle and Means Reconsidered at the Century's Turn*, 26 J. CORP. L. 737 (2001).

191 TSC Indus. v. Northway, Inc., 426 U.S. 438, 449 (1976); *see infra* text accompanying note 199.

192 Jensen & Meckling, *supra* note 190.

193 SAFE HARBOR RULE FOR PROJECTIONS, SECURITIES ACT RELEASE NO. 6084, [1979 Transfer Binder] Fed. Sec. L. Rep. (CCH) P82,117 (July 2, 1979) (adopting EXCHANGE ACT RULE 3B-6, 17 C.F.R. 240.3b-6 (1986), and SECURITIES ACT RULE 175, 17 C.F.R. 230.175 (1986)).

194 *See* discussion *supra* note 122.

195 *See* Carney, *Defining a Security: The Addition of a Market-Oriented Contextual Approach to Investment Contract Analysis*, 33 EMORY L.J. 311, 340 (1984) ("Investors are only concerned with expected future earnings, inspection of information about future prospects might loom large as a major feature of investor protection. It is in the nature of such statements that they are not fully verifiable.").

196 SEC Chairman Harvey L. Pitt, Remarks Before the AICPA Governing Council (Oct. 22, 2001). Such an effort has a good deal of support among business managers. *See Three Fourths of Portfolio Managers Surveyed Find Pro Forma Reporting Useful*, PR NEWSWIRE, Nov. 7, 2001 ("Sixty percent of managers want more information about intangible assets, and six out of 10 want more detailed disclosures about internally generated intangibles, such as the value of brand names, customer lists, among other items.").

197 *Should the SEC Expand, supra* note 140, at 1434-35 (emphasis added).

198 Imagine Johns Manville not disclosing the risks associated with asbestos litigation, or the Denny's restaurant chain not disclosing to investors the progress of litigation related to charges of racial discrimination in its restaurants. More recently, American multinational

corporations have been found to be potentially liable in American courts for human rights violations committed in association with their operations in foreign countries, thus highlighting the need recognized by the Unger Letter to enhance corporate disclosure related to such developments to investors. *See* discussion *supra* note 139.

[199] Martin Memorandum, *supra* note 174, at 2.

[200] Williams, *supra* note 140, at 1251 n.280, stating:

> Recognizing that investors invest primarily to obtain an economic return is not fundamentally inconsistent with requiring expanded environmental disclosure, civil rights disclosure, and other sorts of social disclosure. Expanded social disclosure is extremely useful for the investor qua economic investor, because the information disclosed may portend future economic conditions, even if it is not "economically material" at the time of disclosure.

SEC rules provide a catch all that provides the Commission a great deal of flexibility in setting disclosure requirements. *See* RULE 408, SECURITIES ACT, 17 C.F.R. 230.408 (1988) ("In addition to the information expressly required to be included in a registration statement, there shall be added such further material information, if any, as may be necessary to make the required statements, in the light of the circumstances under which they are made, not misleading.").

[201] Sec. and Exch. Comm'n. v. Great Western Land & Dev., Inc., et al., 1965 U.S. Dist. LEXIS 9834 (D. Ct. Ariz.) (Emphasis added). For a persuasive argument that expanded social disclosure can be mandated by the SEC under proxy rules of the SECURITIES EXCHANGE ACT OF 1934 (the "1934 Act"), the companion statute to the SECURITIES ACT OF 1933, *see* Williams, *supra* note 140, at 1207 ("The SEC has the authority to require expanded social disclosure under section 14(a)" of the 1934 Act.).

[202] On law and economics generally, *see* R.A. POSNER, ECONOMIC ANALYSIS OF THE LAW (Aspen Law & Business 1998); in the context of corporate finance, *see* F.H. EASTERBROOK & D.R. FISCHEL, THE ECONOMIC STRUCTURE OF CORPORATE LAW (Harvard University Press 1991).

[203] On federalism, *see* Easterbrook & Fischel, *supra* note 202; on private ordering, *see* D.D. FRIEDMAN, LAW'S ORDER: WHAT ECONOMICS HAS TO DO WITH LAW AND WHY IT MATTERS (Princeton University Press 2001).

[204] The core support for a doctrine that a regulation can be a "taking" is found in the U.S. Constitution: "Nor shall private property be taken for public use, without just compensation." U.S. Const. amend. V. The Rosetta stone for strong versions of the principle of a regulatory taking is found in Justice Holmes' opinion for the Court in Pennsylvania Coal Co. v. Mahon, 260 U.S. 393, 415 (1927) ("The general rule at least is, that while property may be regulated to a certain extent, if regulation goes too far it will be recognized as a taking."); Keystone Bituminous Coal Ass'n. v.

DeBenedictis, 480 U.S. 470, 502-03 (1987) (Rehnquist, C.J., dissenting) (stating "the holding in Pennsylvania Coal ... has for 65 years been the foundation of our 'regulatory takings' jurisprudence").

205 *See supra* text accompanying notes 4-10.

206 *See* Press Release, United Nations Global Compact, Global Compact and World Bank Institute Cooperate on CSR Program (Mar. 6, 2003) (describing corporate social responsibility program).

207 Business groups have made some headway in extending the "regulatory takings" concept to the international economic arena under the protections offered by the NORTH AMERICAN FREE TRADE AGREEMENT (NAFTA). Article 1110, Chapter 11, of NAFTA states that:

> No party may directly or indirectly nationalize or expropriate an investment of an investor of another Party in its territory or take a measure tantamount to nationalization or expropriation of such an investment ("expropriation"), except: (a) for a public purpose; (b) on a non-discriminatory basis; (c) in accordance with due process of law and Article 1105(1); and (d) on payment of compensation in accordance with paragraphs 2 through 6.

Canada-Mexico-United States: NORTH AMERICAN FREE TRADE AGREEMENT, 32 I.L.M. 289 (1993); 32 I.L.M. 605, 641 (1993) (emphasis added). Several companies have argued that environmental and other regulations amount to "expropriation" and on two occasions have been able to win either money damages through the dispute resolution process established in NAFTA or force a favorable settlement on a member state. *See* Chart of Chapter 11 Cases, Global Trade Watch, Public Citizen, (U.S. chemical company wins $ 13 million in dispute over Canadian regulation on gasoline additive; U.S. firm wins $ 15.6 million in dispute over construction permit for toxic waste dump in Mexico). *See also* Greider, *The Right and US Trade Law: Invalidating the 20th Century*, THE NATION, Oct. 15, 2001 ("Under Chapter 11, foreign investors from Canada, Mexico, and the United States can sue a national government if their company's property assets, including the intangible property of expected profits, are damaged by laws or regulations of virtually any kind.") In a situation similar to the discussion about disclosure here, in 1994 the cigarette manufacturer Philip Morris was able to beat back efforts by the Canadian government to impose a "plain packaging" requirement for cigarettes which would have removed terms like "light," "low tar" and "mild" from packaging. The company claimed the measure would have been tantamount to an expropriation of its trademarks in violation of Art. 1110. The Canadian government recently renewed its effort to impose "plain packaging" requirements and, once again, Philip Morris is opposing them and threatening action under NAFTA. Ronald Corbett, *Comment: Protecting and Enforcing Intellectual Property Rights in Developing Countries*, 35 INT'L. LAW. 1083 (2001); Public Citizen, *Philip*

*Morris Warns Canadian Public Health Proposal Violates NAFTA*, 2 HARMONIZATION ALERT 1 (Mar.-Apr. 2002).

[208] *See supra* text accompanying note 2.

[209] Unger Letter, *supra* note 3, at 2.

[210] In a late 19th century takings case, Holmes defended half price fares on a privately run streetcar system for children traveling to school against a charge of a "taking" by the streetcar company on the grounds that to do otherwise would be to violate the deep "structural habit" represented by public support for education. Holmes wrote:

> Constitutional rights like other [sic], are matters of degree and ... the great constitutional provisions for the protection of property are not to be pushed to a logical extreme, but must be taken to permit the infliction of some fractional and relatively small losses without compensation, for some at least of the purposes of wholesome legislation. ... Education is one of the purposes for which what is called the police power may be exercised. ... Structural habits count for as much as logic in drawing the line. And, to return to the taking of property, the aspect in which I am considering the case, general taxation to maintain public schools is an appropriation of property to a use in which the taxpayer may have no private interest, and, it may be, against his will. It has been condemned by some theorists on that ground. Yet no one denies its constitutionality. People are accustomed to it and accept it without doubt. The present requirement is not different in fundamental principle, although the tax is paid in kind and falls only on the class capable of paying that kind of tax - a class of quasi public corporations specially subject to legislative control.

Interstate Consol. St. Ry. Co. v. Commonwealth of Massachusetts, 207 U.S. 79, 86-87 (1907) (emphasis added; citations omitted).

[211] Brauneis, *supra* note 19, at 642-43 (*citing* Interstate Consol., 207 U.S. at 79).

[212] *Id.* at 701.

[213] Coffee, *The Future as History: The Prospects for Global Convergence in Corporate Governance and Its Implications*, 93 NW. U. L. REV. 641, 697 (1999) (arguing that "accepting any significant disparity in disclosure standards for one market creates an unstable environment in which political pressures are likely to produce regulatory arbitrage - and the proverbial 'race to the bottom'").

[214] *See* Testy, *Comity and Cooperation: Securities Regulation in a Global Marketplace*, 45 ALA. L. REV. 927, 929 (1994) ("Conflicts among national regulatory regimes may encourage regulatory arbitrage as well as ill will among and between nations."); *see also* Licht, *Regulatory Arbitrage for Real: International Securities Regulation in a World of Interacting Securities*

*Markets*, 38 VA. J. INT'L L. 563, 633 (1998) ("Foreign listing becomes a medium through which undesired effects can be exported from one country to another."); Romano, *Empowering Investors: A Market Approach to Securities Regulation*, 107 YALE L.J. 2359 (1998) (advocating regulatory competition). Licht argues that financial arbitrage can ameliorate the impact of regulatory arbitrage, because in an efficient market the price of the company's stock will reflect the value that investors place on the company's choice or, in the case of a dual listing, its mix, of regulatory regimes. In some sense, that is precisely what happened when PetroChina attempted its IPO. The PetroChina Campaign was part of the process by which information about the company was integrated into the market price - a price, as indicated, that the underwriters adjusted downward as poor investor reaction during the road show accumulated.

215 *See* Licht, *id.*, at 635. Virtually all the existing literature on international securities regulation is preoccupied with two basic issues: the question of regulatory competition among national regulatory regimes, and the related problem of extraterritorial application of such regimes (extraterritorial jurisdiction). At the heart of the debate stands the likelihood of detrimental regulatory arbitrage - the so called "race to the bottom' - if issuers migrated to markets with lower-quality regulation. The alternatives to this scenario are a beneficial "race to the top' or to some middle-range "optimum'. From these scenarios different conclusions may be drawn about the need for regulatory intervention.

216 *Id.* at 633.

217 *Id.*

218 Licht, *Managerial Opportunism and Foreign Listing: Some Direct Evidence*, 22 U. PA. J. INT'L ECON. L. 325, 326 (2001).

219 *Id.* at 326 (stating that "piggybacking may also have a dark side in the sense that foreign listing transactions could be guided, inter alia, by managerial opportunism"); but *see* Romano, *The Need for Competition in International Securities Regulation*, 2 THEORETICAL INQ. L., Article 1, at para. 2 (2001) ("There is no evidence supporting the claim that competition would result in a race to the bottom, with issuers choosing the lowest level of disclosure possible.").

220 A substitute form of legitimization does take place in such regimes, as suggested at the outset of this chapter, but it is largely driven by ideology and the arbitrary use of power rather than the checks and balances of an accountable institutional structure.

221 Jacob, *Graft in Asia on Rise, Says Business*, FIN. TIMES, Mar. 13, 2003, at 9 (stating that "Graft is endemic in China: according to the most conservative estimates, the magnitude of corruption ranges from 3 to 5 percent of GDP").

222 *See generally* Barnard, *Social Dumping and the Race to the Bottom: Some Lessons for the European Union from Delaware?*, 25 EUR. L. REV. 57 (2000) (demonstrating how competition between jurisdictions in a deregulated internal market lowers standards, inducing market

participants to flock to the state with the lowest social standards, thus leading to a race to the bottom); Barenberg, *Law and Labor in the New Global Economy: Through the Lens of United States Federalism*, 33 COLUM. J. TRANSNAT'L L. 445 (1995) ("The substantive legal standards implemented by federal authorities may permit social dumping in the form of movements of capital either across the borders of geographic, public institutions ... or across the boundaries of functional, private institutions....").

223 *See supra* text accompanying notes 134-138.

224 F.R. EDWARDS, THE NEW FINANCE: REGULATION & FINANCIAL STABILITY (AEI Press 1996).

225 *Id.* at 10.

226 National Accounts Data, Bureau of Economic Analysis, U.S. Department of Commerce.

227 Flow of Funds Accounts of the United States, The Federal Reserve Board, Release date: Sept. 9, 2003 [*hereinafter* Flow of Funds 09/09/03], and Flow of Funds, Release date: Dec. 5, 2002 [*hereinafter* Flow of Funds 12/05/02].

228 Flow of Funds 09/09/03, *id.* at 51; Flow of Funds 12/05/02, *id.* at 51.

229 EDWARDS, *supra* note 224 at 16.

230 Flow of Funds Accounts of the United States, The Federal Reserve Board.

231 On this division of history between an Industrial Relations era and a Capital Markets era, *see infra* text accompanying notes 268-276.

232 Office of Investment, AFL-CIO, THE VODAFONE HOSTILE BID FOR MANNESMANN: THE WRONG TRANSACTION FOR LONG-TERM INVESTORS, Nov. 22, 1999. I drafted the initial version of this report. *See also* Press Release, AFL-CIO, "Statement by AFL-CIO President John Sweeney on Mannesmann Takeover" (Nov. 22, 1999). The following discussion is based on my personal contemporaneous observations.

233 Press Release, AFL-CIO, "Worker Shareholders Challenge Unocal's Plans For New Investment in Burma and Ask For Commitment to Global Labor Standards" (May 20, 2002) (on file with author).

234 Press Release, "AFL-CIO Calls for Shareholder Vote on Amerada Hess' Acquisition of Triton" (Aug. 2, 2001).

235 *See infra* text accompanying notes 277-287.

236 This can be thought of as analogous to the influence of World War II on the post war civil rights movement. Having fought, yet again, on behalf of the United States in the war, black Americans came home to the world of Jim Crow. This time, however, they joined with many in the labor movement that had been established in the 1930s to break this country's system of de jure racism.

237 W. COLBY & P. FORBATH, HONORABLE MEN: MY LIFE IN THE CIA 62, 74-75 (Simon & Schuster 1978).

238 R.H. SMITH, OSS: THE SECRET HISTORY OF AMERICA'S FIRST CENTRAL INTELLIGENCE AGENCY 12 (University of California Press 1972).

239 COLBY & FORBATH, HONORABLE MEN, *supra* note 237 at 108-40.

240 Today a dim echo of this approach lives on in the activities of the Congressionally-funded National Endowment for Democracy and the State Department's Advisory Committee on Labor Diplomacy.

241 After the events of September 11, 2001, the ascendancy of the national interest/neo-conservative wing of the foreign policy establishment was marked with the appointment of figures like Paul Wolfowitz, Elliott Abrams, Otto Reich, and John Poindexter to key administration positions.

242 Dinesh, *Sudan Sanctions Renewal Draws Focus to Cooperation in US's Terrorism War*, OIL DAILY, Nov. 6, 2001, at 8.

243 Tyler, *A New Power in the Streets*, N.Y. TIMES, Feb. 16, 2003 at A1.

244 Diamond, *Bridging the Divide*, *supra* note 11.

245 *See* Auerback, *Korea's Election Results: Another Decisive Turn Against Washington*, INT'L PERSP., PrudentBear.com (Dec. 24, 2002); Auerback, *Cognitive Dissonance and the Washington Consensus*, INT'L PERSP., PrudentBear.com (Jan. 8, 2002); Auerback, *Thailand's Election: More Signs Of Backlash Against The West*, INT'L PERSP., PrudentBear.com (Jan. 16, 2001).

246 *See* Auerback, *Capital Controls: The Counterattack Has Begun*, INT'L PERSP., PrudentBear.com (Jan. 21, 2003) [*hereinafter* Auerback, Capital Controls]; Marshall Auerback, *Capital Controls: Malaysia Ends A Successful Experiment With No Fanfare*, INT'L PERSP., PrudentBear.com (May 8, 2001).

247 Sakboon, *Aids Activists Step Up Drug-access Drive*, THE NATION (Thailand), Mar. 7, 2003.

248 Alan Greenspan can be seen as a key representative of this perspective.

249 M. DE ANGELIS, KEYNESIANISM, SOCIAL CONFLICT AND POLITICAL ECONOMY (2000) [*hereinafter* DE ANGELIS].

250 *Id.* at 6-7 (emphasis added).

251 *Id.* at 17 (emphasis in original).

252 *Id.* at 30.

253 *Id.* at 6.

254 Kalecki, *Political Aspects of Full Employment*, in 1 COLLECTED WORKS OF MICHAL KALECKI - LAPITALISM: BUSINESS CYCLES AND FULL EMPLOYMENT 351 (J. OSIATYNSKI ed., 1990), *cited in* DE ANGELIS, *supra* note 249 at 4.

255 DE ANGELIS, *supra* note 249 at 13-14.

256 Keynes, *Am I a Liberal?*, in IX THE COLLECTED WORKS OF JOHN MAYNARD KEYNES, ESSAYS IN PERSUASION 305 (1972), *cited in* DE ANGELIS, *supra* note 249 at 20.

257 A. NEGRI, KEYNES AND THE CAPITALIST THEORY OF THE STATE POST-1929, IN REVOLUTION RETRIEVED: WRITINGS ON MARX, KEYNES, CAPITALIST CRISIS AND NEW SOCIAL SUBJECTS 1967-83 19-20 (Red Notes 1988), *cited in* DE ANGELIS, *supra* note 249 at 21.

258 J.M. KEYNES, THE GENERAL THEORY OF EMPLOYMENT INTEREST AND MONEY 269 (St. Martin's Press 1936), *cited in* DE ANGELIS, *supra* note 249 at 29.

259 DE ANGELIS, *supra* note 249 at 83.

260 *Id.* at 6.

261 *Id.* at 143.

262 *Id.* at 90 (noting "the single most important achievement of the [collective bargaining] contract from business' perspective was the establishment of a mechanism that took the control of production away from workers").

263 *Id.* at 143.

264 Minutes of Senate Subcommittee on Employment, Manpower and Poverty (July 25, 1972), *cited in* K. WELLER, THE LORDSTOWN STRUGGLE AND THE REAL CRISIS IN PRODUCTION 3-4 (Solidarity 1973) [*hereinafter* WELLER] (unpublished manuscript in possession of author).

265 WELLER, *supra* note 263, at 3 (citations omitted).

266 *Id.* at 11.

267 *Id.* at 12.

268 *See* E. ROTHSCHILD, PARADISE LOST: THE DECLINE OF THE AUTO-INDUSTRIAL AGE 17 (Vintage Books 1973) (referring to the Lordstown strike as "the most famous contemporary example of worker alienation").

269 DE ANGELIS, *supra* note 249 at 144 ("Friedman's (1968) presidential address to the American Economic Association ... represented the ... undermining of theoretical support for demand management policies.").

270 This explains in part the fierce opposition that emerges whenever economically troubled developing countries attempt to implement protective measures like currency controls. *See* Auerback, *Capital Controls, supra* note 246 (noting "that US trade negotiators are working proactively to ensure that any incipient resort to [capital controls] is to be eliminated as ... future trade deals are pursued).

271 *See generally* H. SHAIKEN, MEXICO IN THE GLOBAL ECONOMY: HIGH TECHNOLOGY AND WORK ORGANIZATION IN EXPORT INDUSTRIES (1990) (discussing advanced manufacturing systems in Mexico). Of course, those textile mills have now, for the most part, moved on to places like Mexico and China as well.

272 DE ANGELIS, *supra* note 249 at 157.

273 Campbell, *Analysis: Brazil's Hopeless Defense*, UPI, OCT. 17, 2002 (noting Brazilian "growth has ... been modest because of the constant need to keep interest rates high in order to sell debt, attract foreign portfolio capital inflows and curb growth in imports and in the external deficit"); Romero, *Brazil Raises a Key Rate By 3 Points*, N.Y. TIMES, Oct. 15, 2002 at C1 (describing "an unexpected move in the middle of the standoff between Brazil's government and financial institutions speculating about the direction of the real [Brazilian currency]"); Wheatley, *Brazil: Business Likes Lula - But Wall Street Doesn't*, BUS. WK., Oct. 14, 2002, at 35; *Soros Slams Antsy Markets Facing Brazil's Leftist Candidate*, AFX EUR. FOCUS, Oct. 8, 2002, at 35.

274 In late 2002, benchmark Brazilian interest rates stood at 25%. Barham, *Heading Out of the Storm*, LATIN FIN., Feb. 2003 at 16; *Interest Rate is Increased After All; New Signal to the Markets Gets Poor Response*, LATIN AM. WKLY. REP., Jan. 28, 2003 at 41.

275 Foer, *Radical Solution*, NEW REPUBLIC, Sept. 23, 2002 at 15.

276 *Id.*

277 DE ANGELIS, *supra* note 249 at 151.

278 *See* Diamond, *Labor Rights in the Global Economy: A Case Study of the North American Free Trade Agreement, in* HUMAN RIGHTS, LABOR RIGHTS AND INTERNATIONAL TRADE 218 (LANCE A. COMPA & STEPHEN F. DIAMOND EDS., 1996, 2003) [*hereinafter* Diamond, *Labor Rights*]; for a sophisticated critique, *see* Stone, *The Post-War Paradigm in American Labor Law*, 90 YALE L.J. 1509, 1566 (1981) [*hereinafter* Stone, *Post-War Paradigm*] (stating "the industrial pluralist metaphor of the plant as a mini-democracy ... [is] mere illusion"). Note that my argument comes at this question from a slightly different angle than Professor Stone, suggesting that it is internal workplace conflict that pushes its way outward to a battle over broader democratic principles, while at the same time generating periodic compromises that are seen as legitimate stalemates or cease-fires between employer and employee. For further discussion of inward legitimation effects of the Wagner Act, *see* Stone, *The Structure of Post-War Labor Relations*, 11 N.Y.U. REV. L. & SOC. CHANGE 125 (1982-83) and Becker, *Democracy in the Workplace: Union Representation Elections and Federal Labor Law*, 77 MINN. L. REV. 495 (1993).

279 29 U.S.C. 151-69 (1935).

280 United Steelworkers v. Enter. Wheel & Car Corp., 363 U.S. 593 (1960); United Steelworkers v. Warrior & Gulf Navigation Co., 363 U.S. 574 (1960); United Steelworkers v. Am. Mfg. Co, 363 U.S. 564 (1960).

281 Warrior, 363 U.S. at 578-80 (emphasis added).

282 INDEPENDENT STUDY GROUP FOR THE COMMITTEE FOR ECONOMIC DEVELOPMENT, THE PUBLIC INTEREST IN NATIONAL LABOR POLICY 32 (1961), *cited in* A. COX ET AL., LABOR LAW 571 (Foundation Press 1977), *cited in* Stone, *Post-War Paradigm, supra* note 278 at 1576.

283 K.E. KLARE, CRITICAL THEORY AND LABOR RELATIONS LAW, IN THE POLITICS OF LAW: A PROGRESSIVE CRITIQUE 539, 561, D. KAIRYS ed. (Basic Books 1998); Klare, *Judicial Deradicalization of the Wagner Act and the Origins of Modern Legal Consciousness, 1937-1941*, 62 MINN. L. REV. 265 (1978).

284 But *see* Stone, *Post-War Paradigm, supra* note 278 at 1577 (Industrial relations system suffers from an "antinomy" such that "the more successful the theory [of industrial pluralism] is as a tool of manipulation, the less tenable it is as a mode of legitimation.").

285 C. KERR, MARSHALL, MARX AND MODERN TIMES: THE MULTI-DIMENSIONAL SOCIETY 48 (Cambridge Univ. Press 1969).

286 Diamond, *Labor Rights, supra* note 278.

287 Turley, *Dualistic Values in the Age of International Legisprudence*, 44 HASTINGS L.J. 185, 186 (1993).

[288] DE ANGELIS, *supra* note 249 at 49. De Angelis is not alone in this view of the emergence of the modern American labor movement in the 1930s. His perspective is not simply that of an obscure Italian commentator, though it echoes the views of figures like Antonio Negri who helped found the "autonomist" tradition with which De Angelis is affiliated. An echo of this viewpoint is found in the United States in the work of Staughton Lynd and others. *See* STAUGHTON LYND ed., "WE ARE ALL LEADERS" - AHE ALTERNATIVE UNIONISM OF THE EARLY 1930S (University of Illinois Press 1996).

[289] It is true that Kerr's view is an exaggeration of trends. Kerr always fancied himself a far-sighted analyst of emerging tendencies in modern capitalism. The most insightful criticism of Clark Kerr can be found in H. DRAPER, THE MIND OF CLARK KERR (Independent Socialist Club 1964). This short book grew out of a series of lectures by Hal Draper, delivered to students at Kerr's own University of California at Berkeley just prior to the breakout there of the Free Speech Movement that would end Kerr's career.

[290] A classic example is De Angelis' misreading of the labor movement's no strike pledge in World War II. While made formally by labor officials, it was broken on a regular basis by many local unions in both the AFL and CIO, most notably by the coal miners, the machinists in defense plants, and some autoworkers locals. Despite the tension between these layers within the trade union movement itself, De Angelis sees the unions as a monolith "subordinating the interests of the rank and file to those of "the country." DE ANGELIS, *supra* note 248, at 58. This view is echoed in the work of Lynd, *supra* note 287. But *see* N. LICHTENSTEIN, LABOR'S WAR AT HOME: THE CIO IN WORLD WAR II (Cambridge Univ. Press 1982) (discussing deep dissent in CIO over the pledge).

[291] KERR, *supra* note 285, at 48.

[292] While memories of the 1992 riots by African American and Latino residents of south central Los Angeles have begun to fade, the economic and social conditions that, in part, sparked this event have certainly not. *See* California Legislature Assembly Special Committee on the Los Angeles Crisis, TO REBUILD IS NOT ENOUGH: FINAL REPORT AND RECOMMENDATIONS OF THE ASSEMBLY SPECIAL COMMITTEE ON THE LOS ANGELES CRISIS (1992) (arguing that "like other urban conflagrations - from Watts to Miami - the 1992 Los Angeles Crisis was sparked by a single incident, yet rooted in grievances and tensions which had accumulated for years" and that "economic troubles only exacerbated the tensions tearing at the heart of Los Angeles").

[293] The most articulate and palatable of such perspectives is J. GRAY, FALSE DAWN: THE DELUSIONS OF GLOBAL CAPITALISM (New Press 1998).

[294] China Gas Blast Death Toll Rises (BBC News television broadcast, Jan 5, 2004).

[295] *Id.*

[296] Kahn, *China Blames State-Owned Company in Gas Blast*, N.Y. TIMES, Jan. 4, 2004, at 3.

[297] *Id.*

## Conclusion

[1] See the discussion *supra* at p. 4.
[2] International Confederation of Free Trade Unions, *"Trade Union Rights Under Threat,"* REPORT OF THE EXECUTIVE BOARD, BRUSSELS, (Dec. 1-3, 1993).
[3] See the discussion *supra* in Chapter 3.

LaVergne, TN USA
05 December 2009
166065LV00001B/8/P